My Animals and Other Family

By

Keith Pugsley

For my lovely wife Gilly, without whom none of what follows would have been likely, let alone possible. Forever young.

Contents   Page

Prologue

The natural world contains about **8.7 million species**, according to a new estimate described by scientists as the most accurate ever. But the vast majority have not been identified - and cataloguing them all could take more than 1,000 years.

If I'm honest there probably haven't been that number of species featured in my life. But animals of several species have featured since earliest times, and in my case "earliest times" means "since 1949". My attempts to catalogue them all as I do here have only taken about two years, yet I do ask you to accept this record as a serious study of the species catalogued.

There is no accurate record of the lives and deaths of the animals mentioned in this work prior to 1996. So my musings on events prior to that year are based on personal recollection and entirely dependent on my own biased opinion. Since 1996 however, and the inception of Black Pig Farm in rural south Bedfordshire by my wife Gilly (a T.V. personality of note and inspiration for this work) those lives and deaths have been scrupulously recorded in the Black Pig and Long Lane Calendar. Those intent on researching the detail of what is written hereafter may inspect this document on request in writing and on payment of a really reasonable fee to the Official Archivist of Black Pig Farm. The author of this work is the Official Archivist of Black Pig Farm.

What follows is an accurate, if sometimes sentimental, homage to the animals and to the efforts, the dedication to duty, and to the sheer bloody hard work of looking after a number of disparate, desperate but mostly delightful animals over a period of 25 years by Gilly, Lady Mallens of Bedfordshire, with a little help from me.

1. Childish Encounters with Animals

"Start small." My father's motto in business. And it's been mine throughout life. "Aim big, but start small." That may be why I've retained my perfect but diminutive stature. Because I started small. I just didn't aim big with it.

It was the same with my experiences with animals. I started small. With white mice. Just a couple to start with, encouraged by my pal at Green Lanes School, Andy Rice (Tim's brother in case you haven't been paying attention) who already had a menagerie of the little creatures at Popefield Farm. His had exotic names, like Harold, Naomi and Fiona. I can't remember what I called mine, but they were housed in a palace of my father's making; the drawer from a chest of drawers, covered with a sheet of aluminium mesh and with a bed of wood shavings and sawdust from the local sawmill in Lemsford Road. This makeshift hutch was quartered at the bottom of our garden in Crawford Road. It must have been a blissful domestic situation for the pure white, soft and cuddly couple, where they could get up close and personal, rub little pink noses, scratch with needle sharp claws. I cannot recall their coming, but I rather suspect they were adopted from Andy Rice, who seemed to have rather a large and burgeoning supply. Anyway, they were undoubtedly related. Which made it doubly shocking when I found that one of the tiny white creatures was clearly pregnant. Probably the female, I pondered. I knew nothing of sexual relations in those days, even less about incest and gestation periods. I was only eight or nine at the time, and not a worldly wise boy.

So perhaps I shouldn't have been surprised, but I was, a couple of weeks later when I came across a small soft pink ball of mousemanity, if that's a word, an almost perfect pink sphere made up of ten to twelve new born, seemingly clinging to each other in blind fear. Each about half an inch long, hairless, eyes yet closed. The proud mum busied herself about tidying the wood shavings, plumping up the hay in my imagination, apparently oblivious to the needs of her young.

Now of course there was no internet in the Pugsley household, or indeed anywhere else in the world, in 1958. Much less a single device on which to have accessed Wikipedia. And our 10 volume Arthur Mee Children's Encyclopaedia had nothing of interest on the subject. Besides, good old Arthur was of a religious and poetic bent, so the only mention there may have been of white mice would have been the pair last seen scurrying up the ramp into Noah's Ark. So the fact that *mus musculus* has a gestation period of 20 days, for instance, clean passed me by. Or that it is usually rampant, indiscriminate about its choice of partner, ignorant of the taboo of incest, sexually mature at 40 days and completely lacking in moral fibre. All these interesting, but to a nine year old suburban child, obscure facts just went over my head. My parents wouldn't have been clued up about the life and loves of *mus musculus* either, because they indulged me for some time in my rodent endeavours.

Mice grow quickly too. Within a couple of weeks they're independent of their mum and quite athletic enough to climb to and through the cage roof, especially if it's made of ½" mesh. You've guessed it. Within weeks we had an infestation. I'm not sure how or whether my mum, not squeamish about mice but not their greatest fan either, ever got over her encounter with the hordes that confronted her on her rare visits to the shed. I'm guessing that dad, ever more practical and resourceful than mum, came up with a suitable Final Solution.

However the matter was dealt with, it must have been with some sensitivity. I do not recall a "Mystery of the Missing Mice", or banner headlines announcing "Rodent Pogrom". And one of my rare remaining recollections of my mousey friends is a touching testament to the concern my parents had for my own wellbeing.

When I was nine years old, cycling down Crawford Road on my way to school, or maybe on my way to Mr. Bayliss' sweet shop on the roundabout, it seems my front wheel had an argument with a raised (or perhaps a dropped) manhole cover and I was thrown over my handlebars to head-butt the highway and eat dirt. I have absolutely no recollection of the incident itself to this day. I suffered severe lacerations to my face and was later diagnosed with mild concussion. My first actual memory of the incident is of waking up in my parents' bed. They were both in the room as I awoke. As were some of my many pet mice, a selection as it were, in a small ornamental glass fronted cage, and a medical practitioner.

"Whose mice are they?" I enquired, to the clear consternation of my parents, and I think the GP, whose head was promptly buried in his *"Home Doctor"* as he looked up what to do in the event of a case of mild concussion.

I later remembered my mice. And I'd been touched by their thoughtful presence in my room. But I never did remember the incident itself.

There were also tortoises in the Pugsley household. Four of them. Mum's was called Timothy. It is of course very possible that all four bore this soubriquet. Nominally, there were four of us, so there had to be four tortoises. They became famous media tortoises when one or two of them, probably female so not Timothy, laid eggs. Famous because, unaccountably, a cub reporter on the Hatfield Herald somehow became aware of them and reported on the strange goings on in the Pugsley household where fecund tortoises dwell, recumbent in their (and I do quote) "specially heated sandbox".

Like most domestic tortoises in the UK of the 1950s, and there must have been millions of them, ours all died an untimely death and were consigned to the grave by 1960. Tortoises were of course easily captured, transported and peddled from pet shops all over the country in those days, but nobody knew that as tropical animals they should live in a vivarium until six or seven years old and then be carefully and sensitively hibernated during the winter months, not just left to their own devices under the bonfire with a string attached to their shell. So the 1950s was a bit of a tortoise holocaust in this country. I only recall the passing of my sister's tortoise, and that only because she had the foresight to bury the creature in a marked grave and then exhume and retrieve its bones and shell precisely one year later. That, and because I swear I saw its ghost, a small helmet-shaped globule of ectoplasm as it flitted amongst the dahlias in the back garden.

Lassie, a pretty tricolour Manchester terrier, plump and perhaps middle-aged by the time I remember her, was the family pet in Crawford Road. I do not recall the coming or going of Lassie, but she was memorialised by the acquisition, in our new house in Ground Lane, of a replacement Lassie II, also tricolour Manchester terrier, much younger and sprightlier than Lassie I. This second Lassie was to become dad's inseparable companion at work in his metal store at Welwyn North where she would travel with him every day. She walked to his command without lead, was always exuberant and playful with me and was occasionally entrusted to my care for long walks in Hatfield Park during the school holidays.

I'm afraid Lassie II came to a tragic and untimely end. Whilst in the care of my Grandfather, who then lived just over the road, she bolted excitedly across the road to greet the returning dad one summer afternoon and was totalled in the street right in front of our house by a speeding car. I don't think dad ever forgave Grandfather. Don't think Grandfather ever forgave himself. Lassie II was never replaced. The ritual of the "finale pidale" last thing at night came to an abrupt end. And dad travelled to and from work unaccompanied for the rest of his working life.

You know when you're asked to give the name of your first pet as unique information to identify you over the telephone to your bank or building society? Well in my case that'd be Ginge (the first G is hard, the second soft, so the name would rhyme with "binge" or "hinge"). He was a handsome white and tan smooth haired guinea pig, given into my care when I was about 12. A very personable little creature, Ginge lived on his own in a hutch in the garden, but he'd come indoors often and sit on my shoulder or my lap to watch TV. I fed him a daily diet of mixed bran and oats, laced with used tealeaves from the pot and supplemented with dandelions and sow thistle nicked from neighbouring gardens or the roadside verge often in pre-dawn raids before I readied myself for school. In spring and summer Ginge was let out in the garden in a chicken wire run to graze on grass and weeds.

Delightful creatures are guinea pigs. But they are neither pigs, nor do they come from New Guinea, so they are properly called cavies, if you are to be politically correct. They are in fact rodents, sort of posh rats. And if they can be said to come from anywhere it's the Peruvian Andes, where they are still raised principally for their meat and are considered quite a delicacy. Low maintenance, friendly and quite voluble when excited, they get on well with rabbits and other rodents and are perhaps a better pet for the child as rabbits can prove argumentative and sometimes vicious. They're clean, intelligent and cuddly, and good company for the lonely child. But they don't live too long. A few weeks if you live in Peru. Four or five years in the wild elsewhere or in captivity. Ginge only made it to two years and his end was tragic. Allowed to roam the back garden in the summer months under supervision, he contrived to hide one day behind a shed where he was inaccessible to humans. He would not respond to calls to return at bedtime and dad tried to coax him out of the hiding place with a broom handle. I think he (dad, that is) became frustrated and angry when Ginge would not yield to gentle nudging from the broom. The nudging became less gentle, more of a poking really. Ginge was eventually recovered from behind the shed but must have been damaged internally. He died in his hutch later that evening and I was distraught. I took to my bed, grief stricken.

I know that dad was deeply sorry for killing Ginge. He came to my bedroom and, while I feigned anguished sleep, planted on my forehead the only kiss I remember from him. I forgave him instantly. But I never forgot Ginge. Or that kiss.

I had a brief encounter with my first chicken at this time; a pretty little speckled bantam that my sister Linda had adopted and named Cherokee. It spent its days pecking around the back garden until it fell prey, I assume, to an urban fox.

These were the pets of my childhood and adolescence, the characters that made up my small family in my early years. I had no others until I met Gilly and her mum's dog Sherry, the beautiful golden retriever that graced the council house in Luton, in which she'd grown up, and in which I as an undergraduate lodged part time. I developed a special friendship with Sherry during my courtship with Gilly and would meet her out of work with Sherry on her lead on Friday afternoons after college. When Sherry died, put to sleep because of some undiagnosed illness at home by a vet that I never thought Gilly's mum completely trusted, we took her to our recently acquired matrimonial home in St.Albans and I buried her there in a shallow grave. Gilly's mum thought she'd not be allowed to bury her in a council back garden. Like she believed she wouldn't be allowed to have me as a lodger. Then again, she might well have been right on both counts, knowing the vagaries of local housing authorities of the 1960s and 70s. By the way, Sherry's grave was not shallow out of disrespect for the dear animal. It's just that I didn't know how to dig a grave in those days. I'd never dug a grave for a dog before, any other animal for that matter. I was to learn that particular skill much later in these adventures.

2. Domestic Bliss with Animals

I married Gilly in 1972 and thought we'd settle down to domestic bliss in our house in Chiswell Green on the Watford Road in St.Albans. For some reason the bliss wouldn't be complete without a family. And for us family did not mean kids. We both felt we needed a dog to complete our version of the traditional domestic bliss. So we went out and got one.

Sam was a sweet little Airedale terrier, the kind with square head, shoulders and body that fits neatly into a box that can be stored on a convenient shelf or in a cupboard. We got him from Battersea Dogs Home, where of course *all* rescue dogs in the world are to be found. We travelled to and across London, making good use of our commuter season tickets, and found the dogs' home with the help of a street urchin we chanced upon just outside Battersea Tube Station. He hurried us through a maze of backstreets and alleys such as we'd never have navigated with the A to Z and brought us right to the door of the home where we were introduced to Sam and brought him, unprotesting, all the way back to Watford Junction and briefly into our lives. It must have been a strange and exciting experience for the little chap, and almost certainly his first experience of public transport.

A happy and spirited chap was Sam. He certainly didn't deserve us as parents. Totally new to, and unprepared for, parenthood, we were naïve newlyweds, living in a small detached house a daily commute away from Big Smokey where we were in the early stages of local government careers. What were we thinking of? And what did we know of dog ownership and the commitment that goes with it? We had Sam for one week. We took him for some fairly uncontrolled walks around the village; he slipped his lead on one occasion and was nearly totalled on the main road as we galloped around frantically trying to catch the little blighter. He did display some slightly unnerving anti-social behaviour, and liked humping the unsuspecting cushions in our conservatory. But he should be forgiven these quite understandable tendencies; he had after all been abandoned once already in his short life, and I suspect he only craved attention.

What was unforgiveable I now see was our behaviour towards him. As mentioned, we were both employed in the city, a drive, train and tube commute away. Sam spent the long days of that week in early summer locked in the garage with a bowl of water. He was clearly bored witless with his new and unfulfilling life with us and wrought havoc re-arranging the garden tools and general paraphernalia one keeps in a carless garage. For about twelve hours a day.

It took us a full week to realise what an irresponsible mistake we'd made. Sam would have to be rehomed, again, this time with someone who could give him the company and attention he so richly deserved. Fortunately my dad came to our (and his) rescue and found him a new billet with a pensioner neighbour of his in Hatfield, and Sam left us actually quicker than he'd arrived. We did learn a valuable lesson from our encounter with Sam; you cannot own a dog and work full time unless someone else can mind him for you. Fifteen years were to pass before we had our next canine friend.

For the time being we reverted to guinea pigs, or cavies. At least I had some experience with these sociable creatures and was confident we could give them a decent life. John (chocolate brown smooth haired) and Roderick (tan and white like Ginge, but rough haired) Pugsley took up residence in their purpose-built hutch, well the one I'd fashioned out of an old kitchen cabinet, some ply wood and chicken wire. It had two floors and a ladder with slatted grips which gave access between the dining quarters on the ground floor and boudoir with nesting box on the upper. On dry days we'd contain them on grass in a mesh compound I made out of four central heating vents joined together with wire hinges. Bijou accommodation indeed. And they dined on the statutory bran and oats mixed with tea leaves, as I'd remembered from my adolescent adventures with Ginge, again supplemented with sow thistles and dandelions in season and vegetable trimmings from the kitchen.

We'd had John and Roderick for some weeks when we noticed the holes. In Roderick, that is. A touch alarmed at this apparent manifestation of some flesh consuming disease (are cavies known to contract leprosy? we pondered) we took both to a vet in St.Albans. There, for about £20, we were informed that male cavies are territorial and apt to fight, sometimes to the death, even if there are no women or other possessions to fight over. John, slightly larger and more butch than the shy and retiring Roderick, had been feasting on him.

Now I cannot recall the arrival or the departure of John and Roderick, nor what if anything we did to curb John's pugilistic cannibalism. I'm sure Roderick recovered from his ordeal, and yet again we'd learnt something about rodents. But they are not known for their longevity and I cannot recall their making it to Eaton Bray when we took the domestic bliss there in 1974.

We were in Eaton Bray for 27 years and started with a succession of cats. Not exactly a clowder, as we never had more than two at one time. So more a succession.

Starting with Tweakle, a pretty tabby farm kitten, surplus to farm requirements, we adopted from someone in the village. That tabbies are almost always male is the first thing we were to learn about cats. That tortoiseshells on the other hand are almost always of the female persuasion we were to learn much later. The second thing we were to learn about cats was that male farm kittens are often very nearly feral. Introduced into our dining room after dark one winter's evening Tweakle promptly shinnied up the curtains and would not be persuaded to come down from the pelmet (yes we had one in those days) for hours. But he soon warmed to us. As an old hippy, I had taken to wearing a loose fitting cotton kaftan about the house and Tweakle would happily sit on my lap or between my legs reclining there in a sort of hammock. We didn't have Tweakle too long. He grew into a handsome and of course entire tom cat who wandered the garden and the streets with impunity. Too much impunity for his own good. He was killed on the road right outside our house and buried in the back garden.

Maude was the next of our feline friends and of course we named her after Gilly's mum. She was black, long haired, with white markings on chest and face, and playful too. She'd hide behind the sofa and then suddenly emerge running out on hind legs, waving her front paws in excitement and delight. I am here talking about Maude of course, not Gilly's mum, who was mousey, plump and not nearly so playful. We had a deal of fun playing with the young Maude on winter evenings. I dubbed her "Madame La Pamela" and swear she answered to this name rather more eagerly than to "Maude".

When Maude became pregnant (father unknown) she also became very serious and matronly. She took on the role of motherhood with aplomb, and gave birth to five kittens in the summer, just before we were to go away on holiday abroad. I acted as midwife, though there was really little for me to do. It seems a domestic cat, however domestic, will attend to the business of birth unaided. So although I busied about with bowls of hot water and a large number of towels, the looks I got from Maude were more of subtle bemusement than gratitude. Maude deposited Maudette, Montmorency, Marmaduke, Montgomery and Margaret on the dining room carpet with some dispatch and not a little satisfaction. And there we left them, to the tender mercies of neighbour Mrs. Bird, as we flew off to Magalluf and ten days of donkey riding on some distant beach. Mrs. Bird fed them, sort of, and tended to their immediate needs. But Mrs. Bird was in her eighties and could barely see. We returned to a bowl of maggots and six self-satisfied kittens that'd had the run of the place for nearly a fortnight. They all survived though, and grew into healthy young cats, which when old enough (about eight weeks) we rehomed. As the last of the kittens (renamed Cosmic and Gizmo) left our front door for their new lives, Maude immediately returned to her old playful ways and sense of humour. It was as if she couldn't wait to get rid of the little blighters.

A year or so later Maude had some mysterious misadventure with a fence, we believe, and came home one day literally dragging her tail behind her. The tail, clearly dead, was not performing its essential function of maintaining balance and direction, could not be persuaded to lift let alone wag, unaided. Anyway my suspicions of life in the tail being extinct were confirmed when the vet lay it out on a table, whilst still connected to Maude, and gave it a resounding thwack with a club hammer. Maude showed not a sign of emotion at this outrage on her once fine and fluffy tail. So the tail had to be amputated. And this little operation led to one of my first attempts at amateur veterinary surgery. No, I didn't lop off the tail myself. I let the vet do that, supposing him to be more qualified than I. But for weeks after the operation (tailectomy?) I was required to drain the pus that gathered in the abscess that formed around the wound on Maude's arse and clean it with saline solution. Not a wonderful experience I can assure you, but a job that had to be done, and I'm not squeamish at the sight of bodily fluids, unless they're my own of course.

The operation to remove Maude's tail also took part of her anal nerve. This meant that, for the rest of her short life she would occasionally drop a small, hard, dry turd onto the carpet, quite oblivious herself of these unwelcome deposits. We pretended not to notice. Well there was no point making her self-conscious was there?

Maude followed in Tweakle's footsteps, victim to a passing car, probably as she crossed the road from the field opposite our house. She was picked up by her unwitting assassin, and buried in his garden in the small estate of "executive style" houses behind us.

She was followed by a pair of females we rescued from a cat charity in Barnet and named Minkie Denise (young, black and white long haired like Maude but still retaining her luxuriant and bushy tail) and Myrtle Fiona (because she was tortoiseshell and Myrtle rhymes with turtle and turtles are like tortoises and so you see what I did just there, that subtle play on word associations etc.?) who was some years Minkie's senior and may have been quite an aged cat. They were completely unrelated and with a large age gap but got on surprisingly well together, as females will. They slept in upturned chairs on the kitchen table and sat on our respective laps (Minkie Denise was Gilly's cat, Myrtle Fiona mine) to watch telly in the evenings. Myrtle was the first to leave us, in the summer of 1985. Natural causes as I recall, and just the passing of time. She had become slightly incontinent, as old ladies will, or just plain lazy, or both, having to be forced through the catflap at bedtime to avoid nocturnal accident. Minkie Denise survived her by several years.

Beatrix the bunny entered our lives when Gilly was a school secretary and found her wandering the playing field. She looked for all the world like a wild rabbit, sort of dun brown verging on grey in colouring, bright of eye and bushy of tail. But as she was so tame and the school was on the edge of a vast London overspill council housing estate, I suspect she was an abandoned pet. Gilly caught her easily, as I recall, and she was no greyhound even then. I built her a rather splendid hutch following plans and specifications found in my otherwise never used Reader's Digest Encyclopaedia of Do-It-Yourself. Very proud of that hutch was I, and it well outlived Beatrix, who must have been incarcerated with us for four or five years.

When Beattie was getting on in years she developed what we thought to be a large growth under her chin. Still inexperienced with animals and naïve with vets and their crippling fees we took her to a vet in Dunstable for an exploratory.

"What you've got there is one very fat rabbit", opined the vet sagely over half-rimmed specs one Saturday afternoon. "I should restrict her diet a bit, get her to apply for gym membership, send her out to earn her living perhaps. That sort of thing. You know a little exercise is called for. She'll be on her way to a heart attack otherwise."

"OK, thanks for that. We'll get her on a treadmill, soon have her sorted," I replied. "By the way, we've had her all these years and she looks like a she. But we've never been sure. Could you tell us what sex she (or he) is?"

"Certainly," retorted the vet, upending Beattie in his arms and rummaging about in her nether regions. "In fact, she's a he. You'd better think of calling him Bertie in future. I can feel a large pair of healthy testes in there."

Whereupon Beattie, or Bertie, opened his mouth and let rip with an earth-shattering and stomach churning scream.

"Wow!" I exclaimed, "I've never heard a rabbit do that before."

"Neither have I," admitted the vet. "I'm afraid Bertie's dead."

"Oh bugger," I think I said, "What do we owe you?"

"What, for killing your rabbit? Nothing, that's on the house."

So that was Bertie's fate, to die of shock in the arms of a veterinary surgeon only moments after coming to grips with his own sexuality. We conveyed the fat and now rather limp form of Bertie the bunny back to civilisation in Eaton Bray and gave him a decent burial in the back garden, close to Maude and Tweakle.

George gerbil was the last experiment with animal husbandry before Badger and Black Pig Farm. He was a present from Gilly to me and I rather think as compensation for the loss of Bertie, of whom I'd become very fond. A small rodent of indeterminate age and doubtful longevity, George lived his days in a small tinplate cage in the workshop. Alone. And for the most part unloved. I cannot remember his coming. Or his going. I only look back with regret at some of the experiences with animals before Badger when we perhaps cared, in a perfunctory way, for their basic animal needs but with scant regard for their emotional expectations. Even today, when I see a solitary caged creature or bird, a pang of regret and longing catches in my throat. For animals, most of them anyway, are social creatures. They have social and emotional needs. I know this now. I didn't think about it then.

Badger Arthur Maradonna Bonecrusher Pugsley (aka Whistbrae Country Boy) entered our lives in March 1986 and changed them for ever.

Our approach to animals had matured manifold over the years and we carried out a great deal of research before embarking on the commitment a relationship with a dog actually entails. Gilly had been badgering me for years to overcome my reluctance to commit. But when my Myrtle died leaving Minkie Denise as our sole charge I finally conceded. The hunt was on for a suitable breed. We studied the *Observer's Book of Dogs,* the *Penguin Encyclopaedia of Dog Breeds*, some Kennel Club magazines and a host of pre-internet sources. We even visited the annual Crufts show that year. We finally settled on the large and hairy Briard as a likely contender and somehow located through a friend of a friend of somebody down the pub somebody who had one, living in Stevenage, and was prepared to meet us.

We visited Chewbacca (for that was his name and if you've seen the film *Star Wars* and know the breed you will instantly see the connection) one wet and windy Friday evening.

I was just taking a pull on the pint of homebrew I'd been offered after introductions when Chewbacca made his entrance. He was enormous, and enormously hairy, more of a mount than a dog. Bit like a dark brown yak from the Himalaya or a mammoth from pre-history. Anyway, he took one look at me and gave a single deep throated bark, of such volume and intensity that he blew both me and my beer away. As I tried to wipe away my embarrassment and the beer from our host's face, the carpet, sofa and wallpaper with the solitary Kleenex I found in my pocket, in walked Murphy, our host's pet number 2.

Murphy was a slate grey bearded collie with a broad dopey smile and totally engaging personality. We both fell instantly and silently in love with the breed and tacitly agreed, there and then, word unspoken, that a dog of Murphy's breed would tick all the boxes.

So we did our best to clean up the mess I'd made with the homebrew, swiftly re-wallpapered the lounge, made some polite noises about Chewbacca and enquiries about the whereabouts of Murphy's breeders, and left the Stevenage couple in peace.

By the end of March we had holidayed in Tenerife and returned to pick up a nine week old bearded collie pup from breeders Alan and Viv Stevens in Coalville, Leics.

We were, perhaps for the first time in our lives, completely prepared for the commitment to Badger that was to last very nearly 16 years. He became our "son and hair", and we romped the Beds. and Bucks. countryside together for the rest of our stay in Eaton Bray. He had his favourite walks down the back of Church Lane (he actually learnt to spell "church" viz. C-H-U-R-C-H because we had to spell it out this way or Badger would break into paroxisms of excited barking if you mentioned the "C" word). Other walks were around the football field ("the footie"), Dyers Lane and the Comp, "Big Field", into Totternhoe and up the Knolls, into Edlesborough, Northall, Dagnall and beyond. We took him on holiday to the Norfolk Broads where he captained the motor launch which came with our rented cabin on the river bank. We visited Mr. Cumpstey, the butcher in his striped apron, for sausages to throw on the barbie. Twice we took him to the holiday camp at Sussex Beach and walked the beaches of the Twitterings and into Bognor with Badger. Badger loved car trips too, and we visited Warwick Castle with him. He stayed one night in Winston Churchill's favourite Grand Hotel in Scarborough on the occasion of my addressing the inaugural meeting of the Association of Local Land Charge Officers. We were, in effect, inseparable from Badger for all the years we had him. And we never went abroad after our second trip to Tenerife in 1987 as we couldn't bear to leave him in kennels.

It was really Badger and the connection we had with him that introduced us properly to the village we had lived in already for fourteen years but had taken little interest in. Badger opened our eyes to the truly wonderful life we were in the middle of but had not noticed. He reconnected us to our idyll.

Minkie Denise was not as impressed with Badger as were we, and she told him so. With tooth and claw. But they rubbed along together acceptably after their initial meeting, when Minkie took to our bedroom in disgust and would not be coaxed down for some days. Minkie died a couple of years later, a victim to ferocious cancer. She's buried in the back garden of Hyumpum, our house on the Totternhoe Road in Eaton Bray, with our other feline friends.

Ten years of walking and talking with Badger in this way went by, rather quickly as it happens, and not uneventfully. Badger was at first a latchkey kid as Gilly still worked full time at the Careers Office and had to drive home during the lunch break to let the chap out. She went part time on a job share in 1987 however and was able to devote a further 2½ days a week to his care.

Shortly after going into partial retirement Gilly applied and was accepted for the position of volunteer at Whipsnade Wild Animal Park (never let anyone hear you call it a "zoo"). As a member of the Friday team she was to spend that day each week giving guided tours of the exotic and domestic species that roam more or less free about the 630 acres of the park, giving animal talks outside various enclosures, voice-overs on the train and exhibitions in the park's Discovery Centre. I should let her tell you of the adventures, sometimes scary, always magical, that she experienced in her five or six years with the Zoological Society of London. From my point of view I was privileged, as her partner, to visit this world-renowned institution and its inmates, large and small, at both dawn and dusk, taking in the splendours of creatures such as Bumps the camel, Anna the limping elephant, Graham Lucas the human rhino.

Then, in 1996, events conspired to change our lives again, this time rather dramatically.

3. Black Pig Farm, an experiment

There were only three of us back then. Gilly, Badger and myself, living in Hyumpum. It was a comfortable existence. Mid 'sixties four bed det. des. res. With most mod. cons. In the village of Eaton Bray, South Bedfordshire. The living was easy, cushioned, perhaps a little routine.

We had both been local government officers for most of our professional careers. Gilly was growing thoroughly disenchanted in the Careers Service, trying to find non-existent jobs for the disaffected and limited teen porridge that was flooding the market in the 'nineties. She was gradually losing the will to live. I too was learning disenchantment, pushing a pen for the local government legal service and kidding myself that I was part of the brave new world of vision and customer service.

Badger was just growing mature, gracefully. A proud and still very lively ten-year-old bearded collie, he went with the flow; undemanding, easily pleased, our son and hair and the apple of Gilly's eye. We had never really wanted children; Badger had more than filled that particular void in our otherwise very stable, very secure and almost smug relationship.

Sunday morning walks to the car boot fair in nearby Stanbridge had become almost a routine in itself by the middle of April. We would stroll, Badger, Gilly and I, the two miles of rural tarmac between Hyumpum and the field Farmer George Bunker reserved for these gatherings. And there, amongst the would-be vendors and hopeful purchasers, we would idly peruse the collections of the unwanted, the useless and the unnecessary, that these colourful phenomena of the 1970's produced.

This particular Sunday morning, bright and cobalt clear, was otherwise unremarkable. As we rounded the bend in the Rye, and leant on the short parapet of the bridge that was to be the undoing of so many winter motorists unaccustomed to frosty morning black ice, we were still unaware of the life changing discovery we were about to make, half a mile further on.

We had walked this way many times before. We had witnessed the passing seasons; the hedgerows burdened with summer fruits and nuts, the ubiquitous horse chestnut and oak, horses idly grazing in their electrically fenced paddocks, cows in the meadow. Et cetera. But on this particular bright but chilly April morning we spotted something new to us, something not entirely in keeping with the otherwise rural ambience.

"For Sale," declared the incongruous looking sign from its post, half concealed by the bramble and rich undergrowth of a drainage ditch, "Freehold paddock with stables, outbuildings and water. Apply to #### for further particulars".

Now we had both of us nursed separate and largely unspoken ambitions over the years; Gilly to care for some of the less fortunate animals that life's vicissitudes leave behind in its wake, and I simply to own a little bit of England's green and pleasant, and live rather like a hermit on it. We had idly dreamed of desert islands in the Indian Ocean, fortresses in Scotland and sun-drenched lagoons in the Greek Islands. But we had concluded that we were neither rich nor adventurous enough to make the break further from home, and both being anglophile by nature, had looked very much closer (i.e. within a five mile radius!) for our own particular Garden of Eden in rural Bedfordshire. This proclamation from the undergrowth announced itself almost as a bolt from that cloudless blue April sky. The opportunity to move on with our, as yet, largely unformulated life plans was not to be denied.

It was almost as in a dream that I dialled the number of the estate agents on the clumsy brick of a works mobile phone that I had taken to carrying with me on these Sunday morning jaunts and tentatively enquired as to the availability of the advertised plot of pasture land. It was still for sale, and the particulars would be put in the post that day. Estate agents in South Bedfordshire in the 1990's were nothing if not obliging in their attempts to clinch an early deal, and Sunday morning opening had become quite de rigueur.

The rest of our walk on that propitious Sunday morning was dominated by talk of our respective plans for "Donkey Dell", the working title for this new and entirely exciting project. What we could not have been aware of as we strolled dreamily along the country lane to the boot fair was the life changing decision we were about to make, the adventures we were about to have and the people and other characters we were about to meet on the way.

A few days later the sales particulars arrived. We drove the mile-and-a-half down the Rye to the "freehold paddock with stables, outbuildings and water" aforesaid and gingerly clambered over the four bar gate (no key to the padlock being apparently available) and walked across the thick unkempt grass.

I think the title for this new project, "Black Pig Farm", was my idea. We'd recently visited a small private childrens' animal farm and been introduced to a small and rather tatty Vietnamese Black Potbellied Pig which was covered with bird shit and didn't look particularly well looked after. We'd both fallen in love with the little chap and Gilly thought particularly that rescuing these creatures, which had once been fashionable to keep, might be preferable to working her days away at the Careers Service. And this plot of four-and-a-half acres might very well fit the bill.

There was a small stable block with two loose boxes, and attached at each end a home built wooden barn construction that would serve for storing hay or straw. In addition a large garden shed (which would become the "Farmhouse") provided accommodation for humans to shelter from the elements. The paddock was lozenge shaped, perhaps a hundred yards at the road frontage but tapering to maybe a hundred feet at the hedge boundary of what we would call "Home Farm". It had served as a small airfield during WWII and I believe Lysander reconnaissance planes were known to use it on covert missions.

Black Pig Farm and its range of barns and stables would, we thought, prove ideal as a plot for recreation and to house Gilly's rescue project, at least as an experimental beginning. There was a family of settled gypsies adjoining the boundary, and the water supply was doubtful, but the land was close to home and the buildings sufficient to house a modest number of rescued pigs. Gilly had just been offered terms of redundancy from the Careers Service, and the £12,000 severance pay would go a long way towards the £20,000 Eastern Gas wanted for it after they'd finished laying a new gas main on neighbouring land and were ready to sell. We decided to take a punt, and on or about Gilly's 45th. birthday on 20 April 1996 we offered the asking price.

I dealt with the conveyancing but the Eastern Gas employed a conveyancer who was obviously as disenchanted with his job as I had become. He was a nightmare to contact and always seemed to be in the pub. Mobile phones were still in their infancy, but this chap seemed to live his life on his. Contracts for the purchase of the land were exchanged on 29 July. Completion of the purchase took place on 23 August. There would need to be an opening ceremony.

I had arranged for a small varnished wooden nameplate announcing in gothic script

"Black Pig Farm" to be made. At lunch time on 23 August I cycled down

the Rye with drill, bits, screws, a bottle of bubbly and a length of red ribbon (lord knows how I cycled carrying that lot) and said nameplate and attached it to the gate post. The ceremony took place when Gilly, holding her recently acquired shepherd's crook, cut the ribbon at 3.00 p.m. in the sunny afternoon and we raised a glass with Badger in celebration.

Black Pig Farm came with its own resident cat. Felix, black long haired with white markings, had been left behind by the former owners. He'd survived scrounging scraps from workers at the nearby factory where he worked as rat catcher and general factotum. Nervous of human company at first he soon made himself comfortable in one of the barns where he found dry hay for a bed and two square meals daily when Gilly did her rounds. The first true resident of Black Pig Farm quickly made friends with us and all the others who were to inhabit the place over the next four years.

My interest in Black Pig Farm was principally its rural location. I'd followed in my father's footsteps in making this radical (I thought) lifetime downsizing change, and revelled in the notion of getting back to the land if even only at the weekends. I bought myself a mountain bike. At the end of a sweaty day in the office in Hemel

Hempstead I would rush home, tear off suit and tie, don my old working clothes and hurtle down the Rye in search of new farming adventures.

First amongst our priorities was getting the grass cut. We had four and a half acres of fast yellowing grass on the stalk to deal with and I really didn't fancy getting out our ancient Qualcast and several miles of extension cord. Besides, there was no mains electricity at Black Pig Farm, so our even more ancient Mountfield and about 100 litres of petrol would have to do the job. What I didn't realise then was that what I was looking at, even in late September, was quite a valuable arable crop, worth £100 on the ground to good old Georgie Bunker who obliged us one fine Saturday morning in the early autumn by cutting, then later turning once or twice, baling and taking our four and a half acres of quite knackered hay leaving a golden stubble that would winter well and grow again in the spring. You see, I was quickly getting the hang of this farming lark.

Then there was the gate. Black Pig was not badly off for fences and the previous owner had gone to some efforts to secure the land against escape of his few equine charges. But a gate between what we called rather grandiosely "Home Farm" (where most of our animals were to be housed) and the "Outfield", was missing. So I set to one Saturday afternoon and fashioned one out of a section of heavy duty walkway which I found in a pile of such next to the "Farm House" (the wooden garden shed). I'd acquired two large and ornate agricultural hinges and a gate hook from the merchants in nearby Leighton Buzzard and applied these, rather artistically I thought, to the gate I'd fashioned by removing alternate slats from the section of walkway. The finished article was, by any description, a wonder of epic proportions, the likes of which old Isambard Kingdom would have been proud. Stout, sturdy, and maybe a tad over-engineered, the gate post itself groaned at the weight as four of us manhandled it into place and I bolted the hinges down. Gilly was mightily impressed with the technology, not to say the craftsmanship. I think her pretence at struggling with the massive construction on daily visits to Black Pig Farm was a really subtle form of praise for my genius and my artistry with these engineering projects.

Black Pig Farm was ready for its first occupants by the back end of September. We'd been visiting Blackberry Farm, the RSPCA rescue centre a few miles distant, and had expressed an interest in any farm type creatures such as pigs, sheep, goats, cattle and equines that needed a new home. Our first catch, landed one warm Friday evening in September, consisted of a Vietnamese potbellied pig and its close pal, a little Soay sheep. Both were in need of a new billet and each would set us back a mere £5. But the RSPCA do not deliver. Neither would have been comfortable, we thought, in the back of Gilly's Citroen 2CV. Nor would my employers have been too impressed with paw, hoof and horn indentations, not to say prodigious quantities of ordure slopping about in the car they so kindly leased for me. So that's where Farmer Palmer entered, stage left.

Alan Palmer (dubbed by us "Farmer Palmer") was in fact a self-employed driving instructor who fancied himself an agriculturalist. He'd taken the tenancy of a smallholding called Blue Gate Farm just outside Leighton Buzzard and stocked it with a motley variety of waifs and strays, the leftovers of animals unwanted by the farming fraternity. He had won Arnold in a rashly conceived impromptu drinking competition at his local pub and was now trying to unload him onto any willing foster parent. Arnold lived in the back of Farmer Palmer's animal trailer and travelled the countryside towed by unsuspecting learner drivers keen to add "reversing with a trailer" to their repertoire.

And Arnold? Well he was a 22 stone Vietnamese Potbellied Pig; black, covered with spiny bristles, with tusks protruding from each side of his massive, benignly smiling, maw. Looking for all the world like an elderly Chinese gentleman, he carried before him an aroma of the spices of old Araby. Some would have considered him dangerous, even ferocious, but he was a recondite good humoured gentleman. He would make an ideal first candidate for Black Pig Farm.

We struck a deal with Farmer Palmer at our first meeting. We would take on Arnold if he would act as transport for the other VPB and the little Soay we'd agreed to take from the RSPCA. So in the afternoon of a warm and balmy 19 September 1996 Arnold plodded warily down the ramp from the back of Farmer Palmer's trailer and stood face to face with Gilly outside the stable. I'm not sure who was the most curious, who the most surprised. Farmer Palmer and I left the two to get acquainted while we motored off to Blackberry Farm.

We returned a couple of hours later with Beau and Pepys, the second and third candidates for Black Pig Farm. Arnold and Gilly were taking tea on the lawn.

Top Tips for the Farmer No.1: Effecting introductions between pigs

Over the course of the next twenty years we were to learn many cunning tricks and strategies associated with animal husbandry, coarse veterinary practice and general rural affairs. The manner in which pigs should be introduced to each other, especially when they are both male, entire (i.e. not castrated), loaded with testosterone, hot and grumpy, was the first of these lessons and we learnt it from Farmer Palmer.

Jeyes Fluid is the answer. A generous helping of a thin solution of the eponymous disinfectant poured by watering can from a great height all over the animal's rear end will disguise the smell and therefore the fact of the animal's essential pigginess. And if both contenders are treated in the same manner they can be expected to act like the gentlemen they actually are.

Well, it worked for Arnold and Pepys who got on like a couple of good mates instantaneously. A good thing too, as both were supplied with a magnificent pair of tusks and, at twenty stone apiece they could pack a powerful punch. They did get into the odd scrape with each other and Pepys came off worse from one encounter when Arnold opened a five inch gash in Pepys' flank. The bleeding was profuse. And it led to one of my very first attempts at the coarse veterinary practice above referred to.

Top Tips for the Farmer No.2: How to repair a five inch gash in a twenty stone pig.

First catch your pig. Which may not be so easy if he does not wish to be caught and is not overly impressed with your attempts at first aid. But if you can counsel or persuade him to hold still for just a few minutes, and you have a sanitary towel and some strong parcel tape about your person, you are probably about as prepared as you can be for this delicate operation. Basically one of you holds the pig still while the other applies the deployed sanitary towel to the gash thus staunching the blood flow. If there is a third present that person can assist by applying copious quantities of the parcel tape to keep the towel in place for at least a few seconds. You will find that the blood flow is quickly staunched. You may find that the sanitary towel was not actually necessary. If you have a tin of antiseptic blue spray handy (available at all good veterinary surgeries, price about £10) you can forget everything I have said about sanitary towels, parcel tape and even holding your pig steady. You just have to be quick and have a good aim.

By and large Arnold and Pepys got on famously; a couple of piggy pals, they roamed the four-and-a-half acre pasture chewing on grass and roots during the day, and shared one of the loose boxes with Beau by night. I'm not sure what Beau made of the arrangement. She, small, brown, curly wooled and horned, had become Pepys' inseparable friend at Blackberry Farm, and seemed as a lone sheep to tolerate, even accept, Arnold as part of her extended family.

A comfortable little rural routine began to establish itself down on the farm. Gilly would do her domestic duties at home, you understand, iron my shirt, make tea, see me off to work, drop in on her mum and stepfather Stan three doors up the road to check they were still alive. Then she'd climb aboard her Citroen 2CV with quantities of pig nuts, sheep nuts, carrots and mash, a large container of water and Badger in the front seat and trundle off down the farm. There, with the help of a shopping trolly I'd rather generously provided, she'd march across the field to the stable block, let the trio of Arnold, Pepys and little Beau out and feed and water them. The rest of her morning would, I imagine, have consisted of a relaxing pooh pick, a gentle mucking out of stables, perhaps some light tinkering with the hay bales and a playful wrestle with the gates, before she left for the more homely and sedate chores in the house.

The afternoon routine was much the same, but in reverse as she put the little trio to bed before sundown with their respective suppers. If I was able to leave the office treadmill on time I'd join her in the evening pooh pick, or perhaps attend to some minor fencing repairs or some tricky amateur veterinary surgery.

In late November Potter joined us from Blackberry Farm. And she and Gilly both became film stars in the making. Potter (we named her after Beatrix) was an adult gilt of indeterminate age, much smaller than Arnold and Pepys, but of the same black and piggy persuasion. She'd ended up at Blackberry Farm when the craze for pet Vietnamese potbellieds was on the wane and she'd simply become surplus to requirements. She'd also been grossly overweight at the time of rescue; Blackberry Farm had her on a diet of one apple a day to reduce her prodigious and dangerous bulk to the slim and sylph-like cigar-shaped creature we met in the stable that bright day in November.

Blackberry Farm was hosting a series of *"Pet Rescue"* at the time, with Wendy Turner Webster, pretty sister of television's Anthea, as front presenter. Potter's rescue and rehoming at Black Pig Farm became one of the highlights of the series; Potter's signature tune being *"I've Never Met a Girl Like You Before"* (the Edwyn Collins version). Gilly and her mum were filmed in at least three episodes both at Blackberry and Black Pig Farms as Potter, grumbling at the iniquity of the situation, was transferred from the one to the other to take up residence with Arnold and Pepys. Wendy caught the rough end of a nip from the protesting Potter at one stage of the operation, when she was being put to bed for the first time in her new quarters. A member of the production crew asked whether Potter could have passed anything on to Wendy that was contagious. Gilly's somewhat sarcastic reply was in the form of a question:

"No, why, has Wendy anything that Potter should be worried about?"

Potter fitted well into the growing community of Black Pig Farm. She gave a little female company to Beau, though Beau for her part didn't seem that fussed. The boys, Arnold and Pepys, were fascinated by her. They would follow her out of the loose box in the morning, watch her pee on the grass and then swoop in (if the motion of a 22 stone pig can ever be described as "swooping") and drink her piss as though it were nectar from the gods. Then all three of them would mooch about in the grass and weeds or take a snooze in the compost heap until tea time.

A Few Words about Pigs

I love them. They are the most engaging of creatures. Amongst the most intelligent of the animal kingdom they are also perhaps the cleanest. They will never dung in their sleeping quarters unless compelled by captivity to do so, and then only reluctantly.

They eat almost anything. It is illegal in this country to feed meat or meat products to pigs, but they will certainly eat anything that is edible, including human flesh. In all our years of keeping pet pigs the only two items we found they would turn their snouts up at with polite disdain were onions, cooked or raw, and, somewhat surprisingly, mushrooms. Pepys, for instance, had a particular predilection for strawberries. With Arnold it was avocado pear. Potter favoured the carbs, particularly wet bread and pasta. Gilly's mum would cook up a delightful compote of mashed potato and grated carrot which they would all devour with great relish and a good deal of noise. We negotiated early on for the Leighton Buzzard Tesco contract for all their throw-away produce; odd shaped potatoes, specky apples, bruised pears, loose grapes that'd broken away from the stalk, mango, paw paw and endless bananas. Most of this was consumed by us of course, and we didn't buy a single potato for four years. But the pigs did get their fair share and grew fat, healthy and happy on a veritable cornucopia.

All animals, in my experience, have their own special personality. Pigs in particular are individualists. Arnold was a gentleman with high self esteem, a gentle sense of humour and a kindly nature. Pepys was perhaps a little timid for his size, and a bit grumpy. Potter was a bit of a loner, with a slightly odd shape. I believe that she had reached such outrageous proportions on her little stumpy legs early in her life so that they had buckled under her. She always seemed to be in some pain as she plodded around the yard on the bent little pins, a muffled groan on her permanently tortured snout. Most pigs are in the end benign and friendly to man. There are a few rogues however who for whatever reason are not so benign. Some are downright nasty. So far we had not come across one.

Enough of pigs for the time being.

"Have you any other creatures with which we might increase the stock of our fast burgeoning menagerie?" I chanced as we had loaded Potter on to Farmer Palmer's animal trailer for the trip home.

"Well, we do have this peacock, you know. You can 'ave 'im for another fiver," came the reply from the faintly disinterested RSPCA volunteer. "One owner from new, as far as we know. 'E's only been 'ere a few days."

So we took the peacock, a beautiful bird, iridescent in blue, green and purple, and stuck him in the animal trailer with the troubled Potter. And we set off for Black Pig Farm.

We called the peacock Tennyson, carrying on with the literary theme. At Black Pig Farm he was to spend the next couple of months locked in the hay barn and fed on a diet of corn, chicken pellets and household scraps. Peacocks are majestically beautiful birds and quite easy to look after. However they are also incredibly stupid and I put this down to my well-rehearsed theory of the inverse ratio of a creature's intelligence being equal to the ratio of the size of its head to that of its body. A peacock's head is tiny when compared to the size of its body. So peacocks, indeed chickens, turkeys, guinea fowl and all birds with small heads and large bodies lack common sense. They just do not know when they are well off. And if introduced to new premises it has to be under cover of darkness, when they are asleep, and they have to be kept in close captivity, in the case of the peacock, for six months or more before they understand that they have moved house at all.

The rest of the history of Black Pig Farm can be conveniently diarised, as follows.

4. Nineteen Ninety Seven

January 1997 Christmas came and went. For us both I think the visits to Black Pig Farm over the festive season were a welcome novelty and a break from the monotonous tradition that Christmas had become. Picking up pig dung and removing it to the dung heap, feeding and watering our little menagerie and keeping them entertained and happy gave us both a purpose during the holiday that had been sadly missing for most of our adult years.

By the end of January I could bear the incarceration of Tennyson, that beautiful and iridescent creature, no longer. On the 28th. of the month I fed him his usual ration of mixed corn and tentatively left the barn door slightly ajar, so that he could get a glimpse of his wider surroundings. Just as tentatively Tennyson peeped out and then took one bold step outside into the winter sunshine, which glinted on the blues and purples of his magnificent plumage. And then, utterly magically, he displayed for me the full beauty of those startling colours at the door of the hay barn. It was as if he were saluting me, paying homage to his master. Or something. Anyway he took three further strides and then launched himself into the winter scene, flew clean over the fence and into the blue yonder. I never saw him again.

Oh he was seen again alright, just not by me. We were soon to be bombarded by enquiries and, rather annoyingly, complaints from neighbours in the vicinity. Peacocks are rather beautiful, but can be excessively noisy. Their cry is a plaintiff but quite raucous shriek which can carry on the airwaves for several miles. Fortunately there were a number of errant peafowl inhabiting the wilds of south Bedfordshire at the time and it was easy to be convincing fending off complaints with an insistent

"But you know our peacock's cry was a semi-tone higher than that which you describe. It cannot be the Tennyson we know and love that is annoying you."

But when Tennyson took up residence in the branches of a large horse chestnut in the back garden of a chronic ornithophobe in Great Billington we really did have to step up to the mark and at least try to remedy the situation. And as I had not yet embarked on my career in hypnotherapy and was not in a position to systematically desensitise the elderly lady to the phobic stimulus, i.e. Tennyson the peacock, the only option open was to attempt recapture.

We roped in Paul ("Pad") Wilson, friend and at the time neighbour for the rescue attempt. I was busy at work at the time but Pad was self-employed as an independent financial advisor so much more in a position to assist Gilly in this endeavour than I. Early in the morning, well before dawn on three consecutive days Gilly and Pad stalked the back gardens of houses in Great Billington, each armed with torch, keep net and mallet. I'd instructed them in the art of peacock capture which, if my theory gleaned from my copy of Robinson Crusoe was correct, should have given good and prompt results. Old Robinson, you see, cast away on his desert island, as Daniel Defoe would have him, caught and tamed tropical parrots by creeping upon them in the early dawn light and stunning them senseless with a club. He then placed them in a net and carried them home to his cave where they swiftly became domesticated or made ready for the table. Well it seemed to me that what works on a tropical desert island with parrots should be equally successful in rural Bedfordshire with errant peafowl. Gilly and Pad would just have to be a little stealthy climbing those trees, and swift and accurate with the mallet. Well, I'm still convinced the theory's sound, but in practice Gilly and Pad lacked the stealth or the swiftness. Or something. Because after these three abortive attempts we (well they actually) gave up. As far as I know Tennyson the peacock may still be freaking out the ornithophobes of south Bedfordshire. He was a youngster, as peacocks go. And a good peacock can do 15 - 20 years if he doesn't meet a fox.

February 1997 In February we were joined by Wally Patch and Honky Pig. We

rescued both from Longford Farm when, for quite different reasons, they were surplus to requirements of the private animal sanctuary where we'd first seen and fallen in love with the Vietnamese Black Potbellied who was not surplus to requirements.

Wally was an adult and ageing Suffolk Cross sheep with an illustrious showbiz background and only one eye. The other eye having been bitten out during a disagreement with a dog while Wally was still a very young lamb, he had been adopted and reared as tame but stage-struck by a company specializing in the training and supply of animals for stage and screen. So as a lamb and young sheep Wally trod the boards with the other luvvies. He was once shawn of his fleece to the *Stripper's Waltz* for an episode of *Alas Smith & Jones* in Trafalgar Square.

Wally was, it seems, being bullied mercilessly by the other ovine residents of the farm. Larger than he and with a full set of eyes they'd taken to excluding him from their company and he spent much of the day alone and miserable. Though we'd gone to Longford Farm in search of another VPB (that's short for Vietnamese Potbellied Pig) we were pleased to take on Wally as our second sheep and perhaps a more suitable companion for Beau. In fact he was soon to take a major role in Gilly's affections. She learned "Sheepish" and was able to communicate with him quite successfully with a series of grunts, baahs and one-eyed winks.

Wally arrived at Black Pig Farm in the back of Farmer Palmer's stock trailer with Honky Pig, another Longford escapee. Far from black, Honky the Yucatan pig was pinkish in hue, with large black dots. He also had a long snout that tapered almost to a point, razor sharp four inch tusks and a mean streak. I guess Farmer Palmer and I should have noticed the warning signs as we towed the unlikely pair through the lanes of Potten End with the trailer slewing wildly from side to side. We had locked

Wally in the back of the trailer with a psychopath. Although the two were separated by a metal divider, there was not much of that left at the end of our trip. The divider was buckled beyond redemption by what we realised was Honky's attempts to murder and perhaps devour the hapless Wally.

At Black Pig, Honky exited the trailer first and we coaxed and manhandled him quickly into the hay barn with a bowl of pig nuts. He was clearly grumpy verging on the maniacal, and the glint in his steely blue grey eyes was quite disturbing. We thought a night in the slammer would perhaps cool him down, make him a little more philosophical about his good fortune and bright future with us.

Wally stepped out of the trailer with a little trepidation and a quiver of the chin after his ordeal. But he soon made friends with Beau and the triumvirate of pigs, Arnold, Pepys and Potter. And they were to get on famously for the rest of our stay at Black Pig Farm.

Honky on the other hand had been our first major mistake. When we arrived at Black Pig the following day it was to find Honky busy in a furious attempt to break, not out of the hay barn, but through its wall into the loose box containing the three other pigs and Beau. Had he been successful, and he had gnawed his way half way through by the time we arrived, I have no doubt whatsoever he would have murdered everything in his piggy sight. Because, as we have found, pigs can be like that. They can be potentially fierce and dangerous animals. I thought at the time that I could reason with Honky. Perhaps coach or counsel him to a better and more positive lifestyle. You know, help him see life more rationally and understand the error of his ways. But five minutes alone with him in the hay barn was quite convincing. Honky would have to go back to whence he came, before he murdered and devoured the lot of us. I escaped the hay barn unscathed, but with the clear impression Honky was trying to open up a main artery in my leg with one of those four inch razors he kept just under the snout.

Now I really like pigs. The nice ones, that is. And most of them are really nice and I can really feel a kinship with them. But a nasty pig just has to go. As soon as possible. And under English law even a nasty pig is entitled to twenty days grace before it must move on. It's to do with "standstill restrictions", you know. If a pig arrives on your farm from another holding you can't move any pig off your holding (including the one that's just arrived) for 20 days. These are requirements of the Animal Health Act 1981 and the Disease Control (England) Order 2003. And by the way you need a licence to move your pig anyway. So vicious old Honky (I'm sure he had behavioural problems rooted in his early litter life and these may have responded in time to counselling and affection but we had other bacon to protect) had to stay somewhere for the requisite 20 days before being repatriated to Longford Farm.

We chose the Gas Board which owned the five acre field next to Black Pig and there was an empty stable with water supply on it. Honky became a squatter, or perhaps an illegal immigrunt, for the requisite 20 days. We frogmarched him there at dawn one morning, helped by Pad Wilson and an estate agent's "For Sale" board he'd purloined for the purpose. Gilly walked ahead with a bowl of tempting pig nuts and Honky didn't seem to mind at all his forced moonlight flit. He holidayed in the "borrowed" stable for three weeks, being fed, watered and his toilet needs attended to twice daily. He only came to the attention of one curious Gas Board inspector in that time, and even he was kind enough to turn a blind eye and forgo any question of rent or service charges.

March 1997 Honky Pig left us on the 9th March. Farmer Palmer kindly acted as

his chauffeur once again, which was gracious of him bearing in mind the damage and mayhem Honky had caused outward bound. He returned to his deep litter quarters at Longford Farm and we shall never know what became of him thereafter.

With the coming of spring our thoughts moved to chickens. A farmyard didn't seem the same without them, and a few fresh eggs might be nice. Enter Fenella and Cordelia, barred Plymouth Rock hens, and Bernard, blind Rhode Island Red cockerel, gifts from one time county councillor and long time country chancer Brian Piggott. Brian was trying his arm at chicken farming at the time and to encourage our little charitable endeavour donated three of his dodgy brood. Bernard appeared blind, but this was just because he had been reared in darkness and hadn't bothered to open his eyes yet. When he found himself in the bright springtime sunshine of Black Pig Farm he soon changed his ways, opened the old peepers and trotted around the place with his two women. The chickens were free, but their housing, in the shape of a rather well-appointed and bijou chicken ark, set us back over £200. The chickens would run about all day, grazing happily on the rough tussocky grass. But they'd always return for their tea of chicken pellets and the safety of the chicken ark.

Rabbits came next. At the end of the month Farmer Palmer brought us two of his offcasts, a breeding pair of black long-haired creatures we named Bertie and Bunty. Again, they were free, but their housing, a spacious and rather heavily built two-bedroomed affair with its own stand, cost us a further £50. There's nothing much you can do with a rabbit, except feed it and, if necessary, eat it. But we'd resolved not to eat any of our charges, so Bertie and Bunty just sat their dutifully in their hutch, until we sprung another fifty quid for an outside fox proof run for the summer.

APRIL 1997 In April your average sheep farmer's mind turns to shearing. Well, we were far from average farmers and we only had two sheep. And one of them, Beau the little Soay, didn't need shearing so much as plucking. But we still had Wally to contend with, and the following is very much NOT the traditional method.

Top Tips for Farmers No.3: How to shear a sheep with nail scissors.

First catch your sheep. If he's a friendly, humanised and good natured sheep like Wally was, this may not be difficult. If he's an average field type of sheep he'll be cantankerous, frightened, stupid and as awkward as possible so you'll need numerous sheep pens, barriers, tunnels, about twenty other people and ideally a well trained sheep dog just to catch your sheep. But supposing you're just shearing the one friendly, humanised and good natured fellow, you'll probably be able to catch him yourself. You'll only need someone to hold him while you do the shearing. So it's easier if your sheep has horns as there's something to hold on to. If your sheep does not have horns, try a standard dog collar and lead. Your helper will still need something to hold on to. Sheep, even friendly good natured ones, do not particularly like to be sheared.

Next, while your sheep is restrained by your helper, and reassured by yourself, take a suitable and close-to-hand cutting implement. It need not be razor sharp, but should be sharp enough to cut through wool which may be drenched in lanoline in a younger sheep. A pair of nail scissors from your manicure set, whilst not ideal, may well suffice. But it will be a long and very hot, sticky, messy job.

Next cut all of the wool off of all of the sheep, taking particular care around the nether regions and private parts. This will, as indicated, take some four or five hours, and you will make mistakes. So it is a good idea to have by you a can of antiseptic Alamycin spray to treat any nicks, cuts or amputations. Because sticking plasters do not stick to woolly stubble.

Finally release your sheep from bondage and dispose tidily of the wool. Alternately just leave it in a heap and eventually it'll blow away.

Even if you are as successful with this operation as Gilly was, helped by next door farming hobbyist neighbour Jane, you might consider next year getting in the professionals. It's quicker and a lot less stressful and messy.

MAY 1997 Our thoughts returned to chickens in May. Those we had adopted had produced not an egg and we felt we deserved to be a little productive. By the way, and I mean no disrespect to those reading this, but it's astonishing to me how many people do not realise that it's only female chickens, that is to say hens, that lay eggs. The male of the species, or cockerel to give it its name, is really pretty useless unless you want to either breed chickens or eat them. Cockerels can be quite decorative, but as we shall see they can be quite nasty too. If it's just eggs you're after, leave cockerels well alone. The vast preponderance of them are used as food for snakes and other reptiles at zoos or go into dog food.

So in May we thought we'd extend Bernard's harem and we bought a couple of hens from Woodside Eggs in Caddington, an establishment renowned for the sale of hens at "point of lay" (just about to lay their first egg). Enter Blossom Dearie and Red May. We added them to the chicken ark in the dead of night, as you have to do when introducing new birds. They will fight otherwise. If you introduce them at night the existing birds will be asleep and not realise when they awake that their numbers have increased. They're pretty stupid too, chickens.

We waited with baited breath and a telescope for our first egg.

JUNE 1997 With June arrived our first egg and our first fatality. Cordelia, one of our first two hens, produced her first egg. Unfortunately soft-shelled, yolkless and inedible, it was promptly consigned to the dustbin. Even more unfortunately in laying that first egg Cordelia prolapsed her cloacca, or egg sack. This small organ in a bird passes for its womb, and if it pops out, as Cordelia's did, it has to be popped firmly and promptly back in, or the hen will die. So, having taken instructions from the trusty manual of smallholdership, I took Cordelia in hand.

Top Tips for Farmers No.4: How to replace a prolapsed cloacca in a reluctant hen.

First take your hen under your left arm with its rear end pointing upwards and into the light so that you can see clearly what you are doing. Next clean the prolapsed cloacca scrupulously with warm soapy water which you will have had to remember to bring with you from your house if you have as yet no water supply or means of heating it. Then coat your middle and index fingers (of your right hand) liberally with Vaseline petroleum jelly or some other sterile lubricant. You will of course have to remember to bring this with you from home or buy it from a suitable pharmacy in your local town if you didn't remember to bring it with you in the first place. Anyway, suitably lubricated, gently ease the by now swollen cloacca back up what appears to be the hen's arse and hold it in place for a few moments. Ignore all protests from your less than patient hen. Then carefully withdraw your fingers from the hen's arse. Breathe a sigh of relief and congratulate yourself on your superior strength in adversity. When the cloacca promptly pops out again repeat the procedure above described. And when it pops out again do not despair, try once again.

When the cloacca pops out for the fourth time, consider taking your hen to the local vet for treatment. He (or she) will examine your hen, tell you gravely that an anaesthetic will be necessary for this complicated procedure, admit your hen to the veterinary hospital for the night and have him call you in the morning. He will then duly anaesthetise your hen, pop the cloacca back in its rightful place, apply a couple of stitches to prevent it popping out again and await the hen's recovery from the anaesthetic. When the hen does not wake up the vet will tell you it's just one of those things and charge you thirty quid anyway. You will at least have the corpse which you can take back to your farm and give a decent burial.

So June wasn't going to be an auspicious month for our feathered friends. Just a week after Cordelia's demise Bernard went AWOL. He didn't turn up for his tea at bedtime on the 11th and as he hadn't advised of any forthcoming holiday arrangements and left no forwarding address we rather assumed he'd been taken by an opportunist fox. We never saw a feather of him again.

We were left with three hens, and the ark looked decidedly under occupied at bedtime. So we approached Peter Healey who tenanted the council's New Ley Farm in the Rye. We'd met Peter and his literally legless wife Ann briefly when we'd towed his animal trailer carrying a prize bull out of danger on the occasion of his own Land Rover being totalled by a youngster charging home down the Rye after he'd passed the driving test. We thought perhaps Peter would have a couple of hens going spare that'd be company for Fenella. He did. A couple of elderly black Leghorns that still produced the odd infrequent egg as they moseyed about his hay barn. Gilly took one under each arm and we hurried back to Black Pig to put them in the Ark with Fenella.

Unfortunately the scheme didn't go quite to plan. In our hurry to squeeze the hens into the ark as dusk fell, one escaped, hopped into the hedge and disappeared, never to be seen again. In the Black Pig Calendar I have named her "The Lost Hen", the only creature to have entered and exited Black Pig Farm without even landing.

We named the one that did land Silver, as she was black with silver edges to her wings. Pretty little thing, but very elderly and with hard horny growths on her feet which were signs of chicken neglect. And I think her egg-laying days were well behind her. But she would add a certain rural ambiance and we placed her gently in the Ark as night fell.

JULY 1997 The grass was as high as an elephant's eye in July. Well it was worth cutting anyway, and this was the first year we'd been in control. We didn't trouble the bluff Georgie Bunker this year as we'd become acquainted with Stuart Holmes,

another of the local farming fraternity who kept cattle and grew corn down the Rye. Stuart was a pleasant and genial blond Eaton Bray boy who was to help us in many ways over the years at Black Pig Farm. He once towed a wreck of a car from the farm drive with his tractor when it had been burnt out there by the local gypsies. He was to cut and make our hay for this first summer and a couple of years to come. The 4½ acres of Black Pig Farm were to yield a couple of hundred bales, much more than we'd need for our few animals for an entire year. So when Stuart had cut, turned, dried, baled and stacked our field of hay we stuffed as much as possible into the hay barn and covered the rest with tarpaulins to keep it dry. We could sell the surplus bale by bale to the "horsey" fraternity in the district.

AUGUST 1997 Our thoughts returned to chickens and eggs (which came first, who knows?) after the hay was stashed safely away. We added to our small flock by buying a couple of Rhode Island Red/Sussex White cross hens from Woodside on the 14th of the month. Enter stage left India and China. They joined the flock with a studied ease and were likely to be our first providers of eggs. This particular cross, coloured a light tan with the occasional black feather, is perhaps the commonest laying fowl you will find. Battery farms all over the country are stocked with them. We waited again, our joint breaths baited, for the appearance of our first egg.

Meanwhile, the end of August 1997 was to prove a momentous time both for us at Black Pig Farm and for the world at large. We took delivery of our first goat, rescued from the R.S.P.C.A.'s Blackberry Farm. She was a pretty, if very aged, Swiss Toggenburg nanny, with delightful creamy beige and white markings. Almost painfully thin and boney-arsed, we were advised by the staff of Blackberry Farm she was advanced in years and might not have long to live. We picked her up and transported her in the back of my Vauxhall Astra Estate to Black Pig on the last Saturday in August. We called her Capricorn. She was an instant hit with Wally and Beau and seemed happy in her new surroundings.

The very next morning at about 10.00 a.m. we were to hear the shocking news of the death of Princess Diana in a car crash in Paris. I was summoned to attend to the raising of the flag to half-mast at the council offices in Hemel Hempstead, and later to open a Book of Condolences. The rest is history. We renamed Capricorn instantly and she became known thereafter as "Capricorn Diana".

September 1997 We were getting along fine with the small but growing menagerie when I noticed all was not well with Wally's left ear. Now if the reader will recall Wally had just the one eye, the left one. I had thought about having the rather unsightly empty right eye socket sewn up, but had been advised that this might harbour infection and cause a rather more serious problem. So I left the eye socket alone. But when his left ear developed an alarming bulge and drooped forlornly at his left cheek, I felt he could ill afford another facial disfigurement. It might be only cosmetic, and only Wally would have been able to see it through the remaining left eye. But I thought I'd help him retain what was left of his good looks. So there follows an account of what you should do about a classic haematoma in a sheep's ear.

Top Tips for Farmers No.5: How to treat a classic haematoma in a sheep's ear.

1.   First catch your sheep. If he's a friendly, trusting fellow, and your wife or assistant is in the immediate vicinity, this can normally be achieved quite simply by giving her appropriate and clear instructions on how to capture, rope, coral and restrain a strong, adult, one-eyed frightened sheep. You may have to supply her with suitably tensioned rope or chain but she should otherwise manage this unassisted if she's a friendly, helpful and trusting wife or assistant.

2.   Next select your operating instrument. If you haven't a handy surgical scalpel and a supply of bandage and wadding to hand, one of those large bodkin needles they use to sew up sacks should do the trick.

3.   Now take the offending ear and stretch it laterally along a suitable fence rail. If this means moving the sheep closer to a suitable fence rail, your wife or assistant will obligingly manage this, though she may need a little coaxing. It will certainly be quicker, cheaper and more convenient than moving the fence.

4.   With the ear stretched along the fence rail, and a wink to your wife or assistant but no warning whatsoever to the sheep, stab the ear briskly but cleanly in the apparent centre of the bulge in the ear.

5.   You should be rewarded with a spurt of evil-smelling pus or blood, or a combination of the two, and the ear should return quickly to its proper size. Your wife or other assistant may then be directed to release the sheep.

6.   Keep your eye on the ear. If on the day following the above procedure the ear has returned to its swollen appearance, you may have to repeat steps 1-5 above. But this time try two stabs with your bodkin in subtly different places.

7.   If on day three the swelling has yet again returned, repeat steps 1-5 above once more, but this time use a sterile Stanley or other suitable razor knife and slit the ear, rather than stabbing it. You should aim for a slit of about half to one inch in length.

8.   If on day four the obstinate swelling has yet again reappeared and the ear is beginning to look a touch dejected and sorry for itself, it may be time to summon your local large animal vet. He should attend promptly for the fifty or sixty quid you're going to bung him. When he does, and you have gone through step1 above again,

ask him, as sheepishly as you like, whether you have acted appropriately and properly to date. He will probably answer something like this

"No, not really. That's just a common haematoma, or a blood blister to you. Quite common in long-eared animals like Wally. Left alone, it would have returned to normal in time. Right now Wally'll need a hefty dose of antibiotics as you've stabbed him four times. That'll be a hundred quid please."

Wally recovered from the knifing incident and does not seem to have borne me any grudge. And I'd learnt a lot about veterinary surgery technique and fee structures.

The rest of the year was uneventful, until

DECEMBER 1997 Farmer Palmer needed land. He had his own smallholding

with an acre or two of pasture and a series of outbuildings called "Blue Gate Farm" (on account of its blue gate). But this rendered nothing like sufficient winter grazing for the ten or twelve sheep and other species he kept. He asked whether he might park ten of his elderly creatures on our field until the grass began to grow in March. In exchange we were invited to choose three of them which would remain as long term inhabitants of Black Pig Farm. The rest would probably go to the slaughterhouse once fattened up on the spring grass. Enter Roxanne Bella, Hortense and Juanita, together with a number of their colleague sheep, to munch on our lush green pasture.

Roxanne, statuesque, elegant and perhaps a little coquettish in the dark brown and cream markings and splayed horns of her Jacob breed, sported an ankle bracelet on her front right hoof. This gave her the appearance, on a dark evening, of a docklands hooker. Gilly named her Roxanne on the strength of her looks alone. I gave Hortense her name. Also a full Jacob and probably one of Roxanne's last year's lambs, she was thicker set than her mum and quite aloof as far as the opposite sex was concerned. Juanita was a Portland ewe, pure white, smaller than the Jacobs and more compact. Older too, in fact I believe Juanita was very old. Hence her single front tooth. And hence her name ("one eater"). These three ran with the rest of Farmer Palmer's flock and Christmas'ed in luxury on the front field of Black Pig Farm.

5. Nineteen Ninety Eight

FEBRUARY 1998 The year had started uneventfully and our menagerie seemed to be thriving. Indeed all was harmonious in the idyll that Black Pig Farm had become, despite the ever present threat of the settled gypsy encampment of GI Joe and his parents next door. Our three pigs, two sheep and one elderly goat cohabited rather well with the smattering of chickens and nobody seemed to be getting on the other's nerves. We did suffer one minor tragedy on the 23rd of the month when Gilly arrived at Black Pig to find Blossom Dearie, sweet brown and white hen, murdered and ravaged, probably by a fox. Foxes are opportunist hunters; they will normally kill all they find, take one bird away and leave the dead to mature in the sun, as a sort of al fresco larder. In Blossom Dearie's case she was taken during the day probably when grazing and quite unaware of the danger.

As February wore on we did begin to notice a change in Arnold. Not in his personality. He always seemed to be smiling, like some old Chinese mandarin, with a sort of inner wisdom and calm. And he smelled wonderful, as if he'd been steeped in fragrant herbs and spices, as he rolled idly in the dung heap, basked in the sun or gently rootled in the weeds. The change was more physical. To be specific we'd never noticed his testicles before. We had assumed he'd been castrated as a piglet, as most male pigs are. But of course the testicles of an entire VPB boar are rarely visible as for some reason they're tucked away inside the pig in that breed. Arnold's had suddenly manifested themselves in no uncertain way and were gradually achieving mammoth proportions, clearly visible on the exterior. But Arnold displayed no ill effects as he waddled confidently about the field, an object approaching the size of a beach ball protruding ominously from his rear end.

As the weeks wore on we continued to keep an eye on Arnold, but the growth was gradual, and, we hoped, benign.

MARCH 1998 On the 16th we added to the motley flock of chickens with Sarah Kezia and Minnie, Rhode Island cross Sussex hens bought from Woodside Eggs and named after our respective maternal grandmothers. And a few days later we were presented with Attila the Bun, a black/white bunny from School Lane, Eaton Bray, where Stuart Holmes, our local beef farmer, had found him romping free; clearly a tame rabbit that'd become surplus to requirements and been abandoned to cope for itself in the wild. Sarah and Minnie turned out like their namesakes; they busied about the farmyard intent on their duties of laying eggs and keeping house in the Ark.

Attila however was a less enthusiastic inmate. He spent his days in a bijou but comfortable two-bedroomed hutch we'd bought for him from an old gentleman who made it his hobby to produce such constructions. But he was either frightened and confused or just plain furious at his capture and incarceration. Any attempt at handling him was met with a frantic and frankly painful paddling of his back feet while he boxed with the front and lethally sharp claws. I named him Attila the Bun because of his irascible temperament and pugilistic skills. Difficult to feed, almost lethal to clean, the grumpy and resentful Attila lived his spiteful days plotting escape and retribution.

Meanwhile the huge scrotal sack between Arnold's hind legs began to burst. He continued to display no outward signs of discomfort or alarm, but when the sack began to split and small drops of necrotic tissue to litter the grass behind him, it seemed only right to seek the advice of a veterinary surgeon. We selected the large animal vet from nearby Leighton Buzzard. The vet himself was quite a little chap; it was the animals he specialised in that were on the large side. But he'd never chanced upon a Vietnamese Potbellied Pig. Much less one with massive necrotic testicles, which is what he diagnosed on Arnold. The contents of his (Arnold's) scrotal sack had simply died from some mysterious and probably ingested airborne infection. They'd have to be removed before Arnold contracted something else sinister, like septicaemia.

The scene was set. The vet promised to return in three days to perform the necessary "dirty" surgery on Arnold. He supplied a syringe of sedative which I was to administer a couple of hours before his arrival. I meanwhile received training from Farmer Palmer on how to sedate a pig. He showed me the recommended method, which is to hold the syringe in the clenched fist of your right hand, needle concealed but pointing downwards (and you need a large needle for a fat pig as they are rather thick-skinned). Then you thump your pig soundly on the rump twice and on the third thump stab your needle up to its hilt into the rump, at the same time depressing the plunger of the syringe. Job done, Arnold looked a little bewildered but not a jot sedated.

The operation on Arnold was conducted under general anaesthetic which the vet administered on arrival. Another problem with a fat pig is that it is nearly impossible to find a vein and the anaesthetic should be administered intravenously if an accurate quantity is to be administered. The vet administered three or four times the estimated dose subcutaneously before Arnold began to show signs of even slight drowsiness, and another couple of doses finally brought the old fellow to his knees.

The "operation" itself consisted of the vet slitting open Arnold's swollen and torn scrotal sack and the removal by hand of about four or five pounds of grey necrotic tissue. The testicles had simply died on him and transformed into this mass of crumbly minced meat. Tissue removed, the vet stuffed the empty scrotal sack with paper wadding, gave Arnold a hefty dose of antibiotics and left him to regain consciousness. We waited with the old chap as he gently snored away the afternoon. When he hadn't come to by teatime we left him on the stable floor covered with an old blanket and went home for our dinner.

Dinner went down in lumps. We were really concerned for Arnold and wanted to see him on the road to recovery. So at about nine in the evening we returned to Black Pig Farm and made our way across the field to the stable in the pitch dark. We lit a storm lantern in the shed and sat by Arnold for a couple of hours. He had stopped snoring and was shivering and groaning in the darkness, almost as if he were fitting. We realised afterwards that he was probably mid heart attack, as suddenly he became perfectly still. He let out a final groan as he expired.

It has taken me several weeks to write these last few paragraphs. The memory of the pain of the loss of dear old Arnold haunts me still. He was such a dear, characterful charming creature and, as the vet who charged over £600 for his work commented, "he deserved better".

Putting the emotion aside for a moment, the practicalities of decent burial had to be considered. I had never buried anything larger than a medium sized dog; Gilly's dog Sherry in fact, who I planted in the back garden of 523 Watford Road in a shallow grave and a bit of a hurry. I didn't even possess a decent spade, much less the skill or energy to dig through the heavy clay subsoil of Black Pig Farm. So I went into a bit of a panic. I asked my colleagues at the council offices whether the cemetery superintendent would be up for a bit of moonlighting in rural Bedfordshire, never guessing that human grave diggers had long been replaced by mechanical ones. In desperation I did go out and buy myself a decent sharp spade and with this pecked about somewhat noncommittally at the ground under the oaks at Black Pig.

It was Gilly who discovered Graham and Wendy DeMeur of Honeywick Farm, a couple well versed in matters rural, who came to our rescue with pick and shovel and helped bury dear old Arnold under the oaks. The interment of Arnold was to be the start of a mutual help friendship with the DeMeurs that has lasted for more than 20 years. It was Graham who taught me how to dig a hole; a skill that both Gilly and I have put into practice so many times over the intervening years. And it was Wendy, the Amazonian of Honeywick Lane, from whom we were both to learn so much do-it-yourself animal husbandry and folk lore in those early days. The DeMeurs were to come to our rescue twice in the very next month.

APRIL 1998 Silver, the little black and white Leghorn hen Peter Healey had bequeathed to us, was very old. Long past laying eggs, her feet were covered in horny outgrowths, the result of red mite infection contracted in the insanitary conditions often endured by barn fowl. I'd tried, with some success, to remove some of the crunchy growth with a pair of wire snips. But that is an operation best left to a vet, in fact best left alone altogether; the risk of removing the whole foot is too high.

At the end of April Silver became suddenly lacklustre and distinctly disinterested in life. She puffed up, as old hens will, and stood in a corner with her head to the wall. Her time had come, or so I felt, but though I knew the theory behind dispatching a sick hen, I'd not practised it. My only experience of dispatching a hen was years before when I'd discovered a poorly hen outside Gilly's house in Bloomfield Avenue Luton (it was clearly an urban hen). On that occasion I took to the creature with a blunt axe in her mum's coal hole and succeeded in bashing its brains in. Certain that was not the recommended method of chicken disposal, I picked Silver up gently, walked with her across the field and placed her on the dashboard of my car where she seemed relatively comfortable for the short journey to Honeywick Farm and Wendy DeMeur.

To my surprise Wendy also knew the theory, but had never practised it. She preferred to trap the chicken's head under a garden spade and then tug the body violently upwards, breaking its neck. Now I knew that was not the correct protocol, so I thought it's time to educate Wendy in the proper method of hen dispatch, which I'd been told about by many but never actually witnessed. Clutching Silver under my right arm, I took her little head between the thumb and index finger of my left hand and with a deep breath, a sharp twist of the wrist and a mighty flexing of the muscles, pulled her head clean off. There was a lot of blood and an elongated neck. Wendy pronounced Silver well and truly dead, despite the momentary movement in her legs, but expressed surprise that this was the authorised method. I hastily assured her that it is not. The head is not supposed to come off. Her spade method is probably to be preferred. It's certainly cleaner.

I took Silver in bits back to Black Pig Farm for decent burial(s).

The first births at Black Pig Farm occurred on 4th April during a furious downpour. It was early on that Saturday morning when we arrived at the gate in the 2CV with water carriers and buckets, ready for a day's "farming". It was already raining but half way across the field the heavens opened. By the time we reached the shelter of the shed I'd rather grandiosely dubbed "the farmhouse" we were both drenched and we hurried inside, not noticing the little huddle of sheep near the dung pile. So it was still with surprise that when we did eventually emerge from our wooden sanctuary we finally noticed Roxanne, drenched to the woolly skin, gently cleaning and tending to her triplets. Of course we were both enchanted, but we'd not brought a camera with us to record the moment. Gilly busied herself with the other animals. I decided on a mercy dash home to get a camera, obviously the most vital requirement. I ran nimbly back across the field and raced home the 1½ miles (if you can truly be said to be racing anywhere in a 2CV).

There I searched for the 35mm. camera I'd had since my fourteenth birthday and checked that there was yet a film in it. Old technology, I know, but the mobile phone had barely been invented and the smart phone still a thing of fantasy. Just before I hurried back to Black Pig with the camera I called Wendy to inform her of the good news. The conversation went something like this:

"Me: Hi Wendy. Guess what, I'm a proud father! Roxanne's just given birth to triplets.

Wendy: Jolly good. What sexes are they?

Me: Dunno. Haven't looked. I've just come home for me camera to record the event. They're still in the field.

Wendy: I see. So you haven't got them indoors? Out of this rain I mean? And have they had their colostrum? Have you sterilised their umbilicals yet?

Me: Pardon? What's colostrum? Where can I get some? What's this about the umbilicals? And should they really be indoors?

Wendy: I think you better get back to them right now. Graham and I will meet you there.

Me: Thanks Wendy, again".

I hurtled back down The Rye, the 2CV doing rather well on two wheels. Galloped across the field. Graham and Wendy were already there with Gilly and the new brood. Wendy took control of the situation, rubbed life into the little boy lamb Roxanne had produced and got them all under cover. In fact, it seems to have dawned on the DeMeurs that we were less than competent on the animal husbandry front. Roxanne and her newborns would do very much better in their care for a week or so. So they were all loaded into the back of the DeMeur Range Rover, Roxanne still dragging her placenta behind her in the dirt, and they were housed in the dry warmth of a fresh loose box at Honeywick Farm. We learnt from this incident the rudiments of ovine midwifery. There are 5 things to remember:

Top Tips for Farmers No.6: How to deliver and treat lambs, successfully.

1.   Ideally the lambs should be born indoors in a cleansed and lined barn or stable to protect the lambs from the elements and from infection. An indication that the ewe mother is about to give birth and needs to be taken in is the size of her udder (which "bags up" shortly before delivery). Also keep a respectful eye on her vulva, which becomes swollen and can drip a little just before the birth act.

2.   Delivery of the lamb(s) may normally be left to the ewe. Even the least experienced ewe normally knows just what to do. She will probably need no help. You will not require a camera.

3.   As soon as the lamb hits the deck the ewe will clean it up and gnaw through the umbilical chord, releasing her child to the world. You should be present with some iodine or a preparatory antiseptic spray. Spray the bloody umbilcal liberally to fend off infection.

4.   Check that the ewe's teats are operating and that milk is being expressed. You may need to fondle and even squeeze the udder to achieve this but the ewe will not normally object or think you're being fresh. Once milk is being expressed, guide each lamb to a nipple and ensure it is "plugged on". Your average lamb is at least clever enough to learn this quickly. Shouldn't need showing twice. This first expression of milk contains the colostrum; all the vitamins and minerals essential to health in a new born lamb. It is vital that they get their share of colostrum.

5.   Within the first week of life you should dock the tails of all lambs and castrate the males. To do this you will need an elastrator and a quantity of rings from your agricultural supplies merchant. You may also need some instruction from a professional. Tails are easy, but you should be sure to leave enough of a stump to protect the female's private parts. It's not that they're modest, just an attempt to protect from infection. With the males, you must ensure that both the testes are contained within the sack you are about to constrict with the rubber ring. This is best achieved by holding the lamb in the air by its front legs and perhaps telling it a joke, or relaxing it with a short story, perhaps a little song. In any event, you do not want to leave one testicle inside your lamb, as we shall see. So do not be shy to palpate the scrotal sack.

For none of the above do you require a camera.

We named Roxanne's children April (after Gilly's middle name, though that's in French), Raindance (because when we first saw her she was dancing in the rain) and Jacob (because he was half that breed). All three were black, as all Jacob crosses seem to be, and as cute as a box of monkeys. They all developed horns and over time Jacob's were to become massive, performing very nearly two complete turns. They returned to Black Pig Farm with their mum a week after their birth, happy, healthy and playful.

In that week, on 8th April to be precise, Farmer Palmer marched across the field with something fluffy, golden and ginger under his arm. Tuesday was undoubtedly one of the most beautiful creatures I have ever set eyes on. Perfectly formed, pretty in the creamy golden coat of a Portland ram but only about fifteen inches from hoof to horn tip, he stole my heart and became an instant favourite. He'd been orphaned at the time of his birth and Farmer Palmer didn't have the time to devote to his upbringing. He needed bottle feeding and careful attention for a while so we took him home and housed him in a box in the lounge. Gilly named him after me, or at least after the me she knew when we first met. I took that as quite a compliment, and an appropriate one. We shared the same good looks, great charm and extremely high self esteem.

Now one thing we learnt from that exercise is that sheep really cannot be house trained. But they make great travelling companions. Tuesday's wish to play and to please was irrepressible. I took him in the car to visit Paul and Jo Wilson and he pee'ed on the floor of their kitchen. He was a welcomed visitor to the offices of Dacorum Borough Council where I was Director and he wow'ed the young girls in the car park where he entertained my female staff with his cute looks and winning smile. But he couldn't stay at home. It was just unnatural. He returned within the week to Black Pig under the guidance and watchful eye of old Wally Patch.

A few days after his arrival at Black Pig he was joined by the returning Roxanne, Jacob, April and Raindance. Jacob and Tuesday bonded as firm friends and brothers in mischief from day one and competed with each other for who could grow the most luxurious, exuberant and curvaceous horns.

MAY 1998 The menagerie was growing slowly but steadily in these early days. On 12th May we adopted Thunder, the black pygmy goat, from cousin Janet and her partner Oz. Born during the crescendo moments of a violent thunder storm and one of twins, Thunder had lost his sibling Lightning to an early and undisclosed illness. The little fellow was living on his own in a shed in Janet and Oz's cramped back garden. It was thought fairer to give him the freedom of our open pasture at Black Pig and Gilly assumed the mantle of goat motherhood for a second time.

Thunder was a playful and a lively fellow. He would jump nimbly onto the feed table and nuzzle and kiss Gilly as she busied herself with the evening feed. He was easily maintained and just needed the six weekly foot trim that I'd learnt to render on Capricorn, a daily helping of goat mix and some juicy hedges and weeds to keep him amused.

JUNE 1998 With the passing of dear old Arnold, Black Pig Farm only boasted two of the creatures for which it had been named. I had acquired a peculiar predilection for pigs and we'd heard of a curious operation in the north of the county where we might get us a few more. Paradise Farm was that curious operation; a small and unobtrusive area of highway verge on the main A6 just outside the village of Clophill. The half acre or so of overgrown verge had sited on it an elderly and ramshackle residential caravan, a ramshackle and derelict gentleman of the road, and a plethora of pigs. The operation looked distinctly rustic to me, and probably not desperately legal. But the skinny and grubby old boy who'd taken up residence in the less than bijou accommodation seemed kindly enough. He explained that he'd unwittingly become a dumping ground for unwanted animals, predominantly pigs, and those predominantly of the Vietnamese Potbellied variety. He was overrun with the little blighters and we could help ourselves.

Now catching a piglet in long grass is no mean feat. They're slippery, quick and cunning. If you're even slightly bow-legged you're not going to be successful. It was more by luck, I think, than judgement that between the three of us and with a lot of ducking and diving, not to mention a bit of blue language, we managed to capture and contain in a cardboard box three of the creatures, each about the size of a large rat. Suitably boxed up we made for home.

Blanche, Bunter and Candace-Marie took up residence in our summer house at the bottom of the garden on D Day. Too small and quick to be given free range at Black Pig, we'd decided to quarter them at home pending their reaching something approaching adolescence and a size at which they could be contained. So for a few weeks they were to luxuriate in their straw bed at the bottom of the garden, being cleaned out, fed and watered twice daily. Delightful little creatures are piglets. They are affectionate, appreciative of one's attention, highly intelligent and as mentioned above the cleanest of creatures. We were to have a lot of fun with our box of pigs.

Ten days later we were to adopt Clarice and William (named after my parents), two bright yellow canaries, cast-offs from G. I. Joe, the gypsy lad who neighboured us at Black Pig Farm. Neither of us were or are particularly into caged birds, but Joe was going to "neck" them if we couldn't take them on. So they were housed in a cage hastily bought second hand and spent their days at home chomping on Trill and millet; they were hardly appropriate for a farm environment.

JULY 1998 This month our experiences were with birth and death ornithological. The miracle of birth is not so dramatic when it's from an egg. But the arrival of two different kinds of duck, appearing as they seemed to from the loins of an unsuspecting chicken, were nonetheless remarkable for the mother, India. The fact that India had exhibited the signs of broodiness in June and we'd capitalised on those signs by placing under her in the dead of night four or five fertilised duck eggs must have had something to do with it. India didn't look too surprised when we arrived on the 9th to find her with her new charges, and she was to prove a competent mother. We named the three Aylesburys Ocean, Lake and River, and the solitary Khaki Campbell (clearly a different father) Puddle.

The very next day we were to notice a tiny bundle of furriness in Clarice and William's cage. We'd spotted the egg, of course, a few days earlier, and hadn't given it a thought, rather expecting it to be a figment of our imagination. But when Dickie appeared I dashed out to the nearest pet store in Dunstable and purchased a small nesting box for Clarice to poach her little sprog. Unfortunately Dickie only lasted a fortnight. Clarice threw off the bonds of motherhood on the 24th when she seems to have lost interest in her chick. Dickie received a decent burial in a matchbox for a coffin and in our back garden.

Meanwhile down on the farm Fenella, last of the Plymouth Barred Rock hens, went AWOL, presumed the victim of a fox, missing in action on the 15th.

AUGUST 1998 August was a busy month down on the farm. Gilly had existed and looked after our various charges thus far with water transported in her car in water carriers. We had exchanged the expired 2CV, Jean Paul, for the Land Rover by this time so that water transportation was a little more practical, but still quite an arduous daily task. In August we went into partnership with Keith and Jane who owned the field next door and hired Roger the Dodger, a dinky 1½ ton digger. Neighbour Keith piloted Roger slowly across the fields cutting a slender trench a couple of feet deep and a couple of hundred yards long. I followed behind Roger and directed operations while Gilly fed lengths of the blue plastic Alkathene pipe into the trench and backfilled with earth. In this way within the week of that hot and sultry August we connected both Keith and Jane's field and Black Pig Farm to the mains and we were to enjoy metred water from a tap for the rest of our stay.

Later in the month Graham De Meur helped with (did) the waterproofing of the stables when the roofing felt gave up the ghost. Later still we constructed, with Graham's help, Quakatoa, a natty little wire enclosure for the ducks, to keep them safe from the fox. And then of course we had the annual grass cut to contend with. Stuart Holmes, the beef farmer who'd befriended us, dealt with the hay crop, leaving the bulk of it in our field covered in tarpaulins. We sold it by the bale even then and made a few quid to supplement the animal feed bills.

But August was also to bring with it another foray into the world of amateur veterinary surgery. Capricorn, our elderly but stately Swiss Toggenburg goat, developed bloat. Now bloat in any animal can be uncomfortable and sometimes fatal. But bloat in a goat can be quite alarming too. It's thought to be caused by overindulgence in protein rich grass and other vegetation, especially in the older animal. And it manifests itself by the animal's belly swelling to unnatural proportions giving it the appearance of a lopsided battleship. Capricorn was quite ancient and bony in goat terms, probably 16 or 17 years old. And after a bellyful of rich August grass (N.B. the goat is a natural browser of bushes and trees from which they get plenty of roughage. Grass is protein rich and more the purview of your average sheep) her belly was distended to unnatural proportions so that she walked with difficulty and a peculiar gait. Clearly something needed to be done to excise what was in effect a ginormous fart, indigestion of monumental proportions. What we did is recorded below.

Top Tips for Farmers No.7: How to treat a goat with bloat.

1.   First run about a bit in a panic in the firm belief that your goat is going to explode and cover you in intestines and other unmentionable body parts.

2.   Next seek advice from your local sheep and dairy farmer who is likely to have the solution to your problem. Peter Healey of Common Farm will do if in doubt, except he's dead now.

3.   The farmer will probably suggest you drench your goat and supply you if you are desperate/lucky with a small quantity of the correct fluid with which to drench your goat in a natty little bottle.

4.   Next catch your goat and drench it. This involves pouring the fluid supplied over the goat's back and shoulders and rubbing it well into the nether regions. Your goat may be a little perturbed, even confused, at your attentions. But you must persist until your goat is well and truly drenched with the stuff.

5.   When the procedure outlined above proves less than successful, report your actions and findings to the farmer and seek further advice. He will probably supply you with a further dosage of the fluid and either lend you a copy of his trusty *Chambers Dictionary, 1994 edition* and point you at page 512, or if he is not a farmer with literary pretensions simply point out that "to drench" an animal is to force a dose of liquid medicine down its throat. And he will probably do this with a sigh.

6.   Return to your goat with guts ache and while one of you holds the goat the other must force the little bottle between the goat's reluctant teeth and pour the fluid down its neck, holding the mouth of the indignant goat shut to ensure the stomach receives the full dosage.

7.   With any luck you'll be rewarded with a cataclysmic fart from the goat's rear end a few minutes later. In any event the bloat will soon dissipate naturally.

SEPTEMBER 1998
Pearl by colour, by nature and by name, was a pretty little cockatiel we adopted from Kay who lived on the corner of The Orchards. She had belonged to Kay's mother but with the old girl losing the plot became surplus to requirements and Kay, it seems, did not have room for her. I took instantly to Pearl; she was a bird of character and of distinction. She would happily come out of her cage and perch on my finger where I'd feed her crisps and red wine. Like Gilly, she was particularly fond of cheese and onion and a beakful of Merlot. Looked after, a cockatiel will live into its twenties, and I think Pearl was well into middle age when she came into our care. But she was no trouble to us at all and we enjoyed her company immensely. As she grew older her claws and beak became a little problematic as they will grow for ever in the wild. In captivity Pearl needed a little podiatry and beak alignment. I attended to her every other week with the application of toe nail clippers and an emery board. So you can count pssitacine beautician amongst my many talents.

The day after Pearl arrived with her cage and vanity case we visited the RSPCA's Blackberry Farm and took delivery of William II (Rufus), Mary, Maise and Puddleduck, four small call ducks, to take up residence in the newly completed Quackatoa.

We lost Attila the psychotic bunny rabbit on my 49th. birthday. He'd always been a grumpy little shit, resentful perhaps of his status as a captive rabbit. Difficult, even dangerous to handle with his ferocious teeth and hind claws that paddled like a pair of scimitars, he made a bid for freedom on that fateful day and escaped our clutches, somehow shaking off the bondage of his hutch at Black Pig. He was remarkably easy to catch, bearing in mind those powerful back legs. But the shock of recapture was too much. He had a heart attack in my arms and expired on the spot. We buried him under that loathsome hutch.

OCTOBER 1998 This was a fairly uneventful month at Black Pig Farm. Which was just as well really as back in Totternhoe Road the situation of Gilly's elderly parent and step parent, her mum and Stan the Ungreat, was becoming critical. Stan was hospitalised it seemed every other week with a blocked catheter, a stroke or some other unidentified complaint, and Gilly had become his unwitting carer and her mother's unpaid taxi service to and from the hospital. Up and down the Luton Road to the Luton and Dunstable Hospital she and her mum would thunder in the 30 year old Land Rover. Then she'd pick up Badger and trundle off down the farm to tend to the animals. Meanwhile I luxuriated in a warm office in Hemel Hempstead, blissfully unaware of the pressures she must have been enduring. Although in hindsight, I believe, Black Pig must have been by then a happy excuse for her to escape the clutches of her mother and her unfortunate choice of a second husband.

At the fag end of the month Red May, the pretty Rhode Island Red hen, suddenly became sick and died of an unknown illness. I picked her up at the close of play late one dark October evening as she languished by a barn. Tipping her up her beak opened and a stream of foul smelling gunk flowed out of her. I believe she was crop bound. I laid her gently on the ground and she died moments later. We were to find this later; that chickens come and chickens go. There is not much permanence or commitment in the life of your average chicken.

On the same day as Red May left us we were joined by a new challenge in our lives in the person of Naseem, a very attractive if smelly pure white albino ferret. Naseem was another of Gypsy Joe's cast offs. He just wasn't catching enough rabbits, so he had to go. If we hadn't taken him on Joe would certainly have dispatched him. So we hurriedly obtained from somewhere a medium sized rabbit hutch to house him and he stayed in the back garden for the rest of our stay in Bedfordshire.

Naseem was an attractive addition to the menagerie. But he was smelly, and his shit stank like no other animal I had encountered. So Gilly had the unenviable task of cleaning out the hutch regularly; essential to keep the stench to manageable proportions. He escaped from the hutch once, and we never thought we'd see him again. But he found his way to Wendy and Graham's at Honeywick Farm and almost ran into Wendy's arms like a homing ferret. This whole affair was quite remarkable as Honeywick Farm was a couple of miles away from our house, Naseem had not met Wendy and they were certainly not acquainted, and Naseem was only missing from home for three or four hours when we received Wendy's call.

"Hullo Gilly. Have you got a white ferret?"

"Well we did have one such. But he's buggered off!"

"Well he's just come down the road. Introduced himself as Naseem. He says he'd like you to pick him up if you have time."

NOVEMBER 1998 Naseem might well have been a touch lonely in his hutch.

Most animals need and crave the company of others of their kind. So it's just possible that Naseem was on the lookout for company, a sort of search for socialisation, when he made his bid for freedom. He was in luck as it happens. A fortnight after the events just described he was joined by Vinnie, a pretty but equally smelly brown pole cat, a gift from Wendy at Honeywick. Vinnie was a solitary ferret as well. The two were delighted with each other's company and became firm friends and blood brothers in their extended hutch. Yes, I extended the hutch by adding to it another of the same dimensions. The two hutches were connected by a length of sewer pipe and hutch one became the couple's bedroom with hutch two their living and dining quarters. They were to stay with us in the back garden. It has to be said that ferrets do not mix socially with rabbits or chickens, or ducks for that matter. They are likely as not to eat all three species, rather than befriend them, as we shall see. So keeping them at Black Pig was contraindicated

DECEMBER 1998 Stan died just before Christmas and this should have been a

happy release for us all. Unfortunately Gilly's mum seems to have had a mental accident at her husband's bedside and was never the same. I shall leave that story for another day. But the impact Stan's death had on Gilly's life cannot be measured. As far as Black Pig Farm was concerned it meant that she had a part time pooh picker to help with the evening duties. Her mum became very efficient at this of an evening for a year or so, even if this was brought to a swift and ignominious end by her taking a dive into the muddy wallow.

6. Nineteen Ninety Nine

FEBRUARY 1999 We were introduced to Blackjack on the 14th. A particularly delightful small black Welsh pony, Blackjack came to us almost as the result of a conspiracy. He'd belonged, as had several of our charges, to Gypsy Joe. When he got tired of the novelty of Blackjack he'd given him to Wendy De Meur of Honeywick Farm. And we adopted him from her.

We were really not horsey types back then, but Blackjack was a small and gentle introduction to the equine world. I built him a stable out of pallet wood and feather edge boarding, with a corrugated plastic roof. Blackjack could come and go as he pleased and he grazed his days away on the pasture at Black Pig Farm with a daily supper of sweet hay. The De Meurs, well specifically Graham, fashioned a two-wheeled trap with bicycle wheels, a couple of shafts and a seat which had done service as a cocktail cabinet. Blackjack had clearly already been instructed on the intricacies of towing a trap and I soon learned to drive him. I once drove that two-wheeled cocktail cabinet from Honeywick Farm to Black Pig and got Jack up to a reasonable gallop on the home straight. It's not much to do with reins, I was to find out. Driving a pony is mainly done with the voice.

MARCH 1999 We lost Capricorn Diana, the aged Swiss Toggenburg goat, on the 6th March. A gentle, pretty and elegant creature, she'd always put me in mind of the Scapegoat of ancient Jewish tradition; the creature upon which all the sins and transgressions of the world were heaped before she was sent out into the wilderness as some sort of caprine atonement. She had always been spare and bony and we'd been warned by the RSPCA from whom we adopted her that her days were likely numbered. She must have been well into her teens and I think it was simply old age that took her in the end. She was euthanized in the hay barn by lethal injection and a kindly vet on an unusually sunny afternoon and buried on Boot Hill with Arnold.

March was a catastrophic month for ducks at Black Pig Farm. We were to lose Puddle, Puddleduck and Maise one murderous night when G.I.Joe's ferret got into the haybarn and simply killed and ate them. Then William II and Mary escaped down the stream that bordered on Black Pig and were never seen again. In fear of further attack from fox or ferret we offered the survivors of this carnage, Ocean, Lake and River, to Wendy of Honeywick farm in the hope they'd survive longer there. The mud at Black Pig had become impossible anyway, and though we missed the duck eggs for which I and my colleagues at the council had developed an inordinate taste, washing the ducks out in the bath at home had become a less than pleasant task for both us and them.

On a more positive note we were to receive, on the 9th, fourteen orphan lambs from farmer Peter Healey to raise and ween. Their mothers having died during or shortly after lambing, these little creatures would need to be bottle fed on milk supplement and then gradually introduced to commercial sheep nuts until they could fend for themselves. In some cases they would be one of three triplets, normally the weakest, taken from its mother and siblings to give all a better chance. For sheep averagely only have two nipples and enough milk for two lambs. We named our new, if temporary, charges after the dots of coloured sheep dye they'd been marked with to identify lamb with mother. So it was that Apple, Violet, Ruby, Blue, Dot, Fat Larry (because she was fat), Prima Donna (because she cried a lot), Nugget (I cannot recall why), Donkey (because as a Charolais sheep with a protruberant Roman nose he resembled one such), Mouse (because he was tiny and also because he resembled one), Georgie (perhaps Gilly's favourite), Gonzales (very slow at eating), Tarzanne (weak, skinny with no muscle fibre at all) and Nel(short for Nelson-because she was clearly blind) were housed in a square of sheep hurdles in our garage. And we became suburban farmers for a month.

We became famous in the village and the envy of our friends and neighbours. A stream of visitors, enchanted children, delighted adults and strangers curious at the bleating, took in the wonders of our tiny farm in a garage. Of course for Gilly the work was immediately multiplied by two at least. Those lambs had to be fed their statutory pint of replacement milk apiece, thrice reducing to twice daily, and Peter supplied industrial quantities of the stuff in powdered form. To this had to be added water at the correct temperature (about 35☐C as I recall) and the same consistency as if it'd come from the udder. Even feeding two hungry lambs at a time this meant 7 feedings three times a day, and this on top of the duties at Black Pig some mile – and-a-half away. Then there was playtime. The lambs spent most of their time luxuriating under a heat lamp to simulate their mothers' body temperature. But twice daily they were allowed a romp in the back garden where they'd gambol around in the spring sunshine, arse around play fighting, eat the miniature ornamental apple tree and the other exotic plants to be found in a suburban village garden and pull washing off the line. When playtime was over Gilly'd call out:-

"Posse, posse, posse!"

in that commanding falsetto I've become used to but they'd never heard. And all the lambs would come running (or rather "bouncing"; playful lambs bounce on all fours rather than run) to her call. The sensible ones, that is. Because not all of the lambs were sensible. Nel, for instance, was probably blind. Definitely not the ticket. Tarzanne was undersized and probably not destined for much in the terms of success in the lamb world. And Gonzales was determined to starve himself to death by the shear speed of his eating. Indeed we originally called Gonzales "Slow Sucker", changing his name to Gonzales in an attempt to encourage him to speed up a bit.

That month with Peter Healey's lambs was at the very least instructive. We were both to learn a lot about lambs, their ways, their dreams and aspirations and their goals in life. Which is predominantly to die. Theory has it that most lambs have as their main goal in life to die, and to die as early as possible. Graham DeMeur once told me that the more intelligent a lamb is, the earlier it is likely to achieve its target of dying. The most intelligent are of course still-born.

APRIL 1999 At the end of a month, by which time most of the lambs had prospered well under Gilly's care and were fully weaned onto sheep nuts, they were to return to Peter Healey. He would keep them for a further year during which they'd have a bellyful of good British meadow grass and then either be added to the flock or go to slaughter. So it was with real regret that Apple, Violet, Ruby, Blue, Dot, Fat Larry, Prima Donna and Nugget left the sanctuary of our suburban garage and took their chances at Common Farm on the 8th. As Gilly's 48th. birthday was approaching I could think of no better present than half a dozen weaned lambs to add to the flock at Black Pig. I chose two particular favourites, Donkey and Mouse, of course. And then the heart took over from the head. I selected the weakest of the rest, the also-rans who probably would not make it either to the flock or the slaughter yard. So the skinny Tarzanne, blind Nel, brain damaged Gonzales (Slow Sucker) and little underdeveloped Georgie stayed a while longer. I paid Peter Healey £25 per head for these little chaps. Defective though some of them were, it was I think the finest present I could have thought of.

Black Pig Farm had become a bit of a dumping ground for waifs and strays of the area. I suppose we were more convenient than the RSPCA at Blackberry Farm. Or maybe we were just confused for that establishment on account of the similarity in names. Whatever. On 4th April we took in Barbara, an elderly hen and the last of Wendy De Meur's after she'd been wiped out by a marauding and murderous fox. Barbara came to us to convalesce from her shock and the inevitable PTSD. She was to live out the fag end of her life with our few hens. Later in the month we added to this few with a couple of classic Sussex white/Rhode Island Red crosses we named McGraw and Goodheart. These make good layers and I had become famous at work for sharing our bounty of eggs when we became "eggbound" down on the farm. I'd developed quite a regular clientele for duck and chicken eggs, and the attention of the Chief Environmental Health Officer who politely informed me I needed a licence to purvey and clearance from him on Food Hygiene and Health and Safety aspects of the endeavour.

On the 6th Farmer Stuart Holmes deposited with us an Old English gentleman rabbit with its traditional brown and white markings. He'd found the fellow in his back garden and recognised it as either an escapee or an abandoned pet. An Old English is quite a special breed and no wild creature. Holmes (named after Stuart and because he wore a deerstalker and monacle just like Sherlock) took up residence in the hutch recently vacated by the psychotic Attila.

The rest of the month became a slow and distressing carnage at the garage in Totternhoe Road. The lambs we'd helped rear, at least the ones I'd bought for Gilly's birthday, were really doomed from the start. Donkey and Mouse were fine strong examples and were to be with us for some years, surviving the migration west in 2001 when we moved to Devon. But the others were all quite weak, and were destined to achieve their goal of an early grave even sooner than we expected.

Tarzanne was the first to go. Try as we might, we never could get her to put on weight. She was nothing but rather dry skin and bone when she suddenly went into an alarming bloat on Gilly's birthday. We rubbed her little belly furiously in an attempt to reduce the swelling. We even took her to the vet in desperation hoping he could work his magic. The vet administered a dose of expensive antibiotics and declared she'd be OK in an hour or so. Well she wasn't. Tarzanne more or less imploded and died in my arms later that evening, probably of heart attack induced by the agony of the bloat. We transported the little corpse to Black Pig Farm, her first visit, and buried her without ceremony on Boot Hill.

Two days later blind Nel expired of causes unknown, though we suspected that she was brain damaged as well as blind. Then, a further week or so later Gonzales (aka Slow Sucker) finally starved himself to death.

MAY 1999 That left little Georgie, Gilly's favourite of the Peter Healey Six, alone in the garage under a heat lamp in Totternhoe Road. When he, too, succumbed to bloat on the first of the month she was distraught but, I think, a little resigned to his fate. We didn't trouble the vet on this occasion; in fact we'd lost all faith in Bedfordshire vets as far as sheep were concerned by this time. Late in the evening on that fateful day I did seriously consider the farmer's last ditch attempt with bloat; an incision with a sharp implement in the abdomen just forward of the hind leg. I just didn't have the nerve and couldn't have borne causing Georgie the extra pain without a certainty of success. Georgie spared me the decision. He died a few moments later, again in my arms, his little head twisting around in his last moment to look me in the face with an enquiring expression, as if to say, "Why me?". That little face stays with me to this day.

The sudden and relentless loss of these four little lambs was of course devastating for both of us at the time. The years and the intervening events have helped to soften the raw edges of those feelings of loss, and what we now know can help to offer an explanation. A new born lamb needs its mother's colostrum, the first and rather gloopy milk that exudes from its mother's teats. This is vital to the success of the lamb and without it the lamb is usually doomed to a short and defective existence. Most of Peter Healey's lambs would have been born outside and they have to fend for themselves from day one. It is very likely that the four "defective" lambs I rescued from Peter Healey had missed out on their vital colostrum and were doomed from the start. Another steep and agonising learning curve to climb.

The rest of this month was characterised by chickens. Loretta was a beautiful pure white Sussex hen who made a bid for freedom. Driving home from Black Pig Farm along the Rye on the 29th May we were overtaken by a speeding lorry, packed to the gunwales with crates of Sussex Whites. As the lorry swerved in front of us, the driver wrestling frantically with the wheel, Loretta (I guessed that might be her name though we'd never been formally introduced) squeezed through the bars of her wooden crate perched high on the truck's flat bed. She glimpsed to right and to left. Chickens can do that without moving their heads, as they have one eye on each side. It's looking forward that's more difficult for them. Anyway, without the least hesitation she launched herself into the unknown in a truly magnificent bid for freedom. She cleared the hedge and landed in the village's cricket field, somewhere near silly mid off I suspect.

I acted with my usual lightning reactions and steely panache, swerved left into the cricket field and retrieved the panting and confused Loretta before she could gather herself. She seemed uninjured. Just a little puffed from her exertions. I conducted a citizen's arrest on the unsuspecting Loretta. We took her straight back to Black Pig Farm and after the briefest of check overs placed her in the custody of the chicken ark. We were one hen up.

On the very next day Barbara, the elderly and traumatised hen from Honeywick we'd taken in for convalescence, puffed up and died, we presume simply old age, and maybe a touch of PTSD. She was consigned to Boot Hill and state funeral.

JUNE 1999 Little Cloud was a cute little Suffolk cross lamb; as his name

suggests, he looked like a fluffy passing cloud as he gambolled in the grass. I think he was a sort of consolation prize from Peter Healey for taking on the responsibility of rearing his lambs in our garage and then selling us the duff ones. Little Cloud arrived, carried across the field by Peter on the afternoon of the 8th. Another orphan lamb, his mother had rolled on him in her death throes and injured his right back leg. Little Cloud was partially lame, but he managed to get about using the gammy leg as a sort of prop, or crutch. So his gambolling in the sun was kind of awkward, his gait stumbling. But Little Cloud was a courageous fighter; he was destined to fight to the very end, as we shall see, and to outlive all his contemporaries by a considerable margin. He kept up with the flock, was uncomplaining and even quite affectionate for a sheep. He seemed to fit in well with the others and become over time a bit of a guru, a legend in his own time, an expert in self-preservation in the rough and tumble of the life of a sheep.

The gammy right leg had a small but suppurating wound in the groin area which needed daily attention in the early days. As farm foreman and amateur vet this was one of my jobs. For the first couple of months of his stay with us I'd have to first catch Little Cloud in the field. More agile then than now, this I achieved with the use of a wheelbarrow. I would chase the little fellow around the field with the barrow, catch him with a rather neat rugby tackle learnt in my youth at the Grammar School, and then dump him on his back as gently as I knew how into the wheelbarrow, which then became a sort of impromptu operating table. From my pocket I'd take a large hypodermic syringe filled with saline solution. Then I'd carefully drain the thick yellow pus from the wound with the gentle palpation of thumb and forefinger, and wash out the cavity with the saline. I quickly became quite adept at this operation.

And whilst Little Cloud continued the pretence of running from me in fear of his life, I like to think he rather enjoyed the attention. Within a couple of months the wound seemed to heal up and my daily routine with him was no longer necessary. But we formed a sort of a bond and a mutual affection that was, again I like to believe, lifelong.

JULY 1999 It was mayhem and virtual wipeout on the 10th when we arrived at Black Pig to find Bunty, Holmes and Loretta, murdered by the fox in Quackatoa and Bertie, Bunty's partner, missing from the matrimonial hutch and presumed taken by the same fox chancing by. We were to lose many chickens, ducks and small furry creatures in this way over the years but this visit from Reynard was particularly depressing. We buried the remains of the little creatures in a mass grave and placed a heavy rock on the top to prevent nocturnal exhumation.

A few days before these murderous events we introduced Daisy to the menagerie. A pretty and lively pure white horned sanaan goat, Daisy was adopted from the RSPCA's Blackberry Farm. She'd apparently been found wandering in the countryside and had the marks of abuse on her, or so we were told. She only had one udder, and it was alleged by the RSPCA that the other had been cut off by her abusers. However, from a cursory inspection it seemed to us that the abusers must have been a bunch of delinquent surgeons, the udder having been extremely professionally removed. And Daisy was a delightfully mischievous little creature, clearly humanised and without a trace of the trauma you'd expect from an abused animal. She had a way of tossing her head at you that could, with the long and dangerously sharp horns that adorned her crown, be a touch disconcerting. She was to wear a pair of Badger's old plastic squeaky Christmas crackers as protective sheaths about the farm. These rendered her safe and respectable in polite company, if they did make her look a bit of a clown.

As for the remaining udder, well that was large and pendulous and very full of milk. A sign that Daisy had kidded in the recent past; she probably had young at home pining for her return. That udder clearly needed attention, I thought, or without it she'll surely burst. Now I'd never milked an animal in my life; never had occasion to as it happens. But, I thought, it cannot be rocket science. So it was that, fancying myself as some sort of latter day Heidi, I took an aluminium jug in one hand and Daisy's pendulous bosom in the other. I had not thought to provide myself with a milking stool so had to kneel on the barn floor with my head nestling on Daisy's right flank. A sort of gentle palpation should do the trick, I thought, ending in a firm squeeze. And that did indeed seem to do the trick. For her part Daisy was unprotesting, almost seemed to be enjoying the attention. I soon had a steady stream of her rich, fragrant and creamy milk frothing in the jug. The udder reduced from its alarming proportions to a limp and flaccid sack. Daisy sighed with relief. I handed Gilly the foaming jug with its contents sloshing about the barn floor, my eyes bright with pride at the obvious achievement.

Of course the following day the udder was back to its swollen proportions and I had to repeat the exercise. I did take a swig of the milk straight from the jug on one occasion; it was warm, creamy, delicious, if a little rich. A few seconds later I felt distinctly bilious and thought better of trying any more. This was clearly a task I would have to perform daily for perhaps the rest of Daisy's life, I thought. I'd read somewhere, I think in one of those dystopian post-apocalyptic novels of my youth, perhaps John Wyndham's *The Day of the Triffids* that unmilked cows that expect to be milked but are disappointed because the farmer has died, explode. I didn't want to have to deal with the aftermath of an exploding Daisy. So I took instructions from the Blackberry Farm vet (remember the internet was not so helpful in 1999 as it is now). It seems that an unmilked animal, if left to its own devices, will ultimately "dry up". So after that I left Daisy's tit unmolested, and it did. But I think my early attentions and concern for Daisy's welfare paid dividends for the bond that grew between us. She was a delightfully playful and confident creature and a fond favourite of mine for the short time we had her.

If Daisy was the rising star down on Black Pig Farm, on the domestic front we were to receive, on 13 July, another of Gypsy Joe's cast-offs; a tiny green and yellow flat-capped canary he'd hatched from an egg. We named her Elsie, after Gilly's mum. She took up residence with William and Clarice in a sort of informal ménage-à-trois in the cage at home. The three seemed to co-exist quite happily, as had their namesakes.

AUGUST 1999 It was just after 11.00 in the morning of the 11th that the few

chickens we had took to their beds in the ark in Quackatoa. We hadn't perhaps noticed, as they already had, or perhaps they'd just sensed it; the sudden change in the atmosphere. The bright sunny day had adopted an eerie orange/ green hue. Light breezes dropped to an incandescent stillness. Some of the larger animals glanced around themselves, uncertain, almost nervous of the portents of gloom. Wally bleated plaintively. The pigs, normally unconcerned with their surroundings so long as they were being fed, gave each other querulous, enquiring looks as if to say "What's this all about then?"

Jacob and his mate Tuesday had been gambolling in the sun moments ago, teasing the crippled Little Cloud and being scolded by little brown Beau for their naughtiness. Suddenly, as if in concert, Jacob and Tuesday turned their attention to me. They stared at me with cold hatred in their eyes, nostrils flaring, sputum dribbling from bared teeth. Now I was not to know that both these strong young sheep were yet entire; I'd ringed them myself in their first week of life but I'd botched the job and they were both monorchidic, with one testicle potent and strangled within. Was it pure unbridled malevolence born of hatred for me and my bungled insults to their manhood? Was it an excess of testosterone? Or was it the solar eclipse that occurred at precisely that moment that caused the two entire rams to charge me at the same time with their not inconsiderable horns? I turned and ran, of course, but was encumbered by bucket and dung rake, so I had to stand my ground. Which was a little futile really, in hindsight. The pair of them charged full on and despite my protests and ministrations hurled me off my feet and almost into orbit.

I lay where I landed, bucket, dung rake and pride dented. I was not going to risk a further bout with a butt. But they didn't seem interested in a return match. The light was returning to the day as fast as it had left. Jacob and Tuesday returned to munching meadow grass. Wally and Beau to their accustomed nonchalance. The pigs returned to the dung heap. The chickens returned from their roost. And I returned to picking up pooh with dented bucket and dung rake and just a little bruised by the encounter.

It was as if the eclipse had never happened. Certainly the animals appeared to have suffered no lasting effects. I even began to doubt the celestial event had actually taken place.

One week later little Clarice canary succumbed to a short and undiagnosed illness or perhaps she was freaked out by a cat as she took the sun outside in the aviary at home. I think it was too late to be put down to the aftershock of a solar eclipse.

SEPTEMBER 1999 *Animal Rescuers* was a short-lived Channel 4 reality TV

prog in the same vein and following on from the popularity of BBC's *Pet Rescue*. It was hosted by the late Linda Bellingham, although in the director's cut she only did the voice over. And it was the second in Gilly's career of successful TV reality docu-dramas. Airing in late 1999 it portrayed her heroic rescue from the obscurity of the RSPCA's Blackberry Farm of what were to become two of the stars of Black Pig Farm; Banquo, the tall and majestic Alpine goat and his mate Fuchsia, lesser in size but huge in personality, a black and white pygmy goat.

Banquo was quite massive for a goat. He had the most amazing and quite deadly horns, like a pair of crossed scimitars that he'd whirl around and threaten you with if he didn't like the cut of your jib. He'd been castrated at Blackberry Farm and treated for the removal of a small benign growth on his neck. We'd watched it on the telly so we had a foretaste of the fellow's feisty character and knew he'd be one to watch.

We had no idea of his antecedents or age, but it was clear he'd been castrated well into adulthood as the male goat does not normally grow horns of any size if he's castrated soon after birth. And Banquo's horns were absolutely massive. A swift swipe from them was to cure Gilly's carpel tunnel syndrome and save her the necessity of a serious operation. I do not recall having the nerve to pair back Banquo's hooves in the time we had him. Just as well as when you're dealing with a large and feisty goat's hooves you can't keep an eye on his horns and I really didn't fancy one of those scimitars up me arse!

Fuchsia was much smaller, about the same size as Thunder, with whom she was soon to pal up. Another characterful little mare though, and with a decent set of horns to hold on to. She soon learnt to copy Thunder's jaunty walk and they were to become inseparable.

So we had a herd. I don't think two goats constitute a herd. Three are probably just a trio. But four must surely constitute a herd. And they got on reasonably well.

Other activity on the farm this month was chicken related. Minnie was killed by a falling pallet on the 9th. I always feel a touch guilty about Minnie. I'd propped the pallet against a fence, out of the way, or so I thought. But I rather suspect it was my clumsiness in passing the pallet which was clearly still very much in the way that caused it to fall on the innocently passing Minnie, braining her and crushing her to death.

We replenished our dwindling stock of chickens from Woodside Eggs in Caddington where we purchased Charleston, a Calder Ranger hen, and Tupelo and Magpie, both Sussex White/Rhode Island Red crosses, on the 22nd of the month.

With the approach of Thanksgiving and Christmas at this time of year, thoughts flew to turkey. And when Goodheart the little brown hen suddenly went broody it seemed, at least to the DeMeurs of Honeywick Farm, like an opportunity not to be missed. Wendy gave us three of her large and lugubrious turkey eggs. She kept a couple of turkey cocks herself so the eggs she gave us were likely to be fertile.

"Just stick them under Goodheart in the ark," she'd told us, "and wait 28 days. She'll turn them herself. Give her a drink of water now and again. And a handful of layers pellets every other day".

"Give them names first," added Graham. "Use a pencil, HB or B. Select your names wisely as you could have the turkeys some time. Uncooked, your average turkey could do 10 years or more!"

We followed instructions, our breath baited. Suitable names for our triplets would, I thought, have to be Turkish. So I selected Mohammed, Sultan and Iqbal. These names were inscribed in large capital letters on the shells. Then we shoved the eggs under Goodheart, who'd already taken up comfortable residence in the nesting box in the Ark. She looked a little perturbed in the beak when I gently shoved the eggs under her, but she adjusted her posture to suit, and soon seemed to get the idea. I would peer into the nesting box at each visit to Black Pig. Goodheart had adopted the mantle of prospective motherhood well.

OCTOBER 1999 Early on the morning of the 4th October I peered into the

nesting box and came face to beak with Iqbal, then a tiny and rather endearing mottled black and grey chick. We waited a couple more days but Goodheart didn't. She must have known from the lack of movement that Sultan and Mohammed were defunct. So the infertile eggs were consigned to the dung heap and Iqbal was to be a solitary chap and our only experiment in the world of turkeys. He grew astonishingly quickly into a handsome if sometimes a little socially awkward cock bird at least three times the size of his surrogate mother.

One of Iqbal's less than endearing habits as he quickly grew to maturity was his sexual union with a bucket. Or a football. Or anything of the approximate size of either. Iqbal spent his days shagging the inanimate. I was to find out many years later that the turkey is naturally a social bird. It needs the company of others more than anything. And it needs sexual conquest on an intimate and frequent basis. Iqbal was expressing not only sexual frustration but also extreme loneliness. It should have been no surprise to us that he soon became an unpredictable and irascible creature, turning his aggression on the unsuspecting chickens in whose midst he'd grown to gigantic proportions. We had to treat Iqbal with some care, always being wary as to his whereabouts and his current mood. And we soon learnt that to approach him unarmed could be to court disaster.

NOVEMBER 1999 By the autumn the two surviving lambs we'd inherited

(bought) from Peter Healey were reaching adult size. Mouse had been ringed by Peter at birth but for some reason he'd missed Donkey, who by this time sported a humungous pair of bollocks. Now we really did not intend to breed, and the presence of an entire and extremely well endowed ram in the flock is generally reckoned in the farming community to be not a good idea. Rams are traditionally "introduced" at breeding time, traditionally early autumn, at the ratio 1 ram to 50 ewes. They then copulate for all they're worth and 5½ months later, or by March whichever is the sooner, the bulk of the lambs are born. Not wishing to go through this procedure we thought we should take action now to prevent the inevitable. Donkey would have to be castrated or, in his case and because the wound caused by such an operation would be so huge, he'd have to have the snip, as it were, that is to say be vasectomised. Here's how to do it.

Top Tips for Farmers No.8: How to vasectomise an adult sheep.

1.   Don't do it yourself. It's probably better done by a professional as they have the right tools and a better bedside manner than you.

2.   Catch your sheep. You may need some help with this. Adult male sheep prefer to keep their bollocks and will need some persuading they're better off without them.

3.   Transport your sheep to the local veterinary surgery where he is to be treated. This may be done in a thirty year old Land Rover but try not to do this in a hurricane or gale. And if you do have to do this on a day of high winds try to avoid being hit on the head by large and falling boughs.

4.   If you were not able to avoid the crushing blow of a tree bough across your forehead in a hurricane at the moment you were loading your heavy and struggling sheep aboard your 30 year old Land Rover take a moment or two to recover consciousness and your sensibilities before driving to the surgery.

5.   On arrival at the surgery try to offload your large and struggling sheep and take it into the surgery with as much decorum as possible. You may expect no help whatsoever from your veterinary surgeon or his staff.

6.   Sit on a suitable chair and take your large, struggling and very wet sheep between your legs so that ideally he is sitting on his bum and quite helpless. By this time you will be dazed, wounded, winded, soaking wet and just as helpless as your sheep.

7.   Sit as still as may be clutching onto your large and struggling sheep with its head on your shoulder and so that you can observe proceedings as closely as possible. Remember, you may have to do this next bit yourself some day, so take it all in.

8.   The veterinary surgeon (he's the one in the white coat and starched collar) will probably administer a local anaesthetic (to the sheep that is, not to you, but keep still in case he misses). He'll then do the easy old bit of slicing open the scrotal sack, locating the necessary pipework, snipping about half an inch out of it (or rather them, as there are two of them) and tying them both off. He'll then sew up the incision and tell you you can go.

9. Return your sheep to the perpendicular. Try to stand up. After half an hour of holding a large wet and struggling sheep between your legs this may be taxing for you. But try anyway. You've got to get home somehow.

10. The return journey is a reverse of the above process, but with any luck the wind will have dropped to reasonable proportions. And your sheep will be struggling no longer.

The rest of your flock should now be safe.

We completed the purchase of Wally's Vineyard on the 18th November. It wasn't a true vineyard as anyone could tell from the complete absence of vines. It was a 2½ acre plot of land adjoining Black Pig Farm that came up for sale by British Gas when they'd finished installing a new gas main down the road. The full plot for sale was 5 acres but we shared the purchase with Keith and Jane who owned the plot to the South of Black Pig. I did the conveyancing and Keith and I erected a fence between the plots to delineate ownership. Black Pig Farm was thus extended from its original 4½ acres to about 7. And we named it Wally's Vineyard after Wally Patch, the one-eyed theatrical sheep. Our little menagerie now had ample space in which to expand.

Unfortunately our first experience post completion of Wally's Vineyard was a contraction rather than an expansion. We lost Daisy, our beloved and joyous little nanny with the one udder. And we lost her under a strange set of circumstances which in hindsight was rather like an amalgam of *Animal Rescuers* and *Crimewatch UK*. Daisy, whose real name turned out to be "Jazzy", was spotted on the small screen by her previous owner during the episode of *Animal Rescuers* in which we rescued Banquo and Fuchsia. We were contacted by Blackberry Farm who had been in turn contacted by the producers of *Animal Rescuers* to whom the distraught previous owners had applied for information as to her whereabouts. Daisy ("Jazzy") had apparently been stolen from the smallholding near Bedford where she had been born and brought up with a herd of goats of which she was very much one of the stars. Her udder had been surgically removed because she had contracted mastitis. She had a brood of youngsters awaiting her return. So we had to reluctantly give up Daisy on 30th November, when she returned to her billet. Her former owners were delighted to have her back in the fold and in their field. They were themselves delightful people and to show there were no hard feelings I attended to the pedicure of their entire flock, a task which for them usually involved the intervention of a vet.

DECEMBER 1999 The last entrant of the year to Black Pig Farm was a solitary cockerel we named Christopher in honour of the inventor of the hovercraft. Christopher joined us on the day before Christmas Eve. I have no recollection of whence he came to us. But he does have the rare distinction of being one of the only two chickens who made it to Devon and Long Lane Farm just over a year later.

7. Two Thousand

We didn't know it at the time, but the Millennium year was to be our last at Black Pig Farm. And in some ways it was to be our most surprising and eventful.

JANUARY 2000 *"Ayup the Duck enters on 26.1.00"*. That's a quote and the first entry in what had become known as *The Black Pig Calendar*, a comprehensive listing of all the creatures to take up residence with us either at Black Pig Farm or at our house in Totternhoe Road. I wish now I'd been more expansive with my introductions as I cannot recall where Ayup came from. Perhaps a rescue from Blackberry Farm? Perhaps deposited with us as some waifs and strays were by well thinking locals who thought we were a kind of overspill for the RSPCA. Anyway, whatever Ayup was he would have been of the duck persuasion and would have taken up residence in Quakatoa. And he would have made up the entire duck population of Black Pig at the time. In hindsight we should perhaps have named him Unique.

FEBRUARY 2000 On the 4th, we took delivery of Barney, a colourful little cockatiel that had been caught in flight by Wendy De Meur and caged with her other motley crew of exotic birds. Wendy thought he'd make a suitable partner for Pearl. Pearl, a spinster of a certain undisclosed age, evidently thought otherwise. She was having nothing of the attentions and blandishments Barney tried on her and insisted, quite volubly as I recall, on separate sleeping arrangements. So we acquired a second cage for Barney and the two tolerated each other's company at a distance of a couple of feet in the lounge in Totternhoe Road. Pearl would still emerge nightly to perch on my finger and sip a glass of red wine with her crisps (always cheese and onion flavour). Barney maintained an air of aloofness. Never joined in the fun. I think he regarded himself as a bit of a loner, a thing apart, something ethereal and to be admired. And though he did grow to be a little more affable over time, in all the years we had him he never emerged from his cage without a fight.

MARCH 2000 The early days of spring brought with them a surprise and a shock or two. Six to be precise. We gave birth at Black Pig to six lambs in quick succession and in as many days. Now the birth of lambs in the early spring is, of itself, not particularly shocking. And we really shouldn't have been that surprised at the births; the mothers to be had displayed the rather obvious signs of ovine motherhood with their udders "bagged up" to bursting point with milk and their respective vulvas swollen and red (on closer inspection). No, what was surprising, even shocking, in the case of Black Pig Farm, was the entire absence of entire male sheep. We only had six males; Wally, Little Cloud, Mouse and Donkey, Jacob and Tuesday. Wally had been castrated as a small lamb and we'd received him as quite an elderly sheep who'd never have known the raptures of love. And I'd ringed both

Jacob and Tuesday myself with the old elastrator, purchased with a box of rings for the very purpose, in the first week of life, as instructed. Mouse and Little Cloud had been ringed at birth by Peter Healey. Donkey had been vasectomised and I had assisted at the operation.

So was this multiple virgin birth? Six immaculate ovine conceptions in rural Bedfordshire? Had we made history? Should I call the newspapers and the *Farmer's Weekly* with my findings? Or had I perhaps bungled the ringings? Perhaps, discretion being the better part of bungling, I'd leave that question hanging and get on with looking after the flock as a good farm foreman should.

In any event, we arrived at Black Pig on the morning of 5th March to be greeted by April and her new, strong and very healthy lamb. We named her Sundae in honour of the day of her birth and her creamy white colour. We were to speculate much later on fatherhood, but in view of the colour, Tuesday is likely to have laid claim to the paternal rights and obligations.

The very next morning we arrived to find Roxanne cleaning up her progeny, a delightfully coal black boy lamb Gilly was to name Dave Nugent, later Dave the Fire, after her friend Eileen's husband, a retired fireman who'd recently succumbed to lung cancer. Now Dave was a pretty lamb who would soon be sporting horns almost as magnificent as his father's. But we did have some worries about his paternity. The only likely culprit, in view of the colour, would be Jacob. So that I believe Dave to have been the product not only of incest, but also of an unnatural Oedipus complex. However, Dave seems to have been accepted into the flock without any recriminations from his colleague sheep, and his stay with us was lengthy and productive. We placed Roxanne and her new born in the hay barn to allow him to gain strength over the next few days.

But the fecund Roxanne had not finished yet. On the following day, the 7th March, we entered the hay barn to find, at her feet, a bedraggled and slimy bit of grubby black wool. This was to be the indomitable and plucky Mr.Parsnip, but when we found him he was barely alive, stunted, looking very sorry for himself and clearly abandoned by his mum. Sheep will of course do this. They seem to know when their offspring is a lost cause. A mother producing triplets will often reject the weakest link and focus on the two stronger siblings. With Mr. Parsnip, appearing as he did a full day after his brother, Roxanne would have not thought him worth the bother or the milk. He was destined to die.

I, on the other hand, just had to give him a chance. I picked him off the floor, wrapped him in an old towel and rubbed some life into him. We transported him as quickly as possible homewards and there I sat and cuddled him in an armchair for several hours, while Gilly went in search of an incubator and some milk substitute.

By the time she'd located an incubator (borrowed, I suspect, from the De Meurs) and powdered milk (bought from the feed merchants) Mr. Parsnip had rallied a little and was showing signs of life. We put him carefully in the incubator, which was a kind of a red plastic box with a gentle heat source to represent the mother's body heat. By late afternoon he could stand on his own spidery thin legs. In fact that's just what he looked like standing; kind of an awkward alien spider, with bent ears and a stubby tail.

Later still we rigged up a heat lamp in the garage where we'd reared Peter Healey's lambs. Unfortunately for Mr. Parsnip we rigged that lamp badly; it was too close to the lamb. Instead of gently warming him through it cooked his little head producing a horribly suppurating burn to add to his already not inconsiderable problems. However, and rather surprisingly in the circumstances, Mr. Parsnip was soon able to join the flock down on Black Pig Farm. And for all his stunted growth, his burnt head and his less than auspicious entry into this world, he was to become perhaps one of the pluckiest and most characterful of creatures. Intelligent too, for a sheep. He would come running at the call of his name and I like to think he had some affection for me as his saviour, the person who could be bothered to give him the two years of life he had.

The aged and now toothless Juanita had not been overlooked in the amorous rampages of Jacob and Tuesday the previous autumn. But Juanita was of an extreme age. I had pulled out the last of her teeth some months before to enable her to chew the grass more effectively as the remaining tooth had worked its way loose and was giving her some problems. But she was having an issue producing her lamb when we found her on the 11th with a pair of feet protruding from her vagina.

Now we hadn't experimented with ovine midwifery and neither had Wendy De Meur, to whom we rushed like a couple of headless chickens in those early days when something urgent and serious occurred. Wendy clambered aboard the Land Rover and we rushed back to Black Pig where we found Juanita looking a little concerned but otherwise no worse for wear. With the two front feet still projecting from her nethers she was easy to catch. Wendy helped us lift her into the back of the Land Rover and we sped off to a neighbour who was well known for her delivery technique. And there, in the back of the Land Rover in a welter of blood and snot Juanita was delivered of a fine strong little lamb. She was white with a greying face and would with time be producing horns like her mum. We carried on the Hispanic strain, naming her Consuela.

Back at Black Pig and later the same day Raindance deposited her brood of two fine strong lambs all alone. Running Bear was a deep chocolatey brown, White Buffalo pure white and fluffy. I believe to this day that Raindance had been gang-banged by Jacob and Tuesday and each had fathered a lamb of his own colour. I know that this is possible, even in the human world, so long as coitus has not been interrupted by more than a few hours. That's my theory anyway, and I'm sticking to it.

65

There was a strange epilogue to the excitement of this month. On the 15th we arrived at Black Pig to find everything in order except for the hen we'd named Tupelo. She was quite dead. We'd become quite used to losing hens and ducks to a fox. But Tupelo appeared to be just dead. Not mauled or damaged in any way. Just dead. I recorded her in the Black Pig Calendar as "eggbound", but there was no particular evidence for this. I took her back home and fed her to the ferrets Vinnie and Naseem. Waste not, want not.

APRIL 2000 We had enough sheep, i.e. more than one, by this time to warrant getting in the shearers. So the nail scissors were relegated to my little manicure set, the one I use for the trimming of beaks and claws. We only had a small flock, and this year's lambs and Beau the Soay did not need the ministrations of the shearer. So it was a quick job once we'd located the local farmer who will do small hobby farmers' flocks. A quick job but a grumpy one. For shearing sheep is a hot, filthy, very unrewarding job for the fee that can be charged. And we must have found, that year, quite the grumpiest of shearers. He spent most of the time cussing and swearing, either at the sheep or at his partner, the sheep handler. We resolved to find a shearer of more equanimity of spirit next year, if one such existed.

MAY 2000 We had another one of those unexplained deaths within the small community of hens on the 4th of the month when we found McGraw dead but apparently unmarked, outside the haybarn. I registered the death guessing her to have been eggbound, and fed her body to Vinnie and Naseem. We were, unaccountably, not having a lot of success with the chickens, but Vinnie and Naseem were putting on weight.

But May was a month where pigs were to predominate. We'd noticed Pepys taking an unnatural interest in the three young girls we'd collected from Paradise Farm two years previously. Blanche, Bunter and Candace-Marie had spent most of that time scampering about Black Pig Farm once we'd transported them there, still in their box but a somewhat larger one, when they were a few months old. They'd been living in the hay barn at night but with free access to the fields, and to Pepys, ever since.

Now a pig is sexually mature at 6 months. And pigs, both male and female, are highly sexed creatures. They are amorous and their love making is prodigious. Pepys however, as our only male, was supposedly castrated at the hands of the RSPCA from whom we'd adopted him. At least that's what we'd been told. We had no reason to suspect there'd be any problems introducing three adolescent sexually mature virgin pigs to Pepys. We were clearly wrong. These three young temptresses would not leave Pepys alone throughout the early days of 2000. It was a daily piggy shagfest of bacchanalian proportions.

Gestation for a pig is 3 months, 3 weeks and 3 days. So though we were surprised and delighted, we were also a little dumbfounded on 18th May when we arrived at Black Pig to the squeaks and squeals from the hay barn. Candace-Marie (and, it seems the "castrated" Pepys) had produced 9 black sausage shaped creatures about the size of a medium rat, or piglets to give them their correct name. Two of these, one male and one female, were lifeless and stillborn. We had five males and two females surviving. We hurriedly separated the living from the dead and persuaded Candace-Marie to take up secluded quarters in a new shed we had recently acquired. There, on a bed of warm hay, she was to bring up her brood in the first days of their life.

Nine days later, on the 27th, we arrived to the shrill cries and squeals of Blanche's brood, again in the hay barn. This time we left the apparently dutiful Blanche to her own devices. She'd given birth without our help and we figured to interfere right now might be tempting fate. If you handle the new-born too soon the mother can take umbrage and reject those handled. Blanche appeared to be making herself and her brood comfortable in the hay barn and the piglets seemed to be enjoying themselves if the squeals and grunts were anything to go by.

When we returned for the afternoon shift we were met with an eerie silence from the hay barn. Blanche appeared to be alone. We searched high and low for the little creatures. And it was only when we did search low that we found them. Blanche had buried them in the hay. After she'd rolled on the lot and killed all but one which was only half dead. Whether this was in a fit of post-natal depression, anxiety or shame, we shall never know. I dug 13 of the lifeless little forms out of the hay where Blanche had attempted to conceal her crime. There were 8 girls and 5 boys. I finished off the only badly damaged survivor in the water butt. Then I buried all 13 near Arnold under the oak trees by the road. It had not been a good day.

JUNE 2000 Next to leave our fold was Juanita, the ancient little Portland ewe

that'd recently given us Consuela. We couldn't be surprised as she had arrived at Black Pig as a sheep well into her dotage. A sheep can be aged in approximate terms by the number of its teeth. Born toothless, they acquire their first pair of incisors at the centre of the upper jaw by the end of their first year. That enables them to crop grass as it shoots up in the early spring. In Devon a one year old lamb with its first two teeth is called a "t-tooth". This is the age at which they are customarily slaughtered, with, as Peter Healey told me, "one good year's grass in their belly."

By the end of the second year the t-tooth becomes a four-tooth then at three it is a six-tooth and finally an eight-tooth at four years old. They have of course no lower teeth, rather a hard muscly pad against which the upper eight teeth grind the grass. An elderly sheep begins to lose its teeth in approximately reverse order at or after the age of ten years. So, at a guess, the toothless Juanita may well have been 12 to 14 years of age when she gave birth to Consuela.

By 4th June she was clearly struggling. In fact she was making no attempt to stand despite our encouragement. When a sheep cannot be persuaded to stand, or is unable physically even with help to maintain a standing position, it really is time to go. Consultation of a vet would have been both expensive and pointless. It was a question of anno domini, a question we would have to ask ourselves and answer many times over the forthcoming years. So instead of the vet we consulted Peter Healey, who attended Black Pig with his shotgun and some pragmatic sympathy. Juanita was dispatched in the loose box and buried in Boot Hill with the other unfortunates.

And though this is a procedure I've had to go through many times now, yet I can never get used to it. It's something about taking responsibility for your decisions about the life and wellbeing of another creature. Having made that inevitable decision, I have to be present at the dispatch. Have to put myself through the agony of the explosion in the brain, the blood and the mucous, the rolling head and the lolling tongue. And then I have to bury the creature decently. It's just what I have to do.

Juanita had survived just long enough to raise Consuela to be an independent and a strong and viable lamb. Faithful and unassuming to the end.

We were this month to have a very short association with an elderly cock and hen we named Napoleon and Josephine and Walter the pigeon. This unlikely trio were dumped on us rather unceremoniously sealed in a cat basket and left on our front door step in Totternhoe Road by Gilly's uncle Dave and his wife Barbara. They'd left us no note. We only knew it was Dave and Barbara who'd left them there when they fessed up some days later. I have no idea where they originated from, but I know precisely where the unfortunate trio went. We took them in their basket down to Black Pig. As we opened the basket to inspect our wares Walter made a bid for freedom and took promptly to the skies, where of course he belonged. He was probably a homing pigeon who'd taken a couple of days rest and would likely now be necked on his return for being late. Pigeon fanciers can be quite ruthless in this respect. Anyway, arriving with us on the 12th, Walter took to the skies on the 13th, never to be seen again.

Napoleon and Josephine at least made it to Quackatoa. They lasted 10 days, being reported missing, presumed taken by Mr. Fox, with Ayup the duck, on the 22nd.

JULY 2000 Pigs grow up remarkably quickly. We'd taken the five males to our local vet for castration a couple of weeks after their birth. This, for the vet, is a quick and simple operation, done with a scalpel and little or no anaesthetic if it's done early enough. I know that your average pig farmer in days of yore was reputed to conduct this one himself, the hardier types being said to have bitten the testes clean off with their nicotine stained teeth. But I'd stopped smoking some years previously and didn't want to take up the habit just to save the vets fees. Anyway, it is an operation I am likely to have botched, even if I'd used the legendary razor blade and fag end. So we left it to the professionals. Mind, the sight of one vet and his two assistants scrabbling around in the dust of the surgery floor as they tried to catch the five quick, slippery and black little blighters was one to behold.

We had of course realised that to keep all seven piglets, even if emasculated, would be foolish. Fights between them would inevitably ensue. Housing would be a problem. Feeding would be a nightmare. So we resolved early on that we'd find homes for five of them and keep two of the castrated males. We called our selections Wilson (after my good friend Paul Wilson who'd already helped us with Tennyson Peacock and Honky Pig) and Mahlon, after me, as that's my middle name. These two would also prove valuable allies for their mother Candace-Marie. She'd always been the outcast of the three and we believe the butt of bullying at the trotters of Blanche and Bunter, who were natural sisters from a different litter.

So we put out the word about five piglets that would be "free to a good home". We advertised their availability in *"Black Pig Monthly"*, a publication we'd subscribed to when first adopting these characterful creatures. We found ready takers for the little beasts and Gilly soon found herself in a series of mercy dashes up and down the motorway to service stations in the West Midlands carrying a box of pigs

The two girls were the first to leave, on 4th July, to Mr. and Mrs. Adams and a new home just north of Birmingham. Gilly had called one of these "Big Gillian", perhaps after herself! Thus breaking the cardinal rule that you do not name anything you might be getting shot of. The others remained nameless, to be christened by their new owners. Two of the boys were taken in the same day by a neighbour in the animal fraternity, Ista, of Great Billington. The remaining boy went to Mr. & Mrs. Harrison of Worcester on the following day, meaning another dash up the motorway for Gilly in the Honda.

Mahlon and Wilson stayed with their mum. For a little too long as it turns out. Although weaned in five or six weeks from birth, the piglet will always look for a free feed from its mother if she's available. Mahlon and Wilson were no exceptions, and of course mum was very nearly always available. The two of them were suckling merrily away at her poor wrinkled little nipples when they were nearly as big as she was. We of course, new to piggy husbandry, knew no better. It was only when Wendy De Meur on a flying visit noticed how wizened and gaunt the still young Candace-Marie had become that she recommended respite care. In fact she took the ailing Candace-Marie away in her Range Rover and looked after her for a full month before returning her, hail and hearty and with her fighting spirit restored, to Black Pig. By this time she had "dried up", to use the colloquial expression; she had no milk to give. And Mahlon and Wilson had forgotten all about the close liaison they'd enjoyed with their mother. The happy threesome trotted around the farm, rootling in the long grass, scoffing the acorns as they fell from the oaks near the front gate, snuggled up together in their shed at night.

Meanwhile we suffered another strange and unexplained death among the chickens. On the 22nd we found Magpie dead but otherwise apparently unmolested in Quakatoa. Again I recorded her as "eggbound", not really understanding the reason for her demise. And once again we fed her to the ferrets. A similar fate awaited Sarah Kezia on the 19th September and Goodheart, Iqbal turkey's surrogate mum, on 23rd November. The deaths would have been alarming, and though the ferrets were glad of the supplements to their diet, the chicken population of Black Pig was suffering unsustainable losses. But as 2000 marched on the rains began to fall and this brought with it mud, filth and depression. And this, coupled with our decision to move westwards, put the loss of chickens at a low priority in our thoughts.

8. Transition. From Black Pig to Long Lane

There follow some extracts from a newsletter I wrote in April 2001 after we'd moved to Devon and Long Lane Farm. I have edited them for relevance to the animals, but they have the advantage of having been written close in time to the events to which they relate.

"The Millennium Year was, for Gilly and myself, a year of unprecedented change and uncertainty. There were many ups and downs. Many gains and some losses. This is an account of some of them.

With June came the decision to move here to the west country and back to my roots, rather than to Wales as first intended. After a couple of abortive viewings, Long Lane Farm soon came to our attention as having all of the attributes of our dream home—close to the coast, 12 acres of prime grazing land for the animals, close to my mum in her advancing years etc. All our efforts went into securing the purchase with lightning dashes up and down the M4/M5 leaving fraught and overworked friends to tend our ovine, porcine, caprine and equine charges.

In August we went out on a limb and secured our future by exchanging contracts for the purchase of Long Lane Farm, with completion delayed until February 9 2001 to enable us to sell our property and the occupants of half of Long Lane Farm to find alternative accommodation.

Meanwhile it started to rain. And rain. And rain. The land at Black Pig Farm is low lying, with high water table and clay subsoil. That means that drainage is less than ideal. Water began to settle and lie in unacceptable quantities very early. By the end of October we had a quagmire and the animals had little or nothing by way of natural pasture to graze. To add to this problem, our hay crop was ruined last year because it was cut so late due to the wet summer conditions. Gilly had a constant battle with the elements to keep the stables clean, animals fed and herself just slightly dry. The mud at Black Pig became too bad for Gilly's mum, who at age 79 is an efficient pooh-picker in reasonable conditions. Gilly had to contend with the elements alone in the evenings, although I could help her with the morning run, feeding and watering Jack the pony while she tended to the sheep, pigs, goats, chickens, turkey and cat.

Meanwhile it rained. And it rained again. And it rained some more. Black Pig Farm became a depressing soggy quagmire from which the animals could derive little sustenance and we little joy. There was not a square inch for them to sit down, and indeed we were not to witness a sitting sheep again until North Devon. Then Gilly missed her footing in the slime and took a dive (in the piked position I think) into the

*pig wallow. She surfaced covered in tears, mud and indescribable filth, and
contracted a similar mouth infection to that from which I had just recovered.*

*In December I commissioned the construction on our new property of a purpose built
piggery to house the 7 black potbellies we were to take with us to Devon. We had
decided that the days of the mud and the muck and the bullets would be over when
we finally reached North Devon. The animals needed to be accommodated in
surroundings as conducive to good living as they justly deserved after the privations
of this harsh and unremitting winter. And I didn't want Gilly to take another dive into
18 inches of slurry and pig shit, albeit in the name of good fun! So having designed
a building and compound that I felt would meet the piggy specifications, and having
located a builder of high repute and not a little aesthetic taste, I travelled down to
North Devon with my good friend Paul Wilson to meet the builder on site and
commission the work. My choice of builder turned out to be excellent, even inspired.
Far from cheap (the final piggery will cost over £8000, to house 5 free pigs!) his
workmanship is beyond compare. The pigs who inhabit it (Blanche, Bunter,
Candace-Marie and her two sons Mahlon and Wilson) have strong, draught proof dry
quarters, with sun balcony and a rooting garden, with views of rural splendour to east
and south over rolling countryside. What is more, they can be put to bed after dark
by either Gilly or myself wearing carpet slippers (us, that is, not the pigs!)*

*The builder (Steve Blackman, working out of Braunton, a tall, bearded and affable
young member of "Christian Surfers") is more often commissioned to work on urban
sculpture, all over the country. He also replaced 3 field gates and constructed two
looseboxes in our stockbarn, to extremely high specification, to house Jack the pony
and Thunder and Fuchsia our two remaining goats. Work continues on the piggery.
Once mains water and electricity have been laid in, there's the sauna and Jacuzzi to
consider, with reading room to follow.*

*In my short sojourn in North Devon one of the most exciting views for me was of well
drained and edible lush green pasture, on the fields soon to be occupied by our
suffering animals in Bedfordshire. I could hardly contain myself with this news, and
took back many photographs and some video footage both of house and land to
cheer up Gilly and remind her mum, of what was in store in the New Year.*

*The first of our animals to succumb to the depressing conditions at Black Pig was
our magnificent Alpine goat Banquo. He basically lost interest in living, lost weight
and faded away with nothing very specific. In extremis the vet attended from
Winslow in Bucks., waded across the mud and slurry that Black Pig had by now
become at 8.00 one wet and dismal evening, and injected the forlorn beast by
lantern light with something that was not to save him. Although he did rally for a
morning, he collapsed in a bony heap in the mud one afternoon, and we dragged
him across the slurry and into a stable. Next morning, in the early hours, he quite*

literally died in Gilly's arms, ten minutes after our arrival. I buried him 5 feet deep behind the caravan on one of the mercifully sunny days of mid January. The inevitable tears were shed at this tragedy. Had we been able to move months before, I believe Banquo would have been with us now. He is recorded in the Black Pig Calendar as "Died on 16 January 2001: a ghost at last".

Nearly one month before D Day (9 February) the enormity of the logistics of moving the contents of 2 homes, three people, two dogs, 17 sheep (some pregnant), 7 pigs, 2 goats, a pony, two ferrets, two chickens, a turkey, two cockatiels, two canaries, two cars, a horse trailer and the contents of various barns some 220 miles struck us with some force. The need for a plan suggested itself. I set to with pens, paper and mindmaps, and about two hours later emerged with a comprehensive plan covering the period from 2 weeks before to one week after the move. This plan, which covered items as diverse and apparently unconnected as emptying and packing the contents of the loft, to checking with Stuart Holmes, the local beef farmer, as to his availability with tractor and trailer on the day of the animal move, was to prove the motive force to break the state of routine and limbo we had drifted into. Daily there were things to do, places to go, people to be seen in the lead up to D Day (or D Days, as February 9 and 12 would become known to us later).

On days 3 and 4 of our plan (31 January and 1 February) I travelled west again in the company of good friend Paul Wilson (Independent Financial Adviser and would-be Chocolateer) to check finally that the animals would all have decent accommodation when they arrived. Leaving Gilly and her mum with the house packing (days 3 and 4 –lounge, dining room, understairs, canary cages), and the by now very precarious and treacherous job of wading across 4 acres of mud to feed and care for the animals, we were like two men behaving badly (in Devon). I have to confess now that these two days of respite from the mud of Black Pig Farm were a short holiday for Paul and me. We met fencing contractor Mark Dallyn on site and gave him instructions on the piggery enclosure. The piggery itself was in an advanced state of construction, despite the horrendous weather conditions that Devon had also been experiencing at this time, and I was well pleased with the quality of workmanship. Then Paul and I fixed and fabricated some chicken cages in the Stone Barn (Honeymoon Hayloft to be) at Long Lane. We noted that in addition to substantial completion of the piggery, the new gates had been hung as requested and the loose boxes constructed in the stock barn. There was really very little preparatory work to complete, the barns themselves having been virtually emptied by the former occupants. We spent some of the time visiting the area, breakfasting in the "Manna House" in Ilfracombe High Street, and carousing the evenings away in the Duke of Wellington, just down the road.

The Duke of Wellington was our undoing on the first night of this short sojourn however. I should explain that my mum owns two cottages in Ilfracombe. Numbers

6 and 9 Church Road. Number 6 she normally occupies herself. Number 9 is guest accommodation. We were sleeping in No.9 but as my mum was at this time in North Devon District Hospital in preparation for open-heart surgery in London, Paul and I were also using the slightly more comfortable No.6 to watch TV and generally relax. Well, after our evening at the Duke of Wellington and a final visit to No.6, we crashed at No.9 to sleep. In the morning it was with some horror that I was to discover that I had left the keys of No.6, and my car keys, inside No.6. The only other set of keys was with my mother in her hospital bed in Barnstaple, some 15 miles distant. My first reaction was, as always, to ask Gilly what to do in a crisis such as this. Over 220 miles away, Gilly answered her mobile phone in the pigloo at Black Pig Farm, where she was desperately trying to lift Pepys, the huge potbelly boar, who had gone lame. Not unused to such cries for help or guidance, Gilly advised me to try and trace Charles Granger, 80 year old friend of my mother, who might be prepared to give us a lift into Barnstaple to retrieve the other key. Some panic and a lot of investigative ingenuity later, we located Charles (ex desert rat and tank corps, WWII) a few streets away, and he readily suggested that he convey us to Barnstaple in his beloved but ageing post war transport—a plucky little blue Reliant Robin three wheeler which he affectionately calls "Del Boy". Soon we found ourselves careening around North Devon's hairpin bends and coastal byways at breakneck speed, piloted by this bewiskered military hero of yesteryear, who had as much confidence and as little concern for the enemy in "Del Boy" as in the Sherman tanks of his youth. The experience was, to say the least, both memorable and eclectic. But we regained access to No. 6 Church Road Ilfracombe unscathed, indeed enriched with deep insight into the real events behind Rommel's defeat. In short, our days in North Devon were as productive as they were enjoyable. We even visited my mum three times in North Devon District Hospital.

Back in Bedfordshire, Gilly was still coping with the ever worsening conditions produced by the relentless rain and the coming and going of our confused and depressed animals. The steady packing of our effects into large cardboard packing crates continued, and Gilly had, in her inimitable fashion, kept well on track and ahead of target. On Day 6 (3 February) we notified the Council Tax authority, insurance company and Post Office of our change of address, transferred funds for the impending conveyancing transaction, had the Land Rover checked over for its longest drive in 30 years and erected temporary holding pens at Black Pig to assist in the collection of animals in readiness for loading. This latter operation was directed by my good friend and neighbour Graham De Meur, and helped by old friend Philip Carter who was to help us in the mega move itself.

At about this time Wally the one-eyed sheep, one of our oldest charges and the apple of Gilly's two eyes, showed signs of decline. Keeping his distance from the rest of the flock, he quickly lost weight and interest in his surroundings. Even more alarming was the loss of his former voracious appetite for everything, especially the forbidden. We began to have serious, but secret and personal, doubts that he would make it to Long Lane Farm. We tried everything, from his favourite foods (rich tea biscuits, bread, broccoli and cabbage) to doses of antibiotics and wormer. After two weeks of worry, a mercy dash to Buckingham for supplies and twice daily drenching with glucose and multivitamins, Wally gradually turned the corner and returned to his bullish old ways. But he continued to sleep in the barn, seeming to have become accustomed to the TLC he received in those weeks he spent as an indoor sheep. The experience with Wally dipped Gilly deeper into despair and despondency, and she had begun to wonder whether any of the animals would survive the move.

Then, just as Wally was turning the corner to recovery, Pepys, our biggest potbelly boar and one of the first animals to arrive at Black Pig Farm four years previously contracted rear end paralysis and was unable to lift himself, other than, with help, his front end. We knew from bitter experience of the veterinary profession in Bedfordshire that there was little or no point seeking professional assistance for this one. The routine became, in those last days at Black Pig, after the animals had been fed and the stables cleaned as best as could be achieved given the conditions, to syringe half a litre of glucose and as much again of multivitamins down Wally's throat, and then lift the pig. At 18 stones of dead-weight pork with a ferocious jaw and alarming tusks, lifting and then feeding him quite literally by hand in a bog and a rainstorm was a task to be undertaken with not a little strength, care and patience. We both received bone crushing bites from the gentle giant whilst administering pain killing aspirins, and my hand is still partially numb from the effort and the broken blood vessels. We knew really that Pepys was going to die, though these words remained unspoken, as we both secretly hoped we could get him to Devon for his final resting-place.

Preparations proceeded apace as we approached February 9. There were still rooms to pack, bales of hay and straw to obtain for the first few days at Long Lane, the horse trailer to insure for breakdown recovery (RAC don't cover it if you are carrying livestock), completion of the purchase to attend to, ferret hutches and bird cages to prepare, the Land Rover to provision, carrying cases for chickens and turkey to prepare, and a squad of helpers to muster for the morning of 12 February when the main animal contingent was to depart westwards. Arrangements also had to be made for caring for our house in Eaton Bray after we left it as we still haven't sold.

Two days before D Day Badger, our 15 year old bearded collie, my son and hair, started to have palpitations and what I now believe to have been mild heart attacks It was self-help again, and the copious use of aspirin to thin the blood, with a promise to consult help as soon as we landed in Devon.

On Day 11 of our master plan, 8 February 2001, the house removal men arrived to pack the house effects onto their lorry. Arriving at 12 Noon, they didn't leave us until 7.30 p.m. by which time all was packed except for 2 sofas, the canaries, cockatiels and ferrets. A small company called CMR working out of Stanbridge near Leighton

Buzzard undertook our removals. If anyone out there needs a removal done, please consider this firm. They provided a service second to none with hard working, careful and willing staff. And for the service they provided us they were ridiculously cheap (at £705 including VAT and insurance, to move the contents of two houses, barns, sheds and a garage 225 miles in a day!). We slept that night in a virtually empty house, Gilly and I on the floor of the bedroom we had occupied for 26 years (bed having been packed in lorry!).

D-Day I arrived on Friday 9 February, bright, blue and promising, a day which together with D-Day II on the following Monday 12 February (not so bright, not so blue) is again emblazoned on my memory.

I had taken the precaution of telegraphing the completion monies on the previous day, so that the legal niceties would not hamper the removal operation. The removal men from CMR arrived at 7.00 am. And by 7.30 the last of the furniture, the cockatiels, canaries and ferrets were all loaded aboard. The lorry set off followed swiftly by Gilly, her mum, our friend Julie Carter (Phil's wife) and the dogs Badger and Jason the Whippet in the Rover Metro.

Left on my own rattling around in a near empty house, I had several hours to kill before Phil, my co-driver in the Land Rover and horse trailer, would arrive to take part in the second contingent. It was a strange and almost eerie feeling to wander those empty rooms that had served as our home for over 26 years, and a slight sense of betrayal clouded an otherwise perfect day. I took seventeen bags of variegated refuse to the tidy tip in Dunstable, and treated the Land Rover to a full tank of the full leaded fuel it was built to run on over 30 years ago (at £1 per litre!).

When Phil arrived in the late morning, we mustered the troops for stage two of the move. Stuart Holmes, a local and very kindly beef farmer (who, says Gilly, looks a treat in shorts!) had agreed to tow out the few animals we were to take in our horse trailer as the advance party. Graham DeMeur, my good friend with backgrounds both agricultural and engineering, was to assist in the mustering and loading. The weather was surprisingly kind, but conditions on the ground were of the utmost bogginess after months of rain and poor drainage. Stuart's tractor cut tramlines two feet deep in the field on the way over, and these were deepened on the way back with a payload of animals in the horse trailer.

First to be loaded were our only two remaining chickens, Christopher Cockerel and Charleston (India had been raped and savaged in the mud a few days earlier by the turkey she had hatched from a fertile egg herself a few months before, and she had been fed to the ferrets. China, a contemporary of India, had mysteriously gone missing without trace, presumed taken by the fox, on the same day)."

(N.B. I need to correct the narrative slightly here. Though I observed with my own astonished eyes the rape and murder of India hen, it was of course Goodheart who had hatched Iqbal and she had died in mysterious circumstances in November. It was only when reading the Black Pig Calendar to put this narrative together that it dawned on me that Iqbal was the serial chicken killer who had been stalking Black Pig. He was destined to solitary confinement at Long Lane Farm.)

"With the chickens crated and on the horse trailer, Iqbal the murderous and rapacious turkey was cornered by me, seized somewhat unceremoniously and bundled into a turkey carrier and thence into the horse trailer. Quackatoa, the fowl compound, was empty, and this was to prove fortuitous for the pig capture some three days later.

Next on board was Beau, the little horned Soay sheep. She went without any bother. Pepys, the potbelly boar, was by now immobile, and couldn't even be persuaded onto his front legs. It took the four of us to drag him physically out of the pigloo on a sheet of corrugated iron and then to roll him squealing and protesting into the horse trailer. Potbellied pigs, indeed all pigs, are known for their inability to withstand stress, so it was with some trepidation on my part and no little indignity on his that this operation was performed. We were determined that Pepys would be buried at Long Lane if he were not to survive the move. Potter, Pepys' long suffering wife, was next aboard, with much objection and squealing, assisted by the corrugated iron sheets and willing helpers as we waded and persuaded through the slurry. Finally, plucky little Mr. Parsnip, young lamb abandoned by his mother, hopped almost willingly aboard. Stuart towed this motley crew (2 sheep, 2 pigs, 2 chickens and a turkey) across the mud and slime of Blackpig's biggest field, tearing great gullies in the clay where the wheels refused to move. We hitched up the horse trailer to the Land Rover, and after disposing of the worst of our mud soaked clothing, headed westwards in our ancient rig carrying a probably illegal load of sorry looking animals to their new home.

We stopped several times on the 6½-hour journey to replenish fuel and oil and to check the water, but the Landy performed wonderfully well really, and the journey became for me yet another adventure in uncertainty. A little like the journey west in Steinbeck's "Grapes of Wrath". I checked on the animals in the trailer only once, and it was a good thing I did. Just outside Swindon the lame bulk of Pepys had shifted aft and was crushing a frantic Mr. Parsnip.

At about 8.20 in the evening and some 10 miles from Long Lane Farm, we met the removal truck coming in the opposite direction. It had arrived at Long Lane by 1.00 p.m. and only just left, having unloaded the cases and furniture, and having been towed up our new drive by local dairy farmer Steve Parkin when it got stuck in the kerbside mud. Gilly tells me the removal men were as magnificent in the unloading as they had been professional in loading in Bedfordshire. It must have been an extremely hard day's graft for all of them. Gilly, Julie and Elsie welcomed our little rig as if we were returning conquering heroes, and I must confess to a little self-satisfaction at our achievement in successfully completing round two of the mission.

We quickly unloaded the chickens and turkey to their prepared accommodation in barns and put Beau and Mr. Parsnip in one of the newly constructed looseboxes in the stock barn. Pepys and Potter would spend the immediate future in the horse trailer parked in the yard where they could be looked after in comfort.

Saturday and Sunday were spent busily unpacking cases and rearranging furniture, making adjustments and generally sorting things out. Phil and I managed to get the Land Rover stuck in the thin mud on the drive, and spent most of Saturday morning extracting it with a system of Scandinavian hoist (the tourniquet method, using a baulk of timber and twisted rope) and the "Ice Cold in Alex" method (winding up the Land Rover on its crank handle, in reverse gear much as John Mills et al did in the film). Julie, Gilly and her mum spent the time making the home more than a little comfortable, while we boys played in the yard.

On Sunday afternoon 11 February I drove back to Bedfordshire in the Metro, returning Julie and Phil to their heavily pregnant daughter. This couple has helped us immeasurably over the years, and has assisted us in both of the only two moves we have made in our married lifetime, with 26 years separating the events. We haven't seen much of them over recent years, but they have remained good and highly valued friends throughout over 30 years.

I spent the night on one of the sofas remaining in our Bedfordshire house. I slept only fitfully. Perhaps I had some intuitive premonition of what the morrow held in store. In my wildest dreams I could not have foreseen the terrible reality.

D-Day II (Monday 12 February 2001) will also stay with me to my dying breath. From modest beginnings, it turned into the most ridiculous day I can ever hope to recall. We had arranged and prepared everything as for a military operation. I was down at Black Pig Farm at 6.30 am. before daybreak, and it appeared to be fine and dry for once. At exactly 7.00 am. the animal removers' lorry arrived and a few seconds later the first of the A Team, Graham and Wendy DeMeur of Honeywick Farm, followed by Paul Wilson of Northall and Stuart Holmes with his tractor and stock trailer. Then, quite unexpectedly and not as forecast, the rain began. Beginning as a slight drizzle, it soon steadied into a dense and relentless downpour. My heart sank, as the possibility of having to cancel the expedition loomed large. After all, the going was mega soft already, with months of rain still sitting on the bedraggled and sparsely grassed Black Pig Farm. But the expedition did take off, and led by Stuart on his tractor towing stock trailer, we gingerly waded across the field in a flash flood, towards the temporary stock pens constructed a few days earlier. The grey dawn sky was leaden, angry and forbidding, the conditions under foot worsening by the minute, and still we waded through the primeval soup of mud, filth and algae. Herding the sheep and two goats onto the trailer wasn't too problematic, since we had taken the precaution of constructing a temporary funnel from stock wire and posts. We were able, with the combined experience of Stuart, Graham and Wendy, to drive most of them up the ramp and into the back of the trailer. The goats needed a little persuasion and Fuchsia a little manhandling, but soon Stuart could count 17 heads on the trailer and the tailgate was duly closed. The treck back across the larger field commenced, but the extra payload of a ton of bewildered and reluctant sheep was too much, not for the trailer so much as for the two wheel drive tractor, and soon the trailer was up to its axles in impossible slime. The sheep and goats were in the dry, and relatively unperturbed if confused. It was mainly I who panicked as the situation was assessed. Our animal transporters had a round trip of 450 miles to perform and would need to hit the road soon if the journey was to be carried out legally. The entire flock was stranded mid field. The rain intensified. Time was wearing on. But Stuart, the resourceful and heroic beef farmer who had provided tractor, trailer and self for the occasion, had another card up his sleeve. He had a four wheel drive tractor and driver on standby should it be needed, and he sped off with Graham to Eaton Bray to collect. Remarkably, for time normally passes with agonising sloth in these stressful and chaotic circumstances, Stuart and Graham returned what seemed to be moments later, closely followed by a very Leviathan of a tractor, with driver Mick Pullen at the controls. This mammoth beast (the tractor, that is, not Mick who is actually quite slight) with its independent 4 wheel drive to each of its 8 ft. by 3 ft. wheels glided effortlessly through the gate to Black Pig Farm (about a millimetre of clearance each side) and through the deepening mud and slurry that the surface of the large field was now becoming. Majestic in its progress across the field, the tractor was quickly hitched up to the sheep trailer and, despite ever thickening clouds and by now thunderous rain, the trip across the field was completed. The sheep and goats were quickly loaded onto the back of the lorry, where they joined Blackjack the pony who had been led across the field and stepped uncomplaining onto the lorry a few minutes after it had arrived.

But the most problematic part of the operation was yet to be attempted. The only animals left at Black Pig were the five remaining errant, fast, fat and very wet black pigs for whom the farm was originally named. Now a pig is a wily animal. Far more intelligent than a sheep. While sheep have personality and a kind of primitive Jungian collective consciousness that makes them follow a joint instinct, sometimes, they have little in the way of independent will. Pigs have a pure brutal cunning, an elaborate instinct for self-preservation, a very hard nose and no conscience whatsoever. With pig capture you only get one chance. The animal senses your obviously murderous intentions with your first move, and once the element of surprise has gone, catching them is a battle of wits, tenacity and pure brawn (excuse the pun), because I forgot to mention, pigs are also immensely strong. On this occasion Bunter and Blanche, the two larger gilts, were reasonably co-operative as pigs go. The temptation of extra rations and perhaps the pigs' natural curiosity to see the inside of the trailer got the better of them. Whilst guiding them in precisely the right direction in the middle of a drenching 18 inch slurry and a downpour was not possible, the general idea must have appealed. Blanche and Bunter soon found *themselves cornered in the straw strewn trailer awaiting their slighter, and faster, colleagues.*

Candace Marie is a wilful pig with long menacing snout, beady eyes and an attitude problem, a result of being mercilessly bullied by Blanche and Bunter (sisters from a different litter) for most of her piglet life. She is svelte in her proportions, lithe in movement and extraordinarily vocal in protestation, even by piggy standards. She travels with her two sons, Mahlon and Wilson, less than a year old and still under her emotional control. If Ma Baker and the Baker Boys have reincarnations, they are surely Candace Marie, Mahlon and Wilson Pugsley. The two boys are smooth like their mum, slick when dry and impossible to handle wet or dry.

Their opponents in what was about to become a lively mudbath struggle, consisted of myself, Wendy and Graham DeMeur, Stuart Holmes, Mick Pullen, Paul Wilson, Helen the cat lady from Edlesborough who had joined us for this part of the fray, and Judy who was to drive the animals to North Devon, and could see we needed the extra help.

Our first attempt was by stealth and cunning to tempt the three little pigs back into their quarters at Black Pig (in the "Shed on the River Kwai") and thence into the back of the trailer. But it is difficult to co-ordinate the stealth and cunning of 8 humans in a flash flood, and try as we may, Candace and her boys were not to be tempted into a fate worse than sure death by a few damp pig nuts and bread. They scattered for safety, to be chased at random by 8 pairs of wildly flailing arms in various directions through the mire and downpour. Then we figured we could corner them as close as may be to a fence by all wielding sheets of corrugated asbestos and iron, forming a sort of moving stock pen. The pigs would only be allowed to go in the direction that the stock pen was moved. That was the theory anyway. Candace had a different perception and plan, which largely involved staying put. Even the smallest of these creatures is unbelievably strong, fast, athletic and slippery, and the moving stock pen idea soon fell to pieces when several stones of hurtling pork breached the pen at its weakest point and bolted for freedom.

By this time the pig squad ("magnificent eight" as I later dubbed us) were wet, bedraggled and filthy with slurry and detritus. It was suggested that I leave the three behind, given the circumstances and their stressed condition, to return in drier weather. This was probably a sensible suggestion, but I knew that I dare not arrive at Long Lane Farm three pigs short, and I think my face betrayed my desperation and concern.

The pigs were in one corner of the home field, near to the caravan, and Wendy hit upon the bright idea of cornering them in the now empty chicken compound, Quackatoa. We planned, as much by telepathy and hand signals, a pincer movement with rear guard action. Armed yet again with the inevitable sheets of asbestos and corrugated iron (for more supplies of which I had to crawl across a fence, in a foot of slurry and rip down some fence panels with my bare hands) we advanced, wearing facial expressions as casual as we could bring ourselves to muster in these outrageous conditions. Wendy and Graham took the left flank, Paul, Helen and I the right. Judy, Stuart and Mick came from the front, all bearing our barriers and shields. We approached deftly, but damply, and for once out manoeuvred Ma Baker and the Baker Boys, as they slunk suspiciously and resentfully through the gate into Quakatoa. Somebody slammed the gate in place behind them and a loud cheer broke forth from the Magnificent Eight. A goal achieved, without penalty!

Inside Quackatoa realisation dawned on the trapped pigs that the game was up, but not before the compound became a launching ground for high velocity porcine missiles. Now a pig is not particularly aerodynamic, but if trapped in a chicken compound it will give up cunning and hurl itself furiously, and quite balletically, at the wire, the gate, or anything else that might conceivably give way to its brute force and weight. We shielded the pigs from outside attraction with the iron and asbestos sheets, but it was clear that the chicken wire of Quackatoa would not stand much of the battering the pigs were prepared to give it. So time was of the essence once more, and Mick Pullen dropped his asbestos sheet, climbed back into the cab of the mammoth 4-wheel drive and reversed the trailer hard up to the gate of Quackatoa. Bunter and Blanche disembarked quite sedately into Quackatoa, and after a couple of rounds of savagery between the warring pigs all five were persuaded onto the trailer. The tailgate was hastily secured once more and Mick towed another motley little collection over the field, through the storm and unloaded them without too many hassles onto the removal trailer.

Black Pig Farm was empty of stock for the first time in its 4-year history. On that dismal and darkling day in February, the day when the worst of the floods were to strike Bedfordshire in torrents that left the roads flooded for over three weeks after our departure, the last of the animals had been removed from the only home most of them had ever known. Black Pig itself was reminiscent of war torn Ypres or the Somme, with gaping canyons cut into the clay by the tractor and trailer wheels, quickly filling to overflowing with the flood water. And we happy few, the Magnificent Eight of Eaton Bray Northall and Slapton, a band of weary and mud soaked heroes and heroines, splashed back across the field to our various vehicles, made our farewells and set off again in different directions.

I have to thank many people for their unstinting help in our great expedition westwards, but none more than this band of stalwarts who really gave of their best on that ridiculous day in February, the day of the Great Great Billington Escape.

For myself, I was so badly besmirched, soaked and covered in mud, blood, flood water and unmentionables, that I wasn't about to sully the neat interior of my little Rover Metro. So I stripped down to my muddy underpants, right there in the Rye Great Billington, and in view of the early morning rat run traffic. I abandoned my clothes in the hedge, and drove home wearing nothing but my underpants and a weary but satisfied smile.

At home (in Eaton Bray) showered, cleansed and rested, I secured the house and after a few brief visits to others involved in the day's events, set off back to Devon. The rain didn't drop below torrential until Swindon, with two foot of floodwater to negotiate in places. By Bristol it had abated, and I arrived at Long Lane Farm, as had the animals a few hours before me, in warm and pleasant sunshine, glistening in the wet but lush meadow grass of our fields.

The next few days were spent unpacking cases and crates and generally putting Long Lane Farmhouse into our way of living. It is pure bliss for us here, and although we agreed that we always loved our house in Eaton Bray, and would miss in particular some of the wonderful people and places of those parts, this place seems to beckon us. We felt that first week as though Long Lane had been waiting for us, like wanderers returned. Conditions for the animals are so much better, even though we live in fear of the spread of Foot and Mouth. It rains a lot, as it seems to everywhere these days. But the rain drains away, and conditions of impossible mud only exist here in the piggery, because that's how the pigs seem to like it!

As soon as we could we consulted the vet at Mullacot Cross Animal Hospital on Badger's condition. Diagnosed with a heart murmur (of which we were aware) and an enlarged heart (of which we were not) he is now stable and on prescription capsules to slow down his heart rate. He will continue with these for the rest of his life. He enjoys his morning walk in our largest field, where he can paddle and drink from the spring. He is remarkably active and lively in his old age, and though he doesn't always see eye to eye with Jason Whippet, we are grateful that he made it here and can enjoy his retirement by the coast, which he has always loved.

On St.Valentine's Day, a scant two days after the animals and I arrived here, my mother was discharged from North Devon General Hospital where she had been since just after Christmas. She was released into our care at Long Lane pending imminent heart surgery at West Brompton. Very weak and debilitated at first, she picked up over the next five weeks, and returned to her cottage in Ilfracombe recently pending admission to West Brompton on 5 April.

In the early hours of the very next morning after my mother's arrival, there were more departures and arrivals. Pepys, the potbellied boar we brought from Bedfordshire in the horse trailer finally went into a coma and died. Sad and prophetic in a way, as Pepys had been one of the first three animals to arrive at Black Pig Farm in 1996, one of the first to arrive at Long Lane, and the first to die here. We dragged him out of the trailer, which he hadn't left since arriving at Long Lane, and stored him in a little barn until I could bury him.

On the brighter side, on this same bright and frosty morning Raindance, one of our half Jacob sheep, delivered twins, two of the prettiest lambs we had ever seen. We had to quickly attend to the mother's milk tubes and ensure the vital colostrum was unblocked, spray antiseptic on the umbilicals, ring the tails (and in the case of the male, his testicles!). Gilly has named them Shawnee and Crow, as Raindance always has North American Indian children. We had been aware that some of the sheep were heavily pregnant before the move, but so grateful that they waited until arrival to actually give birth. Shawnee and Crow would surely have perished had they dropped into the harsh and soaking mud of Black Pig Farm, without us in attendance.

I buried Pepys in the hole 5 feet deep that Gilly and her mum had dug over the weekend. He lies next to the stock barn, behind the horse trailer he arrived in, covered by the only Long Lane earth ever to touch his dear body. Like Arnold before him, we miss him terribly.

April's new lamb, born on 20 February, probably the most handsome, the largest and strongest yet. We have named him Honeylamb, because he is just the sort of lamb Christmas cards are made of—white, with long eyelashes, proud stance and eyes to die for. Honeylamb was followed three days later by Layla, born to Roxanne, the grandmother of them all. Layla is slight, spindly with long legs and ears, and all the charm of the loner, much like her mother. We have left her tail on, so that she can be clearly distinguished from her cousins.

We were blessed in our first fortnight here with splendid weather—bright cloudless skies, frosty mornings, clear nights. Shrove Tuesday was such a day here when Sundae (one of last year's lambs and not yet a year old) gave birth to Pancake, another extremely pretty lamb with mottled markings and retroussé nose. Pancake is Roxanne's first great granddaughter.

By this time of course the Foot and Mouth crisis was upon us. Devon has become a hotspot of disease and infection. We dutifully provide disinfectant footbath and vehicle mat for casual callers, and we dip and spray wherever we go. It's a little ironic really, after the stresses and difficulties we went through to get here, that we have brought our animals to perhaps the most dangerous region of the British Isles. Some rescue operation. However we have to be philosophical. I shall not here enter into a debate on the ludicrous and indefensible manner in which this government has handled the so-called crisis, because I shall make myself angry and you bored. Suffice it to say that we live in fear of losing our wonderful and harmless animals, as far away from the food chain as it is possible to be, to suit the whims of a nonsensical governmental policy based on nothing more than economics and prestige.

The last of our lambs was born to Hortense, a middle-aged sheep and a frosty virgin until last year as far as we know. We never thought she would produce. On the morning of 5 March Hortense separated herself from the flock and took refuge in the top corner of one of our fields, giving all the signs of impending birth. After some *time it became apparent that nature would require a little assistance. The nose and front hooves of the lamb were just protruding from Hortense's vulva, but little else was happening, despite contractions. I swiftly took some advice from Wendy in Eaton Bray and then, stripped to the waste and thoroughly soaped, I performed my first act of ovine midwifery. The lamb I delivered, at first thought to be dead, burst into life as he touched the ground. I cleared his little airways and lay him before his mother, the grateful Hortense, to clean. This was for me an extremely emotional moment. Obviously, I had to name the little chap Miracle. He is black with purest white symmetrical markings on head and muzzle, and he will always be a little special to me.*

These early days at Long Lane Farm have been busy and eventful. There is no routine as such, although my assigned tasks are to feed and water Iqbal the turkey, do the afternoon pooh pick and generally help where help is needed. We have had a few minor crises, like the escape from Alcatraz of Bunter when she decided to go for a walk towards Combe Martin one morning, and shinnied up the bank and over a stone wall. Capture this time was only two handed, but the weather was much kinder! And then Nasseem the polecat ferret escaped from Ferret City, to be caught at the bottom of one of our fields about half an hour later moseying along the hedgerow.

I travelled back to Eaton Bray and Black Pig Farm for a couple of days in March. The house was still fine and welcoming. Even the farm didn't look too bad after the ravages of the move and the winter, but the mud hasn't dried up. It's now covered in places with the bright green algae of stagnant water. The caravan and a barn had been broken into, predictably, bearing in mind the proximity of the gypsy encampment. Minor damage had been done, but in the space of half a day I was able to repair some of the damage and make Black Pig look at least half presentable for its ultimate purchaser. And I brought back with me on this visit the first animal to enter Black Pig Farm—Felix the farm cat, whom we inherited from the former owners when we bought the land in 1996. Felix is a fine, healthy and friendly black and white cat, who had spent the four years with us keeping at bay at least some of the hordes of rats and mice that infest anywhere that animal food is stored. We had thought to leave him at Black Pig when we left, believing him to be used to the territory, and that others than merely us were feeding him. However, we received reports from our friends in Eaton Bray that he was missing us and in some distress at our departure. He had been captured by Helen and Wendy (two of the Magnificent Eight above) and was lodging with Helen pending rehousing. Helen has 21 cats and a couple of goats, and a real concern for feline welfare.

So at the end of this second visit east Felix travelled back with me overnight to Devon. He now lives happily in the stock barn where he has his own armchair and is fed twice daily. Often he will meet me during the pooh pick for a cuddle and a bit of attention, before returning to George's Wood to forage and hunt. On wet nights he holds court with the other animals, and he greets Gilly most mornings when she opens the stock barn doors.

That about brings us up to date here at Long Lane Farm. We wait with baited breath on the news and progress of Foot and Mouth, which is currently about 5 or 6 miles distant as the crow flies. Mr. Parsnip, the pet lamb we saved from desertion by his mother last spring has a prolapsed rectum. Try as I may, I couldn't push it back, though I used half a bottle of Virgin Olive Oil in the attempt. I'm not too clever with bums it seems! We hosted an operation here in the barn when the Vet put him to rights surgically under epidural, so I could probably have a go in the future! An expensive business, but Mr. Parsnip like all of our animals is worth the trouble and the expense; they give us so much pleasure when they're not giving us heartache.

Thank you for reading this. Thanks too and again to all of those who helped and supported us in achieving our dream, and those of you who have shown an interest in our future. We will not forget any of you. And we hope to see you down here sometime. When you are passing. Thank you again, and good luck."

9. At Long Lane Farm

During the Coronavirus Lockdown of 2020 we are approaching the end of our twentieth year at Long Lane Farm. The first twelve months were a disaster, or at least a string of disasters; the death of my mother; the decline of Gilly's into dementia; the wax and wane of foot and mouth disease; the battle of wits with a psychotic neighbour; the tragic death of Jack the pony; the timely but no less tragic loss of my son and hair Badger. And all these stories have a place in my memoirs. But this book is entitled *"My Animals and Other Family"*. The rest of it I intend as a kind of homage to all those animals we have known, loved and cared for over the years. And whilst I will return to the, for me compelling, history of our lives together and how we have grown in those lives, I dedicate this memoir to the animals past and present and to Gilly who has cared for them.

I shall begin with Pigs.

10. Pigs I have loved

With the death of Pepys in the first few days at Long Lane, Potter, his companion at Black Pig, was a lone pig in mourning at the west end of the farm. I have always believed that it was the rapacious attentions of the three young women in Pepys' life that broke his back and brought him to an early grave. Potter had never troubled him in that way; either she was frigid or just old and disabled. I imagine Pepys was relieved at Potter's lack of interest in sex as it gave him some respite from the attentions lavished on him by the three promiscuous maids.

Left to her own devices Potter continued to live in the horse trailer she had arrived in, moseying about the front garden and acting as a sort of house pig receptionist to our guests. She got fed and watered twice a day and seems to have been quite content in Potter's Bar, our new name for the horse trailer in the front garden, in what became grandiosely known as the West End. She had a healthy appetite and put on weight at an almost undetectable rate. Unfortunately her little bent legs must have given her a lot of pain; her waddling was accompanied by a constant complaining cry.

Potter pottered happily enough about the front lawn for nearly two years. Early in the new year 2003 she suddenly seemed to lose the plot. I think she probably had a stroke or other mental accident. She wouldn't eat her pig nuts, and when a pig is off its food you kind of know it is going to die. She still wandered about the lawn for a few days but looked distinctly confused and even grumpier than usual. On the 11th. January she went into a coma and simply died. I dug the grave and buried her in what we then called the Orchard, now the Marauder's Meadow.

Meanwhile, down the East End, living in a kind of porcine luxury in the purpose built piggery with its concrete apron and spacious sun lawn, the remaining five black pigs of Black Pig Farm lived out their lives. It was not an entirely harmonious bucolic idyll down the East End, but the piggery had been well designed and sturdily built with piggy rivalry in mind. There are five bays, or chambers, in the piggery, each with its own front door and rear pop hole. The pop holes open onto a concrete apron which was divided into two by stout galvanised mesh fencing so that the inhabitants of the first three bays would have access onto three fifths of the apron and those using the fourth and fifth bay could be confined to their two fifths portion.

Candace Marie and her two boys Wilson and Mahlon were snuggled up in bays 2 and 3, with bay one reserved for spare hay and straw, buckets and spades for the servicing of the piggery. Meanwhile sisters Bunter and Blanche were housed in bays 4 and 5. All the pigs had access to their portion of the concrete apron during the day, whilst being shut in on winter nights as protection against the elements. During the day each household would have its half day access to the fenced paddock where they could graze on grass and roots, play in the wallow or just rest in the sun. In this way the five co-existed in relative harmony, and the bloodiest of battles were avoided.

Pigs can be astonishingly athletic creatures. For all her 20 odd stone Blanche did make her escape from the piggery one day in our first spring. She must have shinnied up the Devon bank that separated piggery from our back garden and appeared at our back door with a querulous look and a demand for attention. Persuading her back to quarters was no mean feat, but we managed with the help of a bowl of pig nuts and a stout fence post. And Blanche's bid for freedom cost us a couple of hundred quid and some more work for Mark Dallyn, our fencing contractor.

But outside of these minor incidents, pigs need little help on life's highway. They are voracious eaters but easily satisfied on a diet of pig nuts, biscuits, kitchen waste and water. They like virtually everything. Except, it seems, mushrooms and onions. And it is illegal in this country to feed a pig meat or meat derivatives, even though it is by no means a fastidious vegetarian. Pepys had a particular fondness for strawberries and avocado. His two boys carried on with that predilection when supplies from the local greengrocer would allow. They were quite satisfied with grass however and would feast on roots all day. Pigs are quite fussy with personal hygiene, will only pee and pooh as far as possible from their bed, rarely need cleaning out if they are allowed free range, as ours were. And they can be affectionate and playful. They do not need annual shearing, or much other attention. A rub behind the ears, perhaps, and the treat of the odd rich tea biscuit with their elevenses.

One little piece of attention the adult male (boar) can do with occasionally is to his toenails and his tusks. For these grow rapidly and throughout life. Our boys lived their lives on concrete, so their toenails needed little attention. But the tusks have to be trimmed occasionally or they grow into the pig's cheek and can cause quite serious laceration.

Top Tips for Farmers No.9: How to trim an adult boar's tusks without severe injury (to yourself).

1.   First try to catch your pig.

2.   When you begin to realise that an adult boar who does not wish to have its tusks trimmed will never let you, stop trying to catch your pig.

3.   A few days after 1 and 2 above when your pig is less suspicious of you and ideally is asleep, try stealth.

4.   Always go armed with a stout pair of pliers, wire cutters or a welding torch. If the latter, ensure you have a reliable and manoeuvrable power source.

5.   Approach your pig when he is asleep or distracted and always from downwind.

6.   As silently, quickly and accurately as you know how, apply the open jaws of your wire cutters (my preferred implement) to the uppermost tusk of your recumbent pig and clench the arms of the wire cutters with a single confident movement. You will only have this one chance. Do not under any circumstances shout "Hurrah!" if you are successful. Just retreat to a safe distance as nimbly as you know how.

7.   A few days later, when your pigs suspicions have been allayed and he is calmly and peacefully asleep but unsuspectingly presenting the other tusk to view, repeat steps 4 to 6 above.

Nobody seems to know how long a pig is supposed to live. Our three girls rescued from Paradise Farm in Bedfordshire and transported here to Devon in a hail of muck and bullets lived between 7 and 8 years. Blanche was the first to go, after a short illness where she seemed disinterested in her food. I found her early in the morning of 5th. April 2006 lying on her side in her bay apparently comatose and oblivious to the world. We did summons the vet who attended and administered a shot of antibiotics but by this time we sort of knew that Blanche was going to die. The vet advised me to try to warm her up as hyperthermia soon sets in to the body of a recumbent pig. So I covered her with blankets and a duvet, even set up a small radiator in the bay and was prepared to stay the night with her lending her my body warmth. This proved unnecessary. Blanche died in my arms moments later as I tried to rub some warmth into her.

I spent the rest of that fateful day digging a grave for Blanche, just south of the piggery and next to its dung clamp in Oasis Field. We buried her the following morning with full honours having transported her graveside aboard the Enterprise*.

(*The "Enterprise", I should explain, was a funereal bier I constructed from chipboard, two cast iron axles with wheels taken from a mobile chicken shed, and a length of rope for use by the motive power (the two of us) to tow the heavier of our deceased animals graveside. It was a bugger to steer, and a touch over engineered, but gave good service at several funerals until the floor rotted away. Later we used a sack barrow.)

Next to leave the piggery was Candace Marie. She'd always been a feisty little pig, bullied mercilessly by the bigger sisters Blanche and Bunter, but herself furiously protective of her boys Mahlon and Wilson with whom she'd been quartered since our arrival at Long Lane. After the departure of Blanche, who she did not miss and I think secretly despised for the way in which she'd murdered her entire farrowing of 13 piglets a few years previously, Candace Marie had seemed to take over leadership of the pigs. But in the early weeks of 2007 she seemed to slow down, becoming disinterested in life and her dinner. In late March her decline was rapid. She lapsed into coma on the 29th. and died at precisely 10.00 a.m. peacefully on her bed of straw.

Still a little nervous of burying our deceased we dug a grave under the bushes in the front garden, just over the wall from the piggery where Candace had spent the best years of her life. We buried her that evening, after dark, by torchlight.

Nearly nine months were to pass in the piggery with the remaining Bunter and the brothers Mahlon and Wilson. Then in the autumn Bunter seemed to suffer the same fate as her contemporaries. Refusing her food for something approaching three weeks she suffered a stroke and died in her bay on Guy Fawkes day 2007. We buried her at dusk near the septic tank. Her grave is marked by a small pile of soil which became known as Bunter Hill.

Mahlon and Wilson enjoyed the luxury of the piggery undisturbed by women for the next fifteen months. They were always a major attraction for visitors; passing tourists who broke down in our layby were invited to the piggery over the summer months and the boys were an especial delight to the townie children, most of whom had never seen a pig in the rind before.

In February 2009 we were approached by Diana Lewis of the North Devon Animal Ambulance. We'd rehomed several of Diana's waifs and strays by this time and Diana was aware we had abundant fresh green pasture and a friendly retirement home for unwanted or rescued farm animals. She had a pig for us to consider.

"She's a lovely little thing, you know. Three years old. A pet, and the apple of her owner's eye, but a move necessitates her rehoming. Will you take her?"

Well of course Gilly found it difficult to refuse Diana's blandishments and I just love pigs, as I have explained. Plus we had a purpose built piggery with only one of its five bays occupied by the brothers Mahlon and Wilson. Of course we would take the dear little redundant piglet. Shall we collect, or will you deliver?

Flowella Deville arrived on 21 February 2009 in the back of a horse trailer towed by Diana in her Animal Ambulance. She was very pink. She was very large. She was very tall. And she was very long. An adult Landrace, she took up most of the room in the animal trailer she arrived in and took some persuading to leave the comfort of her hay bed and take up position in bay 4 of the piggery. The monika "pet pig" I have to say was a touch misleading in terms of nomenclature. She dwarfed the boys, in whom she seemed to take more an aggressive than an amorous interest; it was clear from the get go that they would not be easy bedmates or even friendly neighbours and would need to be separated from them by the stout mesh fence that had kept them safe from their aunties Blanche and Bunter. My quote is from my own words in the Long Lane Calendar on the day of Flowella's arrival:

"*Seems tame and friendly. Likes her nuts!*"

That she was fond of her pig nuts was clear. Clearer still that she was not so tame and friendly, as I had imagined she'd be. Pigs can be mean. They can be downright nasty. Flowella turned out to be one such. Mahlon and Wilson were terrified of her.

Gilly had the unenviable task of feeding her and cleaning her out, and her wariness soon became cold fear. Be sure, certain pigs will eat literally everything in sight. And that includes human flesh and bone, if available. It soon became a battle of wits between Gilly and Flowella and it was all Gilly could do to keep one step ahead. Gilly would enter Flowella's quarters armed with a long handled broom and the broom was mainly used to keep Flowella at bay. Then, a couple of weeks after Flowella's arrival, I took Gilly to Tiverton Parkway railway station and put her on a train for India and Nepal. I was on my own at Long Lane Farm for the first time and for nearly three weeks to tend to the animals, including the increasingly worrying Flowella.

I quickly got into an established regime with the animals in my care; a routine which I was frequently to repeat as Gilly got the travel bug and left me to my devices while she trotted the globe in search of adventure. My life alone during her sojourns abroad was rarely less adventurous than hers. I was at my wary best in the presence of Flowella, kept her at snout's length at feeding and cleaning out time, and did my very best to reassure the timorous Mahlon and Wilson that all was well; mother would return in a trice and Flowella's attentions were more amorous than predatory. Not sure I was too convincing. Especially on the occasion I contrived to lock myself inadvertently in the service bay of the Piggery, when a gust of wind blew the heavy galvanised iron door shut on me, imprisoning this reluctant farm hand in a dark six by six chamber with no means of escape. It was perhaps the most frightening situation of my adult life; imprisoned in a windowless concrete and steel chamber, quarter of a mile distant from the nearest neighbouring house, with Gilly in either India or Nepal and oblivious to my plight, no food, water or toilet facilities, no communications, no post, not so much as a daily newspaper. I had visions of being pulled out of the piggery bay some 14 days later, a skeleton in wellingtons.

Fortunately for me, my blood curdling shrieks for help, bellowed through the hinge pin of the bay door at the top of my tear stained voice, brought farmer neighbour Steve Parkin galloping to my assistance; he'd just been returning to his house from the fields for a cup of coffee when he heard me. Steve freed me from my steel and concrete coffin and I resolved never again to enter the piggery bay alone on a windy day.

But the problem of Flowella remained. And it soon became clear to me during this enforced and lonesome vigil that she would have to go. I made swift enquiries of our neighbours the Wests at Indicknowle Farm. They kept and bred pigs for the table. They agreed to take her, though pig man Christopher was a little reluctant as he understands the piggy mentality and could spot a rogue a mile off. Flowella would have to remain at Long Lane Farm until the statutory 20 days had passed since her movement there (Disease Control (England) Order 2003) but, subject to that, could be moved to the relative safety of Indicknowle Farm thereafter.

Flowella left Long Lane Farm on 26 March 2009. The reign of terror was over. Gilly and I, and perhaps more importantly Mahlon and Wilson, could relax once more. She joined the small herd at Indicknowle where it was supposed she'd breed and add to the food chain. Her stay at Indicknowle was however to be truncated on account of her irascible and murderous behaviour. Her heart returned to Long Lane Farm in July, together with her liver and a large joint from her back left leg. I forgot to mention that pig man Christopher had also recently qualified as the local slaughterman.

Twins Wilson and Mahlon were now our only surviving pigs. They lived a life of luxury and abandon after the departure of Flowella. Peaceful and undisturbed, save by the odd curious visitor, they were a duo of mollicoddled porkers, spending their days rootling in the meadow grass, wallowing in the wallow, snoozing in the sunshine.

Five years were to pass in this bucolic wonderland before Wilson was to expire. He was found, quite dead, just outside the piggery on the morning of 24 April 2014 and he was still warm. He appeared to have suffered no illness, just a catastrophic heart attack, presumably at first light. We carried his corpse graveside aboard the sack barrow and buried him in Iqbal's Lament, where the advance grave had been dug. Mahlon was alone in the piggery.

Mahlon, the last pig standing. Would have been sixteen years old had he made it to June 2016. But though he'd been quite happy on his own for nearly two years, he died unprotestingly on 27 January of that year. Gilly found him on the morning of that day lying on his side in his bed, apparently comatose. I was invited to say goodbye to the old boy, which I did, with heavy heart. He certainly wasn't going to stand again, aided or at all. I went off to a training course in Bideford, to return at 2.00 in the afternoon. He had died a few minutes before. He's buried just south of the piggery in which he'd spent most of his life, near his auntie Blanche.

11. Goats I have admired

I have a particular affinity for goats. They are hardy, friendly, sociable, much more intelligent than sheep, their close cousins, and above all they are low maintenance. We had arrived at Long Lane Farm with just the two; Thunder and Fuchsia, both charming little pygmies. These two ran happily with the sheep in the paddock but had access to the Stock Barn for shelter and were stabled there at night. For that is the one major difference between goats and sheep that makes shelter for the former essential but for the latter irrelevant; goats have fur, or hair, which is not waterproofed. Sheep grow lanolated wool which is.

For three years and more Thunder and Fuchsia roamed the range, browsing on the hedges and grazing with the sheep on meadow grass. They also received a bowl of proprietary goat mix morning and evening and a six weekly hoof trim. I was and am the hoof trimmer for goats. I'd taught myself this skill in Bedfordshire, practising on the few goats we'd had there. I even had a short career in freelance animal podiatry as the self-styled "On The Hoof". All you really need is a good set of hoof shears or a hoof knife (I carry one wherever I go) and a willing helper to hold the goat. Gilly was invariably the willing helper and she became adept at catching Fuchsia by the horns and restraining her as I attended to her hooves, paring back six weeks or so's growth from each.

Thunder had no horns as he had been disbudded shortly after birth. So holding him steady was not so easy, but I soon discovered the straddle technique, which even a diminutive farmer can use on a pygmy goat. Standing astride Thunder I could grip him between my knees and apply the shears to each foot in turn. I always have a can of alamycin or other antiseptic spray at the ready to treat any foot rot that I might discover by its distinctive smell. It's a bit like athlete's foot in a human. On the whole I'm more at home with a goat's or a sheep's hoof than a human's any day of the week.

The goat herd more than doubled in 2004. In June we were presented with two Anglo Nubians by Steve Edwards, a hobbyist farmer we'd met on the tiny smallholding he rented with a garage and caravan. Steve was into milk and meat production in a small way, supplementing his meagre pension and disability benefits by bringing artisan bred goat, lamb and chicken to the table. We had in fact bought some of his excellent wares in the recent past. The two kids, twins of three months old, that he brought to us in his small animal trailer and walked down our front drive on the 14th. of the month were just too pretty to send to slaughter.

We named them Jasper and Orlando. They soon grew to full size which was considerably taller than the pygmies and we could look them in the eye without stooping. Fortunately both had magnificent horns each side of their bulbous Roman noses as the straddle technique for hoof trimming described above just wasn't going to work for these big boys. The twins were jet black, by the way, though Orlando sported white flashes on what would pass for forehead and chest. They were playful, verging on the naughty, but very attractive and quite startling additions to our growing menagerie.

On 11th. October Chelfie arrived on the scene. A beautiful pure white, if incredibly smelly, sanaan kid, with the beginnings of what were to become a magnificent set of pointy horns, trundled down the drive in the back of Diana Lewis's Animal Ambulance. Diana had rescued this, the last goat to arrive at Long Lane Farm, from the grounds of Chelfham Mill School, where he'd been seen wandering around, apparently lost or abandoned, and befriended by some of the unfortunate inmates of that establishment. Diana had dubbed him "Chelfie" in recognition of where he'd been found, and it was with this soubriquet that he'd already achieved a measure of local fame by appearing in the *North Devon Gazette* under banner headlines. We renamed him Stinker Moran on account of the pungent aroma that was almost visible to the naked eye. For Stinker was young, entire and very virile. All male entire goats have this distinctive aroma; Stinker had it in spades. It's produced hormonally and comes from a gland on the goat's forehead. It's supposedly attractive to the female of the species. Stinker would have to be castrated, if not because of the antisocial smell, more particularly because he'd otherwise becomes bothersome to the ageing Fuchsia.

So Stinker was quarantined in Potter's Bar, the horse trailer that'd become vacant since the passing of Potter Pig. He'd have to stay in the trailer and be fed and watered daily until such time as Diana could get him and his testicles seen to by her vet.

In fact he didn't have to wait long for his freedom. Diana returned to Long Lane a few days later and took Stinker to his destiny. She brought him back the following day as a castrate. A few more days in recovery in the trailer and Stinker emerged to take his rightful place with the other goats. The unbelievable stink with which he'd arrived disappeared in a matter of days and the handsome, proud and rather sweet smelling goat that emerged from the trailer was renamed Aramis.

We had a herd of five goats for just over three years. Though they are low maintenance in general their hooves do have to be trimmed about every six weeks. For these three years I really did begin to understand the plight and the occupational hazard of back ache to the farrier. Twenty hooves times eight times a year equals one hundred and sixty hooves a year or four hundred and eighty hooves over a three year period that needed trimming and spraying. It's not surprising I became quite professional at this task and was once asked by Diana Lewis to attend to the trimming of all the wild goats that inhabit the Valley of the Rocks just outside Lynton on the occasion of their annual treatment regime.

Fuchsia was the first of our Long Lane herd to leave us. She went downhill quite suddenly in the spring of 2007 by which time she must have been at quite a great age. In extremis she was euthanized in her loose box in the Stock Barn during the afternoon of 18 April by Diana Lewis. Diana had never seen me cry, as I always do on these occasions. I buried Fuchsia in our front garden, under a hedge, next to the remains of Candace-Marie Pig.

Jasper followed Fuchsia the following August. He went off his food quite suddenly and we believe his short term illness was probably of an intestinal nature. He didn't respond to a heavy dose of antibiotics administered by Diana Lewis and she returned a few days after this attempt with friendly vet Norman Bussel. Norman administered the lethal injection in the Stock Barn where Jasper languished in his coma. Jasper was buried on 21 August 2007 under a fir tree at the end of Iqbal's Lament.

Orlando didn't seem to miss his brother. He hung in there for another four years, but developed an alarming case of hip dysplasia in his advancing years. It almost seemed as if his legs had outgrown themselves. His walk was as painful to watch as it must actually have been to endure. In July of 2011 his condition reached the limit of endurance. He could no longer stand and collapsed in a helpless heap in the field. Between us Gilly and I struggled to heave the gangly Orlando into the Stock Barn where he spent 24 hours sitting on his haunches until Mark West could get to us with his pistol.

The leaving of Orlando was quite a dramatic affair. He sat on the Stock Barn floor with his now useless long rear legs pointing out in front. He seemed quite nonchalant and was chewing the cud as Mark approached, his high powered pistol cocked. He placed the muzzle of the gun against Orlando's handsome forehead, just above where his brain ought to have been. As he pulled the trigger, a deafening bang! reverberated about the Stock Barn. Orlando stayed sitting upright on the Stock Barn floor, still apparently chewing the cud, with an unconcerned expression on his noble face as black smoke and the fumes of cordite filtered through his teeth.

"Bloody hell! I think he's still alive!" exclaimed Mark as he hurriedly reloaded the pistol and put another explosive shell into the unsuspecting Orlando. More black smoke. More cordite. More unconcerned chewing of the cud. And gobbets of dark red blood ouzed from the beleaguered skull.

Once again Mark reloaded. Again he held the gun to Orlando's shattered skull. Again he pulled the trigger. This time Orlando collapsed in a heap on the concrete floor. He was quite dead. At last.

When I write about it, it seems like Orlando's death ordeal lasted a lifetime. In reality the whole thing was over in seconds, but those moments were as if in slow motion, and they will stay with me until my own last moments.

I buried Orlando with a heavy heart and in a very large hole, in the wood, near the Window on the World, on the day after his death, 8th July 2011.

Thunder, the little pygmy goat we'd adopted from Gilly's cousin in the Bedfordshire days, had witnessed all of the above. He'd seen the coming and going of Banquo, Fuchsia and Daisy, the departure of Capricorn Diana, the arrival and departure of Jasper and Orlando, the advent of Stinker Moran and his conversion into Aramis. And though he'd grown a little grey in the face over the years he'd enjoyed astonishingly good health and caused us no bother or expense at all with vets.

Twice, in his later years, he seemed to waiver in his determination to outlive us all. Twice we dug the anticipatory grave. Twice it was filled by another departing creature. When Thunder finally did succumb it was to anno domini and probably a heart attack in the Stock Barn overnight. And he did this on 15 September 2013 on the day of our return from France. House sitters Jo and Steve wielded the spade on that occasion and Thunder was well and truly planted by the time we got home, in a grave they'd dug him beside the Greenhouse. Dear old Thunder was well over 16 years old.

That left Aramis as our sole surviving goat. He's grown more affectionate and less obstreperous over the years. I trimmed his hooves last week. I put him to bed last evening at dusk with his ginger nut, apple and bowl of goat mix. I shall let him out in the morning. He's also well over 16 years old now. Don't know how much longer we'll have him, but he seems hale and hearty despite the years.

12. Fowl that have flitted through My Life

Many domestic fowl have crossed the hallowed portals of Long Lane Farm over the years. Before I tell of these feathered friends, I have a few tips for the prospective fowl fancier. Just a few essentials that I thought it helpful to pass on to those interested in the breeding, rearing and caring for such creatures as ducks, geese, chickens and the odd (ours was very odd) turkey. And I have gathered these tips under the general heading

Top Tips for Farmers No.13: Eight things you never knew about domestic fowl (probably)

1.   The male of the species is always bigger and more attractive than the female. That's how you recognise them. They're also noisier, can have a tendency to be chauvinistic, aggressive, self-opinionated, argumentative and rapacious. And otherwise than to impregnate the female of the species for those of you wishing to breed, they have no use at all. They are better left alone. Or eaten. Or fed to reptiles at the zoo as are many millions of male chicks annually.

2.   Males do not lay eggs.

3.   Females do.

4.   Eggs are rather delicious and come in various sizes which take different times to boil. They range from tiny (quail, a minute or two) to medium (chicken or duck, three to five minutes depending) to large (goose or turkey, up to eleven minutes) to huge (emu, which I've never boiled but I believe up to half an hour might be about right, and you'll need a lot of Marmite soldiers for this one).

5.   Eggs (laid by females, remember) will only hatch into chicks if they have been fertilised by a male through the procedure known as coitus non interruptus, with which I am sure the reader is acquainted, if only anecdotally. So that your eggs will only be fertile if you have a male bird of the appropriate species in your flock.

6.   Eggs, fertile or unfertilised, may be cooked and eaten in a variety of ways; boiled, fried, scrambled, poached, baked, pickled, coddled, raw. They last and are edible unrefrigerated for up to three weeks, refrigerated for some weeks more than that. But if you eat a fertilised egg do not expect it to hatch out. It's very much an either/or scenario.

7.   Eggs, if fertilised, will hatch out under a bird or in an incubator in 21 days (chicken), 28 days (duck or turkey), 28-30 days (goose) and 43-50 days (emu). Any egg that you have eaten will not hatch at all (see above).

8.	Finally a word about the fox. Chickens, ducks, turkeys and, well all domestic fowl really are prey to the fox, particularly in rural areas. Your enclosures need to be as fox proofed as possible. You can do this by digging in a chicken wire barrier at least six inches below the surface of the perimeter of the chicken run, for example. Or by tying little bags made out of ladies' tights containing human hair around the perimeter, as the fox will be deterred by the smell of humans. Or simply by pissing around the perimeter on a regular basis; this is better done by the male of the human species. Whatever you do to deter the fox, you are unlikely to keep a chicken for more than a year, if you are lucky and your fox is a bit old and knackered. Larger ducks may survive a little longer. Geese and turkeys have an even chance. But, as we shall see below, the days of your domestic fowl, particularly in the countryside, are numbered. So do not get too attached to them or you will live a life of grief.

These are some of the birds I have known. I have put them in separate chapters and called them for convenience "The Bird Tables".

13. Bird Table One, Chickens and the Odd Turkey

Iqbal the turkey, Christopher Cockerel and Charleston Hen arrived at Long Lane Farm in the decrepit horse box towed by the ancient Land Rover driven by Phil Carter on 9th February twenty years ago. Iqbal was put into solitary confinement in Iqbal's Lament, an old pheasant enclosure, where he was, on account of his irascible temperament, sharp claws and beak and prodigious weight, only to be approached armed with broom or shotgun. It was one of my jobs to feed and generally tend to Iqbal during that first year in Devon. Christopher and Charleston, infinitely more equable in temperament, were allocated quarters in the old hen house left behind by the previous owners.

All three were slaughtered by a fox in the early hours of the morning nearly a year later in early February '02. Iqbal was skinned, portioned and curried by Gilly with the comment "I've fed him for three years. Now he'll bloody well feed us". Tasty but tough, we both had indigestion.

Just before the dramatic departure of Iqbal and the two remaining Black Pig chickens we rescued Claude cockerel from a farm in Heddon Valley. Claude had been ostracised by the other cockerels present in the chicken run and came to us for respite care. Two days after his arrival we adopted three wives for him from another farm in Parracombe. Frances, Daisy and Mona joined him in the old chicken house on 29th January '02.

The bliss in the chicken house was not to be long-lived. Daisy only made it to July, when she "puffed up" for a few days and then died in her nesting box. Claude was murdered by fox or foxes unknown in December. Frances survived into January '03 but then caught a cold, "puffed up", was hospitalised in the piggery and died on the 27th. Mona achieved 1st March but then followed her sisters to a speedy and puffy demise.

Snow White and the seven dwarves

Snow White was a hen who arrived at Long Lane Farm with seven variegated chicks, all of different colours and breeds, on 10th May '02. She and her adopted brood were a present from Wendy DeMeur, who'd hatched them at Honeywick Farm in Bedfordshire. We named the chicks after the dwarves, viz. Doc, Dopey, Sleepy (three males, who grew into cockerels) and Sneezy, Grumpy, Happy and Bashful (who were hens). Snow White was perhaps not to know that she was to be the founder of an entire dynasty, albeit a short lived one.

Snow White went missing and was presumed taken by the fox, on my birthday in September 2003, to re-emerge two days later when she was found sitting on a clutch of eggs (see later) under a hedge near the Old Pump House (Camelia Cottage).

She hatched these further nine chicks and was seen resident with them near the Oil Tank. Having named them, rather inventively we thought, Supreme, Marengo, Coronation, Kiev, Chasseur, Korma, Madras, Vindaloo and Phal, she disappeared four days later, together with eight of her brood of nine, leaving only feathers and a memory remaining, with the sole surviving orphan. Orphan Annie, as this lucky survivor was re-named, was put into a budgie cage and lived happily in our lounge for a time. Later still re-named LouLou, when too large for the budgie cage, she found new quarters in the old greenhouse. She escaped the Great Chicken Slaughter of 6th November 2003 because she was lodging indoors at the time. But she came to grief in late December when she was declared missing, presumed taken by fox.

Snow White was one of our most prolific hens. But what happened to all her offspring, other than those accounted for above? Read on.

June was a solitary chick hatched to Snow White in the Old Hen House and named for the month of her hatching in 2003. She disappeared at the time of the Great Chicken Slaughter five months later.

Of the seven dwarves there is not much to tell. Once grown into adulthood they took to the wilds, roosting at dusk in the trees behind the Stock Barn. Their fate was sealed largely by their own choice of habitat, and they'd all perished before the end of 2003. Grumpy Hen left in June, Doc the Cock on my birthday in September, Dopey and Sleepy in November, about a week after the Great Chicken Slaughter which they miraculously survived.

Bashful, the pure white fluffy Silky hen with luxuriant feathers and a cap, hatched out the chick Baby Jesus in the Ark on 8th December '02 when she was barely eight months old herself. Bashful was infinitely more sensible than her sibling dwarves and, ever mindful of her creature comforts, took to the Ark's nesting box to perform nesting miracles. Baby Jesus came from a random egg we shoved under her. She had a habit of hatching out random eggs and performed this little trick on a duck egg on 25th August '03 producing the short lived Derek Duckling (see Bird Table Two, Ducks).

Bashful was the last of the seven dwarves to leave us, departing in late December '03, presumed taken by Mr. Fox

Sneezy contributed to the burgeoning supply of chickens at Long Lane Farm during 2003/2004. She hatched 9 chicks (3 white, 3 speckled, 3 black), we know not where, on 1st August 2003. We collected the little creatures up and put them in one of the loose boxes in the Stock Barn as we were running out of space for chickens. We named the whites Tammy, Patsy and Dolly, the blacks Tex, Mex and Lex, the speckleds Hoss, Adam and Little Joe. This was regardless of sex, which is not easy to determine in the hatchling.

Sneezy's life was otherwise unremarkable, save for his death, which was in the Great Chicken Slaughter of 6 November 2003. Mr. D'Arcy brought us her head in his mouth as some sort of conciliatory offering. Her "children" Patsy and Lex met the same fate.

Happy the hen was responsible for the "birth", in the stone trough next to the old greenhouse, on 19th August '03 of Blissful, Ecstatic, Gleeful, Joyous, Smiley, Chuckles and Guffaw, plus the ill-fated Jacques (Cousteau) who, despite my best efforts as foreman to drown him, survived. Also of Kevin and Roger who for reasons only known to a chicken were promptly adopted by the Baby Jesus. Most of these surprise offspring from Happy the hen took up quarters in a loose box in the barn. Kevin and Roger pitched in their lot with the Baby Jesus and Salome in the Ark.

Happy was another of those victims of the Great Chicken Slaughter of 6 November 2003. Neighbour Pam Parkin found her remains and brought them to us for formal burial. Her children Chuckles and Guffaw had also lost their lives in the mayhem of that night.

And what of the remoter issue of Snow White; her grand and great grandchildren deserve here some mention. Read on.

The Baby Jesus, Salome and Auf Wiedersehen Pet!

The Baby Jesus, Bashful's daughter, took after her mum in terms of parenting skills. She adopted random children and was perhaps a little neglectful in their care. Moses was the product of a random egg placed under a broody Baby Jesus in the chicken ark, where she took up her hatching quarters in June '03. Unfortunately that is where little Moses was found just over a week later, dead under his mum in the Ark's nesting box.

Salome, a pretty white chick, was another "born" out of wedlock to Baby Jesus in the Ark of a random egg on 10th August '03.

Then again, Kevin and Roger, technically Happy's offspring so far as we know, were immediately chicknapped and adopted by the Baby Jesus on 19th August that year. They lived with her and Salome in the chicken ark whilst most of the chickens by now had taken up residence in the loose box.

Baby Jesus just disappeared, early in the New Year of 2004. Having not been seen for several days we had to presume she'd been taken by Monsieur Foxy.

Meanwhile Salome, the only chick to have been hatched by Baby Jesus and to have survived any length of time, was, as we have seen, joined in the safety of the Ark by Roger and Kevin, Happy's redundant hatchlings. These two had escaped from the overcrowded conditions of the loose box in the Stock Barn where most of the barn fowl were lodging. They were named in honour of the electrician and the carpenter respectively who were at the time engaged on converting our Old Stone Barn into the Pleasure Dome. They kind of took to Salome; looked to her for succour and support (the chicks, that is, not so much the sparkie and the chippie).

And Salome was bent on a better life. In the April after her hatching she hatched herself 7 chicks, in The Ossie. No doubt the result of some loving but illicit relationship with one of the barn fowl, we collected the little chicks and put them for safety with Salome in the Ark. There were another six eggs as yet unhatched which we collected and put in the iguana Frederick Chappell-Pugsley's vivarium in the hope they'd perhaps hatch. Good job they didn't in a way as I'm sure Fred would have made quick work of them. We named Salome's brood Oz, Dennis, Neville, Bomber, Moxey, Barry and Wayne, the Auf Wiedersehen Pet! Seven. Kevin and Roger didn't seem too put out by this incursion of a bunch of noisy kids to the Ark, but they did gradually make their way to the, by now, less crowded conditions of the loose box with the other barn fowl. By July they'd all be gone, except the persistent Salome.

Wayne was the first to leave, as in the TV series. It seems that, unlike his namesake, he was somehow crushed to death in the Ark at just nine days old.

Dennis was decapitated by a sparrowhawk in Badger's Wood and found headless near Hagrid's House in the early evening of 22nd May.

Bomber left us, appropriately, on D Day. He may have been by the Ark ladder when it was drawn up the night before to keep the chicks "safe" from the Fox.

Barry and Moxey, still small chicks, were missing at midday on 9th June. We could only presume daylight action by Mr. Fox again. This left only Oz and Neville. But later, when they were put to bed in the Ark, only Oz presented. So the loss of Neville that bloody day had to be presumed too. Oz was alone in the Ark. And he was to disappear the very next day, probably taken by buzzard or crow.

The Auf Wiedersehen Pet! Seven had gone, almost as quickly as they'd arrived. But their mother, Salome, had taken refuge with the other barn fowl in the loose box, so she lived to tell the tale. As did yet Kevin and Roger, and Sneezy's daughter Dolly who'd thrown in her lot with the boys.

Kevin and Dolly had been missing for a couple of days when their absence was noted on 21st June. Presumed taken by fox, this left only Salome and Roger as the surviving barn fowl.

Roger finally fell foul of the fox outside the east hall window in July, leaving Salome on her own.

Evidently a survivor, Salome the errant hen lasted another nine months before she was, predictably, caught by the fox in July '05, or so we believed at the time. All we found of her was a tangled mass of feathers in the Oasis field, just south of the piggery. We still have some of that prolific hen's eggs, though they're well pickled by now!

The Happy and Sneezy broods

Hatched in August '03, Happy the hen's brood all did well to start with, except for the runt of the litter, little Jacques. Clearly not destined for old feathers, I tried to terminate Jacques by submerging him in a tank of water for a few minutes. Sounds cruel, but I still didn't have the technique to "neck" him. Anyway, after my third attempt at drowning the little fellow Jacques simply wouldn't give up. He obviously preferred to die in the relative warmth of the chicken shed with his siblings. Which is what he did. He didn't survive the night.

Blissful succumbed to a sudden and unexplained illness. She died in the loose box in September.

Chuckles and Guffaw lost their lives during the Great Chicken Slaughter with their parent Happy and others, on 6th November.

Smiley just went AWOL for some days in December, and had to be presumed inside the fox.

The rest of Happy's brood dodged the fox for a further six months, but in early June 2004 he was on the silent deadly rampage again and seems to have surprised Ecstatic, the white bantam cockerel. All we found of Ecstatic was a sad little pile of white feathers in Barnfield near the Donkery.

Two days later the last of Happy's brood were seen, or rather not seen, to be missing. Gleeful and Joyous, together with Sneezy's last two Tammy and Hoss were presumed taken by fox at the same time as Ecstatic.

The first of Sneezy's brood to exit stage right was Little Joe. We recorded death by misadventure on 7th September '03 when he was found floating in a water tank outside the Stock Barn, evidently whilst seeking a drink.

Patsy and Lex of course died with mum in the Great Chicken Slaughter in November.

Mex was another of those chancers. When seeking a drink from the water trough at the back of the Stock Barn he must have tumbled in and drowned a few days later.

Tex the black cockerel was taken by the fox in broad daylight the following February.

Tammy and Hoss went missing, presumed taken by the fox, in June '04.

There is no sign of Adam, Sneezy's last chick. I mean no sign at all in the Long Lane Calendar. He seems to have gone missing unnoticed, lost in the mists of time. Sorry to have missed you little fellow.

Hatherleigh Market

While all this mayhem of arriving and departing chickens was playing itself out, as a special treat on Gilly's 53rd birthday (it would have been Adolph Hitler's 105th, but I wasn't taking him) I took her to Hatherleigh's Tuesday market. There, wearing my used car dealer's camel coat and a trilby at a stylishly jaunty angle, I cut a swagger as I bid for four cardboard boxes containing mystery prizes. Each of the birds I'd purchased cost the average of 25p. When I opened the boxes I was confronted by, firstly two slightly annoyed Khaki Campbell ducklings (we named the male Donald and his female partner Campbell), three absolutely livid Sussex cross chicks (we were to name Tracey, Sharon and Debbie), six completely unperturbed Wellsomer chicks ("the Wellsomer Six") and 6 rather amiable Aylesbury ducklings ("the Hatherleigh Six"). All were berthed in their various boxes in the old greenhouse pending some further growth. What, you are bound to ask, was to become of this wealth of birds? Well it goes something like this:

Sharon only lasted a month. She "puffed up" for a couple of days, looked distinctly down in the beak, was hospitalised back in the greenhouse and died in the old hen house in May, about a month after her arrival.

Three weeks later on the evening of what I was to call the Night of the Long Knives all the Wellsomer 6 and Debbie and Tracey were taken by Mr. Fox. Only four barn fowl (residing in the Stock Barn) and the ducks (residing in the relative safety of the piggery) were left.

I shall deal with the fate of the ducks in Bird Table Two below.

The Brontë Sisters

The Brontë sisters joined our little and diminishing flock in July 2004. This was at a time when our flock had been decimated by the fox during the night of the long knives and we only had the few remaining barn fowl left, camping in the Stock Barn. Jane Howarth had set up a small charity at her place in Chulmleigh to rescue battery hens when they'd reached the end of their productive life and were due for the chop. This charity has now grown to unimaginable proportions, Jane Howarth sports an MBE, and her rescue hens are well beyond the average pocket. But in the early days she was selling the poor featherless and traumatised creatures for about 50p a throw. We travelled to Chulmleigh with friends Jill and Robert Hunter and several chicken transporters one wet day in July. For £3 we separated Jane from six of her charges and brought them back to Long Lane where they took up residence in the refurbished Old Chicken Shed with its "fox proof" run. Between them they'd managed three eggs en route and we celebrated our mission with egg mayo sandwiches.

Jane's surname reminded the literary amongst of us of the Howarth Parsonage where the Brontë sisters had grown up and written their famous novels. So in honour of Jane Howarth and her sterling work for charity we named the members of the new flock Jane, Emily, Ann, Charlotte, Gloria Stits, and Annabelle, or, collectively, the Chulmleigh Six. For a while we were inundated with beautiful atomic orange yolked eggs.

Gloria Stits only lasted about three months, but then she was one of the lesser known of the literary sisters. And she avoided murder at the claws and teeth of the fox. She simply "puffed up" for a few days, as chickens are prone to do when they catch cold, and died in the chicken run.

Jane went in much the same manner, early in the new year '05. Her "puffing up" was swift and her death in a nesting box not unexpected.

Annabelle lasted until the eve of Gilly's birthday in April 2005. Then, having "puffed up" for two days, she simply collapsed in a heap. Mark West dispatched her for us the same evening, as I still hadn't learnt this art to perfection. Gilly had by this time started to cremate the lost birds on a brazier in Barnfield. She burnt Annabelle once the rain had stopped. So the three Brontë sisters whom literature has forgotten are perhaps only commemorated here. You will find no mention of them in Wikipedia for instance. I've looked.

Emily was the first of the more illustrious Brontë sisters to leave us when she did the usual trick of "puffing up" over a few days and then died in her nesting box in the Old Hen House in mid-December.

Anne was last but one of the Chulmleigh Six. She died suddenly in the middle loose box of the Stock Barn, apparently after laying her last egg. There'd been no sign of previous illness. It was May 2006.

Charlotte, faithful long lasting and prolific hen, perhaps the most illustrious of all the Brontë clan, was taken by the fox in in the Toad Garden just outside her quarters early in the morning two years later while I was shaving in the bathroom. It was broad daylight. I heard and almost witnessed the crime. She was last of the Chulmleigh Six.

Matilda and the Pirates

Matilda hen was a present to Gilly on her 54th birthday (Adolph's 106th) from Mark West at Indicknowle. Mark waltzed proudly down the drive with her under his arm, a beautiful, plump and as it turned out extremely motherly hen. She was also sort of compensation for the loss the previous day of Annabelle, one of the lesser Brontës (see above). This is what you do when adding a chicken to an established flock, enter it after dark when all the others are asleep. When they awaken at first light they do not notice the newcomer, nor do they realise that their number has been augmented. They're quite stupid really, hens.

Matilda settled into the background as just an average hen. A year passed during which Matilda gave of her bounty and produced almost daily a large white egg with its deep orange yolk for our breakfast. Then quite suddenly in June '06 she became broody. The gestation period for a chicken in the egg is three weeks. Matilda took precisely that time to hatch out the first of her brood in the Old Hen House.

Sparrow and Pirate were the first to emerge, on 15th July (we'd just seen Johnny Depp in *Pirates of the Caribbean*). For her own safety we moved mother and children and the remaining eggs to a chicken run in the Greenhouse.

Next out were Keira and Captain, a day later (can you spot the pattern here with the names?). Matilda trod heavily on little Kiera and she wasn't expected to survive.

Last to emerge was Bloom (after Orlando) and I rendered him a little assistance as he was having trouble with his shell. Keira seems to have survived the treading incident with her clumsy mum and Matilda carried on with the business of bringing up her brood of five in the Greenhouse. After a week or so the chicks were big enough to join the other occupants of the Old Hen House.

Alas her efforts were in vain because four of the chicks, Sparrow, Keira, Captain and Bloom, went missing on the last day of the month. We had to presume they escaped from the Old Hen House and were taken by the fox. Only Pirate remained with his/her mum.

Less than a week later Pirate disappeared. We'd put him and his mum back in the Greenhouse in an effort to ward off the fox. And it wasn't a fox that got him in the end as there was no sign of entry to the Greenhouse. It's a mystery to this day what happened to Pirate. Did a rat take him? A weasel perhaps? The hand of God?

Matilda lasted another couple of years. She gave us plenty of eggs over that time, but didn't take to the hatching box again. So when she died she was childless, taken by the fox in broad daylight and left in the hen run. Or perhaps she just died of old age. Or grief. Her actual fate is unknown.

Ashleigh Fuckwit, my nemesis

The entrance of Ashleigh the big cock from Diana Lewis' Animal Ambulance on 22nd September 2005, was timely. Gilly was able to present him to me for my 56th birthday present one day later. A beautifully coloured (white, black, red and I think a hint of blue) and proud cockerel, he'd have looked equally as well in the show ring as the cock pit. He was temporarily quartered in the greenhouse pending being introduced to the other chickens over which he clearly regarded himself a cut above. Though I could not but admire the plumage, I sensed from the get go an air of arrogance and disdain towards me, his master and benefactor.

My first impressions were right. Ashleigh clearly hated all humans, particularly the male of the species and most particularly me. I learnt never to turn my back on him, but always to face him with either a broom or spade in my hands. He'd run and jump at me with spurs extended, itching to engage me in a fight to the death. He put me in hospital once; jumped me from behind and stuck me with his spur right through the wellington boot and into my ankle. The triage nurse at North Devon Hospital recorded my visit at 3.00 a.m. one summers Thursday morning as "Says he's been bitten (?) by a cockerel".

I added the soubriquet "Fuckwit" to Ashleigh's name after a couple of attacks. And Ashleigh Fuckwit became known as the psychotic terrorist to avoid at Long Lane Farm. I had many a battle with him at bedtime (about 6.00 p.m.) and can recall distinctly battering him about the beak with a garden hoe until he was reeling. But still he came back for more. Ashleigh Fuckwit was a dangerous animal, the terror of the West End of the farmyard and one to be avoided at all costs by our animal sitters for the four years he was to remain at Long Lane. I realise now that I should have done for him once he'd done for me. But, instead, he terrorised the chicken coop and the both of us for those four years, and saw off one or two foxes to my certain knowledge before my batterings with the garden hoe took their toll.

Ashleigh, the once vicious psychopath of the chicken house suddenly started acting strangely subdued one morning. For a few days he seemed as if in trance, almost as if he had suffered a stroke. On his last day he wouldn't come out of the chicken shed. I grabbed him gently and placed him in the greenhouse, where he died, peaceful but unrepentant, in the sun. I removed his left spur, the one he'd done me damage with, with a hacksaw and buried him in Iqbal's Lament. I still have the spur as a kind of reminder that the better man does, in the end, generally win.

Chick's chicks and other adoptees

In June of 2008 we let our cottage in Ilfracombe to Neil Rumson, a former hypnotherapy client and a truly gentle character who was fast to become a very good tenant and an important personal friend. Neil asked if he might fence off a small part of the little garden at Number 9 Church Road and keep chickens. I encouraged Neil to indulge this whim, gave him half a dozen fence stakes and some chicken wire and invited him to convert my dad's old shed into a chicken coup, which he did, adding a rustic gate of his own construction and inserting four standard laying hens to the coup.

For a few days all was well. Then he started getting complaints from the neighbours and one of the hens started eating its own eggs. So, inevitably, Neil (by this time we had dubbed him "Chick" Rumson, a name that has stayed between us now for so many years that Neil will always be "Chick" to me, though he's probably forgotten why) quickly began to go off the idea of keeping chickens and we adopted the cannibalistic Jutta. We stuck Jutta in the old chicken shed at Long Lane in July where she was welcomed in a sardonic sort of way by Ashleigh Fuckwit, the lone survivor of our last and most rapacious attack from the fox.

A couple of months later on my birthday in '08 Ashleigh and Jutta were joined (or rather rejoined) by Cleopatra, Josephine and Mrs. Simpson, birthday presents from Chick. Either he had been given an ultimatum by his neighbours or he simply couldn't withstand the pressures of fatherhood. Ashleigh was of course delighted. Domestic bliss was to reign in the chicken shed for some months.

Then Cleopatra fell off the perch one night in June '09. There were no noticeable signs of illness, though she may have been a little "puffed up" of late. I discovered her lifeless form when cleaning out the Old Hen House.

Two days later we received another five hens, all surplus to the requirements of our neighbours, Trevor and Elissa, who were overrun by an assortment of elderly chickens. We named this batch Apollinaire, Placide, Pascale, Davide and Rundall, in honour of newly made French neighbours and a local author of my acquaintance.

Davide was very thin and had the appearance of being very much the senior citizen. Within the week she was off her feet and dying in the hen house. I took her indoors to warm her up as hyperthermia in an elderly chicken can sometimes be cured in this way. But there was little response from Davide. I replaced her in the nesting box where she died over night. I buried her at dawn in Iqbal's Lament.

Another fox-fuelled massacre took six of our remaining seven hens one bloody night the following June. Jutta, Mrs.Simpson, Josephine, Placide, Pascale and Rundall were all taken from what until now I'd thought was a fox proof run, overnight. Only Apollinaire was left, because she wouldn't go into the hen house the previous night having what I can only think was a premonition of doom. Gilly took the one body we did find and placed it near to where we knew was the foxes' lair in the Oasis field; a kind of offering, or perhaps a piece of paper like Neville Chamberlain's. But there was an heroic postscript to this particularly gruesome episode. A few hours later Mrs. Simpson returned! She must have escaped the murderous onslaught of Reynard and hidden till morning. I could hear her crowing at me from the hen house.

The last of our chickens, Apollinaire and the heroic and doughty Mrs. Simpson, met their death at the teeth of a stoat or weasel. I found them dead in the chicken shed one November afternoon in 2010 at animal bedtime. They were put out in the field for the fox to consume in the morning. We were chickenless yet again!

The Margarets and the Annes

But we didn't stay chickenless for long. Towards the end of November Sue West of Indicknowle acquired a bunch of retired hens from a battery farm in Fremington. These poor creatures spend the nine or ten months of their commercial egg producing lives in appalling conditions cramped up in a twelve-inch square box with literally thousands of others in a darkened shed. They're force fed and required to produce an egg per day. When production falls below this stringent target and the hen begins to take a day or two off, she's for the chop. The Fremington Five were part of a contingent of these often featherless, sometimes blind, birds. Sue let us have five of her birds as she knew we'd been recently bereaved. They would have been about eighteen months old, bald, traumatised and extremely grateful in their own unexpressed way to have been delivered from the concentration camp conditions of the battery. We named them all, individually, Margaret. I had attempted some reinforcement to the sophisticated anti-fox-and-weasel battlements of the Old Hen House, where they took up nervous residence, and I hoped they'd be safe from marauders at least for a while.

The first of the Margarets lasted barely a fortnight, however. She was killed, either by stoat or weasel, in the hen house. Gilly put her corpse in the Orchard for the fox, or at least to keep him at bay for a while.

The second suffered a similar fate just over a month later while I was walking in the footsteps of Livingstone on the Zambesi in January '11. Gilly took off one of her legs for the stoat that had murdered her and left the rest of her remains in the Orchard for the chancing wildlife.

Steve Edwards, the hobbyist smallholder from whom we'd adopted our Anglo-Nubian goats Jasper and Orlando, was downsizing his flock in the October of 2011. We relieved him of five hens, four we called Anne to distinguish them from the Margarets and a little cripple named Lotte. We placed these in the Old Hen House and shut the remaining three Margarets out until tea time, when we mixed the two mini flocks as a sort of experiment. Which seemed to work.

Lotte, the little grey crippled hen, could walk or rather hobble no longer by New Years Day 2012 and we asked Mark West to dispatch her.

Margaret the third was found dead in her nesting box in the hennery one foggy morning in March. I walked across the fields in a thick fog to place her over the fence in the bottom left corner of Oasis Field for the fox.

The Annes all survived 2012 but all met their own fate during 2013, by the end of which we'd be chickenless again.

The first Anne was dispatched by me in April in the Stock Barn where she'd stayed overnight with an expectation of death in the early morning. She'd either been egg-bound, crop-bound or just very sick.

The second, a little brown hen who hadn't given an egg in all the time we'd had her, eventually died after a protracted illness one month later, in the field where we had been putting her in the sun for her last few days. She finally clapped out one sunny afternoon in May.

Exit Margaret the fourth on 1st July 2013, after a long time going down hill and transfer to the Piggery for her own safety. She died in Bay One, normally reserved for straw and tools, while Gilly was on her way back from Guémené.

The last Margaret had probably been marginalised by the loss of her sisters as she soon succumbed to bullying by the remaining two Annes. She seemed to go into a deep depression and, after a short illness, died in the Stock Barn while we were in France in September. She was buried by Jo and Steve, our house-sitters.

The last two Annes, left us on the same day, one taken, the other beheaded, in the chicken run almost certainly victims to the fox, on 23rd. November 2013. Once again we were chickenless.

Edward and the Mrs. Simpsons, our last efforts with chickens

About six months after the Anne and Margaret episode above described had come to its natural end, in the middle of June 2014, Steve Edwards decided to call it a day on his hobbyist life and retire. He'd unloaded most of his stock by the time we hove into view one sunny Sunday morning, to take delivery of Edward and the seven Mrs. Simpsons, a handsome well-fed cockerel and seven hens. We'd rescued them from the pot as it happens for these birds were "eaters" rather than "layers"; Steve was just about to dispatch and cook them. We transported the new incomers to Long Lane Farm in a variety of cardboard boxes. Soon they were clucking happily about in the Old Chicken Shed and well fox-proofed run (?!).

They all made it into the new year of 2015, but the final chicken family to occupy the Old Hen House gradually dwindled over the next twelve months and by the end of the year there was but one of the Mrs. Simpsons to celebrate Christmas alone.

The first Mrs. Simpson left in February, puffed up in the loose box in the Stock Barn where we'd relocated the birds during the damp and drizzly winter months. Thoroughly wet and miserable, she just gave up on life. I knew just how she must have felt as I get the same sort of feelings myself in February. Edward did not seem to grieve over his loss; he still had his other six wives to console him.

Mrs. Simpson No. 2 went missing at tea time in May, presumed taken by Mr. Fox as she wandered in Oasis Field.

Edward Cockerel was discovered in August, headless and dead (naturally!) in Boot Hill, presumed caught by the fox in Barn Field where there was evidence of his feathery capture and kill. He'd presumably been transported to Boot Hill for consumption in broad daylight. I placed his carcase over the fence out of reach of the Chilluns for Reynard to finish at his leisure.

Mrs. Simpson No. 3 made it to September when she was just missing at bedtime. Again, activity by the fox was suspected. Mrs. Simpson No. 4 was taken by the fox presumably right inside the Stock Barn, where we found a mass of feathers one October morning.

Mrs. Simpson No. 5 was living with her pals free in the Stock Barn, which had by this time become the fox's larder and charnel house, when she succumbed to his attentions one night in November. The only forensic evidence of the crime was a pile of miserable feathers.

Mrs. Simpson No. 6 was, rather predictably, taken by the fox in the Stock Barn leaving a load of feathers and one remaining Mrs. Simpson in early December. The fox had spaced its visits to the Stock Barn with great precision; it was almost certainly bringing up a litter of young which was feasting on our flock.

When the last the Mrs. Simpsons was taken in much the same way leaving the tell-tale pile of feathers and a wing in late January 2016, Gilly decided to call it a day on chickens. The eggs really weren't worth all the grief. We haven't had a chicken since.

14. The Black Pig Sheep and what became of them

Sheep come in all shapes and sizes. Many have passed through our hands over the years but not so many have left their mark. They are not known as individualists and have a tendency to stay with the flock where possible. But a humanised sheep, that is one that has been reared on the bottle and has known human company from birth, can be quite affectionate and personable.

They are high maintenance at certain times of the year, need shearing annually and their feet checked for rot in damp conditions (if you see a sheep in a field with a pronounced limp pound to a pinch it's just foot rot or strip, the condition of soreness caused by long damp grass or mud between the cleats). They need protection from fly strike three weeks after shearing. And occasionally they need checking for lice, ticks, head fly and maggots. In winter after the grass has been nibbled to the ground and the new grass has not begun to sprout your average sheep might like some hay or ewe nuts to supplement its diet.

Otherwise sheep can averagely be left to get on with their lives unassisted. They wander around the pasture eating and shitting at will. They do not seem to have any great ambitions, creative urges or philosophical thoughts to ponder. If they have one goal in life, it is to die. As friend Graham de Meur once told me, the more intelligent a sheep, the earlier it will achieve its goal. The most intelligent are stillborn!

We arrived at Long Lane Farm with seventeen sheep. This is what happened to them:

Beau, the little brown Soay and first sheep of my personal acquaintance, arrived in the back of the old horse box we now call "The Love Shack" (it now serves as a reserve log shelter), towed by our ancient Land Rover and accompanied by Mr.Parsnip, two pigs a cockerel and a turkey. She spent her first night at Long Lane in the Stock Barn with the others and then emerged into the sunshine and long meadow grass of Barnfield to munch away in peace. It must have been a little lonely for her until the main contingent of sheep arrived a few days later. But she merged into the background with the other sheep and I think appreciated her new quarters.

A fortnight after our arrival foot and mouth disease was announced in Devon and we were constrained to live through the nightmare of daily visits from MAFF inspectors and veterinary surgeons from all over Europe, foot baths for our visitors and all the other restrictions on our freedom that came with that regime. Beau and the other sheep were not particularly perturbed or even bothered by our plight. I'm sure they had no idea how close they came to achieving their goal of extinction over those nightmarish six months.

Beau was fine about foot and mouth. But she only made it through until late November when she had a stroke or other mental accident of old age. She was helped along by lethal injection by a local vet on the Stock Barn floor on the 18th and buried in Boot Hill.

Mr.Parsnip bucked the sheepish trend.

He had more personality packed into his poor little deformed and stunted body than a flock of one hundred you'd see grazing in the field. You may remember Mr. Parsnip, born to Roxanne and abandoned in the barn at Black Pig. I truly believe I gave him the only two years of life he would have by sitting and cuddling him and coaxing life into the dear little chap in Bedfordshire. But that little life was to be fraught with incident and intervention. While still in Bedfordshire he showed signs of internal damage or underdevelopment and had to be "tubed" by Anne Healey, Peter's legless wife at Common Farm. This was a relatively gentle and homespun operation performed on Anne's kitchen table with the passage of a tube down little Mr.Parsnip's throat to ease the digestive tract with castor oil and allow him to dung properly. He survived that little indignity unscathed. He survived too the third degree burns inflicted on his poor little head and neck by the inappropriately positioned heat lamp I'd rigged up in our garage to give him the semblance of motherly love. He even survived the weeks of olive oil being applied to his burns and withered skin in the lead up to our departure from Black Pig Farm.

In Devon Mr.Parsnip enjoyed the open fields and rich grass and even seemed to thrive for a while during that first spring when he was delightfully oblivious and unperturbed by the plight of Foot and Mouth which beset us. Quite suddenly though, just as the dust was settling and the stream of MAFF vets and administrators by whom we'd been beleaguered over our first six months at Long Lane was beginning to subside, Mr. Parsnip prolapsed his rectum. It just popped out one day, about 2 inches of rectum that should really stay within the body as it does with most sheep. And people for that matter. I was the first to notice it I think. And the first to be concerned that Mr.Parsnip's rectum would probably do better if it returned to whence it came. I'd had a go with a chicken, if you remember the occasion of Cordelia's prolapsed cloacca. Well in a sheep a cloacca doubles as a rectum. My success with Cordelia and her prolapse was not exactly legendary. I really did not think I should attempt to push Mr.Parsnip's back, though I did give it a try. So we summonsed Simon the vet from Mullacott Cross Veterinary Hospital.

The operation took place one sunny afternoon in the summer. Under the cold glare of the neon lights in the operating room (my "workshop" at Long Lane Farm) Simon, resplendent in his surgical whites, the gleam of his scalpel reflected off the sweat on his nervous brow, attacked the escaped rectum with the ease and the expertise of his years. I busied around him like some latter-day ageing veterinary nurse, mopping his fevered brow, staunching the flow of blood, generally getting in the way, as Simon swiftly and rather accurately sliced a couple of inches off Mr.Parsnip's rectum, stitched him up to prevent further relapse and administered a hefty dose of antibiotics to prevent infection. The whole thing was over in moments. Mr.Parsnip joined the rest of the flock a couple of hours later after the local anaesthetic had worn off. He seemed to be none the worse for wear and returned immediately to the high spirited and indomitable creature we'd come to love and respect.

Some six months later Mr.Parsnip did take a downward trend. It was not very surprising bearing mind the dramatic start to his life and the events of the preceding two years that he should contract double pneumonia in the winter of 2002. We quartered him in what was the Old Stone Barn (later to become the Pleasure Dome) to receive the kindness of close care. But there was nothing we could do for him, and he achieved the goal of all sheep just over a year from when he landed at Long Lane Farm, on 26 February 2002.

Wally Patch Gilly's favourite at Black Pig, the only sheep with which she could truly converse (in "Sheepish"), found his mark as the undisputed leader of the flock at Long Lane. He'd survived early bullyings over his gaping eye cavity at Longford Farm, depression and anxiety over the declining weather and ground conditions at Black Pig, and of course the incident of my amateur surgery on his haematoma stricken ear. At Long Lane he proudly took command of the burgeoning flock and led them fearlessly into two shearings and treatments for fly strike. He enjoyed two good summers too, until, in the spring of 2003, he seemed to be showing his age. He lost weight and condition in February and was helped into a loose box in the Stock Barn late in the afternoon of the 25th. It was a mercifully short illness. Wally was dead in the morning.

Friends Julie and Phil Carter from Luton in Bedfordshire were staying with us that weekend. Phil helped me, reluctantly it seems as he does not handle death or animals with relish, tow the stiff corpse of Wally Patch gravewards aboard the *Enterprise*. I'd already dug the grave at the Window on the World, the little glade between Badger's Wood and what has become the Marauder's Meadow. He lies there now, not far from Potter Pig.

Tuesday, the beautiful golden Portland ram we'd adopted from Farmer Palmer and named partly after the day of his birth and partly in honour of the name I'd adopted for myself in adolescence, was my favourite. By the time we'd arrived at Long Lane his horns had reached a stupendous triple spiral and he'd mosey around the field in all his undoubted splendour nonchalantly cudding on rich meadow grass and showing off to the females. In fact it was the mystery of the new born lambs at Long Lane that had brought to our attention that all of the pregnancies cannot that year have been phantom. These were real lambs that were being produced by anonymous members of our less than sterile flock. We would have to mount a veterinary investigation as to paternal rights. Either that, or just have the suspects

castrated. We were a rescue operation, not a religious commune, after all. The pregnancies would have to stop, pronto.

So we decided on the less expensive castration route. Professional veterinary services would have to be brought to Long Lane Farm to undo the bungled elastrations I had apparently carried out. The suspects for this treatment were Tuesday, Jacob and his half brother (and possibly his son!) Dave the Fire. Donkey had been vasectomised in Bedfordshire, so he and his massive bollocks were in the clear. We were satisfied the other males had been properly seen to shortly after birth.

One afternoon in the summer of 2001 Simon and a crew of veterinary nurses attended at Long Lane Farm and the deeds were done. They're quite quick operations really, carried out under sedative or local anaesthetic on the lawn, with me sitting astride a garden chair with each sheep legs akimbo between mine as the vet wielded the scalpel and the nurse the local. All done in an hour or so in the warm sunshine on a grassy lawn.

Tuesday was not to benefit much from the operation, even if the females were. On the afternoon of 17 May 2002 there was a violent thunderstorm and torrential rain. When the storm was over and I was inspecting the farm for damage and depredation I found Tuesday cast on his back in Boot Hill, near to the galvanised iron gate that stood open between Boot Hill and Barnfield. He was quite dead. Still warm and soft to the touch, but quite dead. There was not a mark on his beautiful body but his mouth was full of blood. I have always suspected he was the victim of lightning strike, arcing through the gate and earthing through his dear body. But I will never know the truth.

Donkey avoided the treatment on the lawn that first summer because his lack of potential for fatherhood was beyond doubt. I had attended and assisted at his vasectomy in Bedfordshire after all. Donkey was to present no danger to the girls of Long Lane Farm; rather he was to provide rather a useful service. He still retained his animal desire for sexual relations of course and his ability in this area was undiminished. He became the Teaser of the flock, sort of *"Have Love Will Travel"* satisfying his own lusts and the needs of the more amorous ewes without augmenting their number.

It may have been his amorous adventures that were to cause his premature end. One bright sunny morning in May 2004, on the 4th to be precise, I found Donkey thrashing about in the Stock Barn, stumbling wide eyed but aimlessly about, crashing into the concrete walls in obvious terror and confusion. He was bloated to inconceivable proportions. I rushed off to Stapleton Farm a couple of miles away and Adam Stanbury for advice on what I might do to remedy Donkey's plight.

"Sounds to me like he might be bloated. Something he's eaten perhaps. Or a twisted gut. You could try tubing him, give him a drench. But you'll need to be quick. He could explode!" offered Adam. He also offered me a tube and funnel and a bottle of proprietary drench he kept by him for this condition in his dairy herd.

I made for home on two wheels, hurtled through the open gate, galloped in my wellies to the Stock Barn door. But I was too late for poor old Donkey. He lay prostrate on the Stock Barn floor, sighing his last. He hadn't exploded exactly, in fact he was as bloated as when I'd last seen him. The shock and the pain of his distended condition had apparently given him the equivalent of a violent and fatal heart attack. A few moments later he was still. Out of his agony at least.

I dug a hasty but deep grave for Donkey in front of the old greenhouse. But I still had to deflate his overblown body before he would fit comfortably in it. This I achieved by puncturing his abdomen with a sharpened screwdriver (the instrument has to be inserted in the groin area at the top of a hind leg where it joins the animal's belly; a trick I'd heard in Bedfordshire where I'd also heard that a well-placed screwdriver can save the life of an animal *in extremis* from bloat). Donkey's abdomen returned to more or less average proportions as a stream of gas and green bile shot from the puncture wound. But Donkey was no more unfortunately. He lies in that grave in front of the old greenhouse.

Roxanne was the next of the Bedfordshire sheep to leave us, on the 14th September 2005. Our oldest living sheep at the time of her death, she'd come to us from Farmer Palmer as part payment for hosting his flock during the winter of 1997/8. Although old and due for dog meat at the time, she proved to be the most productive of sheep, founding a veritable dynasty at both Black Pig and Long Lane.

At Black Pig she gave us the triplets Jacob, April and Raindance. One year later she gave us Dave the Fire and the unfortunate but plucky Mr.Parsnip. At Long Lane she produced Layla in the opening months of 2001. And she was to be grandmother to Raindance's White Buffalo and Running Bear, Shawnee and Crow, to April's Sundae and later Honeylamb, possibly to Hortense's Miracle and definitely great grandmother to Sundae's Pancake.

Roxanne, pretty and rather sassy full Jacob (one of the only three we were to possess) noted for her ankle bracelet and her obliging womb, died peacefully during the night of 13/14 September 2005, probably of pure old age and worn out by a lifetime of motherhood.

Dave the Fire, Mr.Parsnip's big brother, was one of those many sheep that gently merged into the background at Long Lane. Nothing remarkable about his life really, but he dutifully acquiesced in eight years shearings and the ignominy of late castration before he succumbed to slow illness over the autumn and winter of 2006. He seemed to lose condition and the will to live over those nine months and then rapidly over his last fortnight. He eventually took to the donkey shelter and refused to stand for five days. When a sheep is "off his feet" he is ready to be dispatched to the

unknown. When his time had come, on the 18th March 2007, he was dispatched by lethal injection administered by retired vet Norman Bussell of the North Devon Animal Ambulance.

Sundae, April's first born and Roxanne's granddaughter, left us on 15 February 2008. Her death remains a mystery, but her destiny was to be half consumed by foxes or perhaps a badger. Gilly discovered her half eaten corpse by the road hedge in Oasis field when doing her morning rounds. She had put the remains in a dumpy bag and towed her to Iqbal's Lament by the time I returned from my early morning swim. She was buried in the wood, and in the digging of her grave bones of an earlier interment (possibly those of Black Crow, who had died about seven years previously during foot and mouth) surfaced, evidence of the charnel house Long Lane Farm was becoming.

Raindance was the first of Roxanne's triplets of 1998 to leave us and at nearly twelve years old had caused very little problem at all. She'd melded into the flock at Long Lane and given us the two little North American Indian children Shawnee and Black Crow, conceived illicitly at Black Pig. In February 2010 after nine years in the background she contracted whatever it is sheep contract just before they die. She was "off her feet" as they say here in North Devon. And she didn't seem willing to get back on them. We duly summonsed Mark West of Indicknowle Farm, having given up over the years contacting a vet for ovine issues as they seem to have little effect. Mark advised us to take Raindance in out of the rain. We did manage to manhandle her into the back of the Landrover and transport her to the Stock Barn, where she died, without explanation or farewell, on contact with the barn floor. She still had a full set of teeth.

April's departure was similar to that of Raindance, just under a year later. Another of those first triplet children of Roxanne and the mother of Sundae in Bedfordshire and Honeylamb in Devon, April spent most of her life in the background at Long Lane. When she died, it was of a short and undefined illness, or simple old age. She would have been 13 years old had she made it to her birth month. But like Raindance she simply went downhill in the winter of 2011 and, despite a little special attention and sheltering in the Ossie for about a week, she was found dead there on the morning of 14 January 2011, two days before my departure for Africa and Victoria Falls. Gilly dug her grave unassisted, thoughtful for my wellbeing so soon before departure to the Dark Continent.

Jacob had the longest and most eventful life of those triplets of Roxanne, and perhaps the kindest of deaths. After Wally had died Jacob was seen by many of the others as a sort of elder statesman, deputy leader then leader of the flock. He'd endured faulty castration by elastrator at my less than experienced hands in Bedfordshire. He'd fathered, illicitly and most probably incestuously, a number of the flock (Running Bear, Dave the Fire, Mr.Parsnip, maybe Miracle). He'd been properly castrated by the vet at Long Lane. He was the only of our sheep to suffer head fly, a condition peculiar to horned sheep which requires urgent attention if brain damage is to be avoided. And he'd suffered the added ignominy of horn removal by cheesewire saw. This latter operation was conducted by myself with the help of Farmer Steve

Parkin to assist in the holding of the sheep while I wielded the cheesewire. Necessary to alleviate the pressure of Jacob's spiral growing horns on his cheek and jaw, the operation was carried out in the Stock Barn quite late into Jacob's adulthood. I still have Jacob's horns.

Jacob was well over 17 years old and our first born at Black Pig Farm when he was found dead on the hot and sunny afternoon of 15 July 2015 after a full and I hope satisfying breakfast.

Hortense arrived at Black Pig with Roxanne and like her was a full Jacob sheep. I always believed she might have been Roxanne's daughter, perhaps her lamb of a previous year. Unlike Roxanne, however, Hortense was not generous with her favours and as far as we knew her only lamb was the large and leggy Miracle, to whom she gave birth (with my memorable assistance) in the first weeks at Long Lane. Apart from giving us Miracle, Hortense stayed very much in the background, caused no fuss and was never ill or in need of my particular brand of amateur veterinary treatment. She endured ten shearings and the usual annual foot treatments. Over time she developed what might have been small cancerous growths on her back and belly but these were soon excised at shearing time and seemed to give her no cause for concern. Which is why her sudden death on the last day of July 2011 was a tad surprising. We found her that afternoon in Boot Hill by the hedge. It is true that she had developed advanced arthritis in one leg by the time of her death, but I'm not sure what exactly it was that finished her off.

Mouse, who with Donkey had been brought up in our garage in Bedfordshire, was with us for 15 years. He once developed a haematoma to the ear which I treated in the same way as I had Wally's, lancing it with a sharpened and sterilised bodkin while Derrick our builder friend held him still in the donkey shelter. He graced the front of our corporate Long Lane Christmas card aged 14¾. Not long after this historic and festive event he went blind and fell into a lingering decline. By this time, perhaps wise to the futile attempts veterinary surgeons had made to save members of our flock, we asked Mark West to dispatch him in Boot Hill with his high powered pistol. Mouse made it to 8th January 2013 when he was trolleyed to Badger's Wood and buried close to the Cosmic Ordering Service.

White Buffalo and **Running Bear**, Raindance's first two children, stayed firm friends and very much in the background at Long Lane. They grew fat and healthy and lasted many years. Buffalo was the first to leave us, on 13th. August 2013. He was 13 years old when Gilly found him that morning unable to stand in Barnfield. Between us we got him to his feet, but he couldn't remain standing unaided. We duly summoned Mark West, who'd become our dispatcher (executioner) of choice by this time to dispatch the old boy, but he died on his own shortly after noon on a hot bright day.

Bear had a pretty uneventful life and was always the more timid of the native American twins. His willy was badly sliced by the sheep shearer one year (he'd mistaken him for a ewe) but seemed unconcerned about this after a copious dressing with the old alamycin spray. He outlived Buffalo by a further three years but was a victim, I think, of the extremely long and wet winter of 2015/16. He finally succumbed to old age and that dreadful weather six days before his sixteenth birthday, on 5ᵗʰ March 2016. Gilly found him that morning lying on his side in Dungroamin, the mobile shelter we'd stationed in Boot Hill. He was clearly unconscious and we let him die peacefully in his own time.

Buffalo was the last of the Bedfordshire sheep to leave us. He was, I believe, the second (to Jacob) oldest sheep we owned which we can determine the exact length of his life.

But before I leave the exposition of the lives of the Black Pig sheep, there are two other notable characters I must mention.

Consuela

Consuela surprised us at least three times in her long (for a sheep) life. Firstly by her birth, which I have described elsewhere, but which you will recall was in the back of our ageing Land Rover, where she was delivered of Juanita, her very aged mother, by a friendly female farmer in Bedfordshire. Secondly by surviving the grief and trauma of the loss of her mother at the hands of Peter Healey and his shotgun, an incident which had ended in the very near decapitation of the unfortunate Juanita. Consuela travelled to Long Lane Farm a traumatised and no doubt grief stricken orphaned adolescent. The third surprise which Consuela was to present us with was the pretty little white ball of fluff we were to name Margarita, the morning after that first shearing in Devon. Consuela had travelled to Devon in the very early stages of pregnancy (I suspect Tuesday as the putative father, because of Margarita's colouring) and deposited her lamb just after the trauma of being sheared.

Apart from these traumatic and exciting events in Consuela's life, she was again very much one of the sheep in the background. By late 2014 she still had her daughter Margarita by her side but she was in steady decline. In November she was off her feet and we asked Mark to do the honours in her dispatch. Mark thought she just might come out of her decline and preferred to help us get her into the Stock Barn and out of the relentless November rain. We tended to her for a couple of days in a loose box with a bed of dry hay and some sheep nuts. But at first light on the morning of 23ʳᵈ November we found her dead.

Little Cloud

Little Cloud was, of all our sheep, the most determined to stay alive. You might recall he came to us from Peter Healey as a little orphan cripple, probably rolled upon by his mum in her death throes. I'd bathed his open suppurating wounds in a wheelbarrow at Black Pig and he'd grown to adulthood with an attitude of self-preservation, also with an unwritten bond with me.

Though Little Cloud's wound eventually healed and my daily ministrations in the wheelbarrow were no more needed, the leg, his rear left, was always useless, save as a sort of prop. He could keep up with the flock and run quite fast if he thought he was in danger, but his gait was at best peculiar. The left, useless, leg acted as a sort of oar to propel Little Cloud along and help maintain a semblance of balance, and at this he was really quite good. Unfortunately the effort and the years must have put terrific pressure on the right hip. By the winter of 2012 his dysplasia was pronounced and he had some difficulty standing, especially on soggy terrain.

One particularly wet and windy afternoon in December Little Cloud took a fall outside Dungroamin. He must have been thrashing about in the mud and slime for hours before we became aware of his plight and hurried to his rescue over the blasted heath of Boot Hill in a downpour. We found we couldn't lift him back to his feet and he was drenched to his aged skin. We summonsed Steve Parkin who was doing his rounds on his quad bike at the time and Steve was able to manhandle the bedraggled heap of wool and flailing legs onto the back of the quad and ferry him back to our Stock Barn.

I really didn't think Little Cloud would survive the night. We propped his shivering, nearly unconscious, form in the sitting position between two bales of straw, tried to mop some of the filth from his struggling little body, left him to his own devices with a bowl of sheep nuts and some water until morning.

We quite expected Little Cloud to expire overnight. But at first light we visited the old chap in his makeshift bed and found him, still shivering, but alive. He spent three days on the Stock Barn floor, contemplating his plight and, no doubt, making his peace with whatever God sheep pray to. On the fourth day we found Little Cloud on his feet, still looking sorry for himself, but apparently ready once again for the great outdoors. We let him out of the loose box and he joined his mates in the cold December sunshine, nibbling greedily at the sheep nuts and hay we provided for winter fodder.

I believe the experiences of that winter in the rain bolstered Little Cloud's spirit and determination. He lasted another year and a bit. But his legs and hips had taken a battering over the years. In the spring of 2014 he began to need more and more help standing and staying on his legs. Gilly or I would start the day by helping Little Cloud to his feet, steadying the old boy before his day with the flock.

Finally he could stand no more. Early in the morning of 6th May we had to summons the executioner for Little Cloud. Mark West attended our plea within minutes and with his high powered pistol. But even at the point of death Little Cloud had no intention of leaving us with a smile. He tried to escape death even with two slugs in his brain. It took a third and a fourth from Mark's powerful gun to lay the old boy down, such was his determination to carry on. He is buried in Badger's Wood, close to Hagrid's House.

Lest anyone reading this memoir should think for one moment that I take the death of these animals lightly, I should point out that the decision to euthanize one of our wonderful animals has always been hard for me. But I feel the need to be present at the pulling of the trigger, as the one who has made the decision that the time has come. And still I feel the bullet screaming through my soul as it tears into the brain of the stricken animal. It's as if I am experiencing the sensation of being shot myself, every single time.

15. Bird TableTwo, Ducks

Martin and Leslie, Aylesbury ducks, came to us from Combe Martin, a couple of months after we landed at Long Lane Farm, in April, '01. Leslie was a sedate little fellow, quiet and at ease with his sexuality, possible a little gay. Martin on the other hand was a rapacious bully. Fortunately for Leslie, Martin was clearly straight; he reserved his pent up amorous attentions for ducks of the female persuasion. But there were some tense confrontations between this pair during the year they spent celibate in the piggery.

In June of the following year we started a new adventure with the introduction of three ducks and two submissive drakes. I'm not sure where these came from, as it was a little early in our association with Diana Lewis of the North Devon Animal Ambulance, but let us say that is where they came from and that they were rescued ducks. Enter Jessie, Mabel, Digweed, Hughie and Louie (not Dewey) to the piggery at Long Lane Farm. It was clear from the start that Martin would have to go as he became furiously competitive for the fresh new female blood that Jessie, Mabel and Digweed represented. Martin went to our neighbours, the Wests of Indicknowle Farm, in July. He would do happy service as a stud duck for a number of years.

We'd had our new brood exactly a year when tragedy struck the ducks in the piggery. Hughie was savaged by the ever invisible fox and died later in the day. Louis (not Dewey) was missing, presumed taken by the same indiscriminate fox. The three ladies remained. I assumed at the time that the boys had fought some battle with the fox in defence of their honour. But perhaps they just ran, or paddled, away. Either way, the remaining ducks were only to enjoy their new found domestic bliss for three months. The fox returned for Leslie, Jessie, Mabel and Digweed after dark in September '03. We must have been late putting them to bed in the safety of the piggery. We were Duckless in Gaza again!

It's probably not entirely fair to blame Bashful the hen (see Bird Table One) for her promiscuity and indiscriminate behaviour as far as the baby duckling Derek was concerned. She must have had some human intervention or help in the provision of a fertile duck egg, whether that came from the piggery where we had ducks roaming about, or perhaps from the Indicknowle brood. Anyway Derek was duly hatched by Bashful on 25th August '03 and then promptly abandoned, no doubt because of his looks. Thereafter he largely depended for his survival on that human intervention. We fashioned a little carrycot for him and took him shopping with us to Tiles R Us in Barnstaple. The men in the tile shop were amused by the little creature when we placed him on a counter and asked him to indicate his preference for ceramic bathroom tiles. And we'd named him Derek after our builder friend Derrick Hamley who was to fit those tiles in our east bathroom once he'd installed the new bath, and who was well known to the staff of Tiles-R-Us.

Derek duckling was to enjoy one more shopping expedition with us in his short life. We introduced him to the bemused staff of Shoe Zone in Ilfracombe's High Street on the occasion of our search for new wellington boots. They didn't have boots to fit Derek. But he wasn't to need them. He died quietly in his box by our bedside on 1st September, after adventuring down the staircase, surprisingly noisily, late one night.

Speeding forward now to Gilly's 53rd. birthday in April '04 and the treat I had in store for her at Hatherleigh Market. You may recall (from Bird Table One) that in addition to a number of chicks I bought her, sight unseen, the two slightly annoyed Khaki Campbell ducklings we named Donald and Campbell and the Hatherleigh Six, a brood of Aylesbury ducklings.

The first of the Hatherleigh Six to leave the stage was Bumblefoot. We named him that posthumously because that is the name of the condition which caused his sad demise. He'd contracted the condition (which consists of white infected pustules on the bottom of the duck's foot) some weeks previously and I'd eventually taken him to a vet at Mullacott Veterinary Hospital when he could barely walk. The vet did his best to alleviate the situation but by the time Bumblefoot's feet were in shreds there was really no going back. He was gently put to sleep in August '05 and buried in Badger's Garden. The rest of the Hatherleigh Six were individually named in commemoration of the death of their comrade. So we suddenly had Seville (drake), Satsuma, Tangerine, Clementine and Minneola (ducks).

Meanwhile Campbell duck had left the piggery to lay and tend to her own clutch of eggs under a hawthorn hedge in the car park. She'd been sitting on the eggs for a good two weeks when suddenly, on 19th October 2005, she was gone. And so were her eggs. There was no trace of her. Just one mangled egg and a few feathers. Once again the fox had to take the blame.

Tangerine was taken in broad daylight in the middle of the afternoon in September '09 and Satsuma, after a very short illness, died in the car park near the asbestos bags, one year to the day after Tangerine. Clementine, who'd been saved from the brutal attentions of diminutive Donald and the male geese in the spring of '09 to walk with a curious gait, didn't appear for her tea on one evening in January 2012 and was presumed yet another victim of the fox. The pile of feathers in Oasis Field was a bit of a giveaway.

We'd had Donald the cheeky little Khaki Campbell duck, for over nine years when he finally overstepped the mark and aggravated Mick, the big and aggressive gander, to distraction. Mick beat him senseless and crushed him against an iron gate. He went quickly downhill and died after nine years in the piggery, at animal time, on 3rd June 2013.

Seville (drake) and Mineola (duck) left us duckless when they were taken at dusk as we were putting the animals to bed one evening in mid-December 2013. The fox must have taken them and all sign of them. We'd had these two for nearly 10 years. These were the last of the Hatherleigh Six.

We kept a few vagrant ducks elsewhere than in the piggery, mindful of personality clash and terrorist competition. Daniel and Delilah were little Aylesbury ducklings hatched to Salome the motherly hen in the Ossie where she'd made a makeshift nest of straw. Of course Salome didn't lay the eggs, we did. Laid them under her anyway when she went broody for the umpteenth time. They appeared in the first week of December '04 and both went missing, Daniel aged two days and Delilah seven, leaving not a trace. Salome promptly abandoned the nest and took up residence elsewhere, as was her habit.

The Russian Invasion of Long Lane Farm in the summer of '05 was Diana Lewis' idea. For it was she who introduced Georgia and the Georgettes, a pretty Muscovy duck and her brood of six. They'd been neglected and abandoned in Landkey and came to us for adoption and, well, a better life. We named them suitably Katherine, Rasputin, Tsar Nicholas, Nikita, Lenin and Rudolph, and quartered them in a loose box in the Stock Barn until they put on a little weight. They seemed to settle in rather well. Tragically, they'd all be gone in a matter of weeks.

Nikita didn't last the week out. She died, either of hypothermia or as a result of maternal crushing.

Lenin's death two days later was just as unexplained.

By the time little Rudolph was found dead we'd moved the survivors to the empty chicken ark "for safety". Rudolph joined his brothers in the Toad Garden, leaving only mother Georgia and three (Katherine, Rasputin and Tsar Nicholas). Rasputin was painfully small for his age and I suspected he'd be the next to depart. Sure enough he was found dead in the ark the following afternoon, having been fine in the morning, although painfully tiny.

The Tsar Nicholas made it into September but was then the subject of misadventure. He was found under a fence between the chicken field and Barnfield one morning, probably murdered by a weasel.

The last of the Muscovy ducks, Katherine and her mum, simply disappeared after dark one night and were presumed taken by the fox. An extensive search revealed no sign of their remains.

By the time 2018 rolled around Gilly had been running down the operation of Long Lane Farm for some years. The only newcomers had been the donkeys in 2014. The piggery had been empty since Mick the goose had left us for pastures new in 2017. It looked lonely, overgrown and a little forlorn. It needed a bit of life injected into it.

Early in the new year I was at Bridgeman's the agricultural merchants buying feed for the donkeys when a message on their notice board caught my attention. "Ducks for sale. At point of lay." The telephone number given turned out to belong to Richard, one of Bridgeman's delivery drivers. And the ducks that were for sale belonged to old George Hopkins. George lived in a shack with a couple of caravans in a field he'd inhabited for 44 years, near Berry Down Cross about a mile away from Long Lane Farm. I knew old George as a sort of remote neighbour. I'd written his will for him recently so I knew he was ailing and well advanced in years. I called Richard's number and he told me the following; George had been taken into the care of his son in Barnstaple; he, Richard, was caring for the fowl (chickens, ducks, guinea fowl etc.) living in the caravans and barns at Yetland Holdings (the field George had until recently spent the better part of his life in; there were a number of fowl including ducks which he, Richard, had been tasked with the disposal of; were we interested?

Well the conditions at Yetland Holdings were as you'd expect of an eighty plus year old man who'd been living rough for the last 44 of those eighty years. Richard, George's daughter, Gilly and I waded through pools of stagnant mud and over hills of chicken and duck shit to gain access to a tumble down barn with a dirt and shit floor by torchlight to round up the ducks.

"How many d'ya want?" asked Richard as he slid in the slime and distributed bucket loads of layers pellets and corn in the gloom.

"How many ya got? How much d'ya want for'em?" I chanced.

"Six in this barn, but one of them's lame. She was run over by the tractor! Tenner apiece." grunted Richard.

"We'll take the lot. Give you fifty quid, Limpy Lou comes free. We'll rescue her!"

"Done!"

"Think I have been!"

We scrabbled around in the mud and shit, grabbing random ducks, some in mid-air. We didn't really examine our purchases until we'd got them back to Long Lane Farm, where we put them straight into the middle piggery bay with some hay and feed.

The following morning we let the Yetland Holdings Six out with a bowlful of chicken pellets and named them, rather appropriately I think. Sir Francis was a large pure white Aylesbury drake. Penguin was already so named by Richard, because he looks just like one. Limpy Lou was a poor bedraggled and mud spattered little thing, with her one broken leg hanging limply behind her. She hopped about in ungainly circles and I kind of knew she'd not last long in this world. Scarlett has pretty blue on brown markings. Birdseye is named after the Captain, has slight blue markings on brown. Marijuana was, just like the substance, golden brown.

In July we were presented with four more young ducks by Christopher West, pig- and bird-man of Indicknowle Farm. About five weeks old, they had been hatched by

Christopher in an incubator but were surplus to requirements. Rather than kill and eat these pretty little creatures, which would have been the normal fate of a surplus-to-requirements duck, Christopher presented them to us. We named them Chris North (dark speckled), Chris East, Chris South and Chris West (all light speckled). We quartered them with the other ducks in two bays of the piggery and they all seemed to get on like a house on fire from the get go.

Limpy Lou, the one-legged duck, was, predictably, the first of the flock to exit, stage left. She'd never been able to keep up with the others and it was quite painful to see her try to swim in the road drain. I had to help her out a couple of times. And her disability did not apparently detract from her attractiveness to the two drakes Sir Francis and Penguin, who saw her as easy meat. I'm afraid she was gang-banged frequently. She was found one dreary wet October afternoon bedraggled, miserable, badly underweight and quite dead in bay two of the piggery which she was accustomed to inhabit, at animal time.

In the spring of 2019 we lost three of the "West" ducks in quick monthly succession. Chris East was not available for his tea of layers pellets at bedtime (6.00 p.m.) on 6th May. An extensive search of the fields and wood revealed no trace of beak or feather. I thought at first she may have been broody and left the piggery to bring up her clutch. Or maybe she'd disappeared with the wild ducks living in the Oasis. In any event we never saw her again.

Two days later Chris South, who'd exhibited suspect behaviour for a couple of days also disappeared without trace.

In June Chris West disappeared in much the same anonymous way and without a trace of a feather. We had to suspect a killing spree on the part of Mr. Fox. We had lost so many other birds this way.

Final duck to leave this way in July was Marijuana, the golden brown duck. Again, our suspicions of fox, crow or sparrowhawk were never confirmed or denied. We just had to suspect fowl (foul?) play as the other ducks were seeking refuge in the Stash, as if they were freaked out by an attacker, which was unusual.

Our remaining ducks, those that had escaped the carnage of the spring of 2019, seemed safe for nearly a year. Then, in the middle of the 2020 coronavirus lockdown, we lost Sir Francis, our large white Aylesbury. The scenario was familiar. He was just not there for his tea, and despite an exhaustive manhunt around the Oasis and Boot Hill not a trace of him has been seen since. We can only blame the fox. Again.

That's brought us very nearly up to date with the bird situation here at Long Lane Farm as at September 2020. With one strange and unexplained exception. If you've been following the narrative and keeping count of our latest acquisitions, you'll have noted we have four ducks. But in fact we have five. And for the life of me I cannot explain the mathematics. We still have Penguin, Chris North (last of the "West" ducks), and three other pretty light brown ducks. It's as if Marijuana has returned from the grave. Anyway, that's what I'm going to call her from now on because I cannot bear mysteries, me.

16. Furry Creatures

Vinnie and Naseem were probably the very first creatures to arrive at what was to become the strange menagerie of Long Lane Farm. When I make that assertion I am of course assuming that CMR's removal lorry was reversed down the drive when it arrived on the afternoon of 9th February 2001, and that Vinnie and Naseem's hutch, which had been loaded last onto the lorry, was the first thing to be removed. I hadn't arrived myself by then, if you remember; I was to arrive later the same evening with Phil Carter, the Land Rover, our ancient animal trailer and the motley crew of animals it contained. So I do not know exactly what happened to Vinnie and Naseem on their arrival. Their hutch, or what was in fact an arrangement of hutches, found its way into the old greenhouse, which at that time was devoid of tomatoes or anything else horticultural. The old greenhouse was to do service as a sort of solarium rest home for any creature for whom we had nothing more suitable by way of accommodation. Vinnie and Naseem must have been a tad confused by their ordeal in the darkness of the rear of the removal lorry, but they seem to have taken rather well to their bright and airy rural surroundings. They spent their days in the two hutches, joined together as they were with a length of sewer pipe, and Gilly would feed them morning and evening, cleaning them out at weekends.

In case you have forgotten, Vinnie was a European polecat, brown and black, with a sweet and curiously intelligent demeanour. Naseem was pure white, a domesticated version of the polecat that we have learned to call the ferret. Also rather handsome in his own specific way. But all ferrets, polecats and polecat-ferrets look pretty similar and are known for their distinct and pungent aroma. They are tame and can be handled, if you don't mind stinking like a ferret yourself, as the aroma seems to adhere to you. And it stays around for a while.

Ideally ferrets should belong to ferret enthusiasts. They should be put to work ferreting out rabbits and other vermin. Ours just lounged about in their hutch(es) and whiled away their time. Must have been bit of a boring existence in hindsight. Naseem escaped twice. Once in Bedfordshire, as described earlier in this memoir, and once at Long Lane Farm. He made his way down to neighbouring Steve Parkin's place where a bemused Pam Parkin had a word with him and suggested he retrace his footsteps. Which he did, to his credit, skirting straight back up the field boundary and his cosy billet in the greenhouse. I did say they are intelligent little fellows.

Wild polecats live about six or seven years. The more sophisticated and domesticated ferret can do about the same. I have no idea of the exact ages of either Vinnie or Naseem, but Vinnie left us on 17th July 2002, after about eighteen months of life in the greenhouse. He was found dead in his hutch that morning, presumably of natural causes.

Naseem only lasted three weeks on his own. On the morning of 11th August I found him acting most strangely in the hutch. I think he'd had the ferret equivalent of a mental accident, perhaps induced by grief for the loss of his pal. I rushed him to Mullacott Veterinary Hospital a few miles away, where the vet took one look at him and declared he should be put down. He's buried next to Vinnie.

The only other "Little Furry Creature" to arrive at Long Lane Farm in those early days was of course Felix the cat. I'd returned to Bedfordshire to pick him up a couple of months after our departure from the home counties. Now Felix was a barn cat. He'd always lived in barns in Bedfordshire; was probably born in one. He'd lived in the barn at Black Pig Farm before we bought it and throughout our 4 year experiment there. He wasn't going to change the habits of a lifetime. And whilst I'd persuaded him to accompany me west to the wild North Devon countryside in a cat transporter and Mini Metro, he could not be persuaded to give up the freedom of life in a barn. So when I arrived home that dark and chilly night in March I had to kind of introduce Felix to the North Devon equivalent of barn life by shoving him in a derelict shed that'd done service as a piggery in olden times.

Well Felix wasn't impressed with his allocated quarters, even though I'd insisted they were but of a temporary nature.

"Temporary? Bleedin' temporary? I should bleedin' cocoa! I'm off!" Or at least that's what I imagine was Felix's reaction to my suggestion that he make the most of it, you know, knuckle down, play the white man, make do and mend. Anyway by the morning he was nowhere to be found. He'd gone while the going was good. I thought I'd never see him again.

A couple of hours later I was doing my rounds down the farm's East End when I heard, or thought I heard, a gentle purring voice.

"This is more like it, mate. This'll do for me! Plenty of dry hay, rats to chase, a water supply. I need for nothing more. I'll take it. The tin roof could do with a little work of course, and there's room for structural improvement, but I'm sure you'll see to that when you have the time. Oh, and I'll take the bed, breakfast and evening meal option if you please. No newspapers. Saucer of milk every now and then would go down a treat. Miaowwww! Etc."

So Felix settled down in the Ossie (so called because Gilly once had intentions of opening a wildlife hospital in the shed in the car park). This was to be his domain for the remaining twelve years of his romantic and eventful barn life. In that time the entire Ossie was rebuilt around him by fencing contractor Mark Dallyn. Gilly kept to the bed and breakfast agreement, feeding Felix morning and evening. She even changed his bedding annually as the Ossie has been used more for the storage of hay than as a hospital. Felix paid his way by catching voles, mice and the odd rat which he dispatched with relish. Never demanding, always grateful, he was the cheery and affectionate face of the East End for Gilly and all of our visitors.

Felix's health was trouble free nearly to the end. He once sustained an injury to a rear leg and we consulted Norman Bussel, retired vet and volunteer with the Animal Ambulance. He knew a lot about cats did Norman. His wife Pauline ran a commercial cattery and Norman would have been resident vet at that establishment in addition to his association with the Animal Ambulance. Anyway, and rather surprisingly, Norman prescribed a few days rest for Felix and nothing else. Cats can, he told me, be prone to leg injury. It's a bit like feline sciatica, rights itself if left alone. And he was right too. A couple of days later Felix was fine. But that was my one and only experience of a vet telling me to leave well alone, and for no fee whatsoever.

When Felix finally did meet his maker it was quick and dramatic. He died on 20th February 2010 after rapid decline over the course of a week, kidney failure and lethal injection administered at Mullacott Veterinary Hospital. He's buried next to the well in the front garden and marked by a black concrete cat. We'd had Felix (full name Felix John India) nearly 14 years. We'll never have another like him.

In the 'naughties we had a series of rabbits, all adoptees from the North Devon Animal Ambulance. Now I'm not sure why we took on these little creatures. I mean, North Devon is not known for its lack of wild rabbits, and living with a 12 acre smallholding we could happily while away the days gazing at hordes of them gambolling free. So why we chose to keep four of them incarcerated, at first in the old greenhouse and later in one of the loose boxes in the Stock Barn, escapes me. Perhaps we were persuaded by Pauline Bussell of the NDAA. Pauline is particularly fond of rabbits herself. We'd rather eat them really.

Pauline first introduced us to Starsky, a young black long haired rabbit of the Lion breed. We called him Starsky at first because he was destined to live in the hutch we'd brought from Bedfordshire and which had remained dormant in the Ossie since our arrival six years previously. He was an attractive, little chap, and as his breed foretold, bore a striking resemblance to a lion, with a flowing main and bright black eyes. Starsky entered Long Lane Farm and the hutch on 5th January 2007, at first as a temporary visitor pending more permanent arrangements. He was estimated to be about four years old.

Now here's the thing about domesticated rabbits. They're normally bought as an introduction to animal husbandry for a young child. The young child normally isn't as interested as its parent would like to think it should be in animal husbandry, or if it was, soon becomes bored with the idea. The rabbit, which is normally a lone rabbit, is normally consigned to some cramped and evil smelling hutch in a god-forsaken corner of the back garden, and it's lucky if it even gets fed and watered. A really caring and compassionate young owner might even clean it out once in a while, if cajoled sufficiently by its indulgent parent. But for the majority of its life it has become an unwanted burden; it is neglected, ignored and probably intensely bored to the point of suicide, if it only had the means. Starsky's life was destined to be very similar to that described because Gilly would, with her other charges, have little enough time to devote much love and affection to a solitary rabbit hidden away in a dark hutch in a dark barn a hundred yards from the back door.

Which is why Starsky was joined a couple of months later, on 8th March, by Ma Larkin, who was to be his lop-eared companion for a while. Ma Larkin was none too glamorous or enchanting, but at least she represented the female company Starsky must have so dearly craved. No shenanigans mind! Starsky had been de-tackled by the Animal Ambulance to prevent further burgeoning of the rabbit population. Starsky's outlook on life was further enhanced at this time by fresh residential surroundings. We stuck him and Ma Larkin in the disused greenhouse in our back garden where the pair of them could enjoy plenty of space to exercise, two square meals daily and a room with a view. Starsky took to his new company and surroundings with enthusiasm. He could be seen busying himself with domestic chores, pottering about in the garden, effecting do it yourself improvements. The garden became his passion. Particularly digging it up. In fact Starsky became so adept with his rearrangements, so absorbed in his excavations, that we changed his name. He was no longer confined to a hutch. He spent most of the daylight hours digging. We would call him Diggory. It's a name that stuck.

The domestic bliss within the greenhouse lasted about eighteen months. Then it was rent asunder. In the early morning of 19th October 2008 as I was watching a rerun of Strictly Come Dancing and generally recovering from the aftermath of the Saturday night dinner party, Gilly visited the rabbitry and came back howling. She'd found Ma Larkin with a large and gory hole in her head, the results of an encounter with an unknown predator. I put on my deerstalker and examined the scene of the crime with my magnifying glass. My suspicions were that the culprit would have been a stoat or perhaps a weasel. Either way, Ma Larkin would have to be dispatched soonest as she was beyond repair. I took out my trusty, but aged, air rifle and put a slug between her eyes. I buried her in the wood.

Diggory was clearly traumatised by the event, and he was distraught with grief and loneliness over the next couple of days. We tried to reassure the little chap and put out a call for rabbit reinforcements to the Animal Ambulance.

One week later, on 26th October, we were presented with Priscilla and Pop Larkin. Priscilla, luxuriant in his pure white fluffiness, we decided was probably gay, a female impersonator of the most flamboyant and outrageous kind. Pop Larkin was of the brindle persuasion, sober, reserved and extremely formal in manner and outlook. They would make excellent and varied companions for the recently bereaved Diggory, perhaps take him out of himself. And to encourage Diggory out of the post traumatic stress disorder his recent experiences must have induced we rehoused the three rabbit companions in one of the loose boxes in the Stock Barn. There, with the hutch to sleep in, and a supply of toys treats and other distractions to keep them amused, we felt they'd be as happy and healthy, and as amused, as it was possible for any three rabbits to be.

The average rabbit doesn't take a lot of looking after. You need to keep them fed and watered (easy) and reasonably clean (not difficult but boring, and this is where your average kid in charge of a rabbit falls down most severely in its loyalty to its pet). You need to keep a watchful eye on the claws and teeth, as both grow throughout life and, kept in captivity, your rabbit's teeth and claws can be a bit enthusiastic. I found the occasional application of wire snips or pincers ideal for both tooth and claw. You can always consult a vet if you like, but wire snips or pincers are cheaper and just as effective. I became the local consultant rabbit chiropodist and orthodontist for those few years in the 'naughties'.

Peace reigned in the rabbitry for just over a year. The three boys rubbed along together nicely and they provided amusement to the few junior visitors to Long Lane Farm without involving Gilly or me in undue hardship or backbreaking labour. But then a mystery dressed up as a tragedy was to break up the little rabbit heaven towards the end of 2009. On the morning of 28th November the beautiful and enigmatic Priscilla was found dead on the floor of the loose box. There was not a scratch on him. He'd showed no signs of illness (rabbits don't as a rule) and wasn't of an extreme age. I assumed heart attack. I buried him in the empty Iqbal's Lament alongside a few other recent departures. But when just two days later Pop Larkin was also found in the same late and unmarked condition I began to suspect rat poison. There is always a certain amount of rat bait in a Stock Barn; there has to be as animal feed attracts the little blighters. We try to conceal the poison where our animals cannot get to it. I believe the two unsuspecting rabbits, inquisitive as to the contents of a sachet or two of the poisoned blue corn, just helped themselves. Unless of course Pop was simply pining for the loss of Priscilla and topped himself. Just in case there had been anything between the two of them I buried Pop Larkin next to Priscilla.

Diggory was alone again. Worried about the rat poison I took him and the hutch out of the loose box. He was to spend the rest of his life as he'd started it, alone in his hutch, in the Ossie. And so, sadly, Diggory ended up as do most domestic rabbits, consigned to a lonely hutch in a distant barn, loveless and largely forgotten by the world. When he finally died, on 23rd June 2011, there was not a mark on him. I buried him in a disused badger set by the old henhouse in the wood. There was a tacit understanding between Gilly and I. We'd never keep anything again that needed incarceration in a hutch. In fact we burned the hutch.

17. The Sheep of Long Lane Farm

We've had a burgeoning community of sheep over the years at Long Lane Farm. A few of these were born here, others rescued and adopted from Diana Lewis' North Devon Animal Ambulance, yet others adopted from local farmers without the time or will to bring up and care for an orphan lamb or an aged crone. Some just wandered in. At least one was rustled! And every one of them has been lovingly cared for from birth or entry to death by Gilly, with a little help at times from myself. They've all been sheared at shearing time (between April and June) and treated against fly strike three weeks later. They've all been manicured and pedicured (often by me, sometimes by the shearer), treated with antibiotics when under the weather, buried at home under the soil and shillet of Long Lane Farm.

Here is the cast of characters in order of appearance:

Shawnee- born 15th February 2001 to Raindance. Little horned sheep with an unusual grey face and otherwise white wool. The adult Shawnee once contracted "white eye", a condition in sheep which renders them temporarily blind. There is no treatment and no explanation for this condition, but Shawnee recovered her sight without assistance and lived a full but virginal life until 30th November 2015 when, by now one-horned (she lost one in a fight) and clearly arthritic, she went blind again and finally off her feet. By the end of November that year she required assistance to stand. On the 30th she could stand no longer and was dispatched by Mark West with his rifle in Boot Hill.

Crow- Shawnee's twin brother in name, born the same day but of a completely different black with white flash colouring. A spindly little creature, bit like a spider really, Crow was only to survive a few months. He achieved the golden aim of all lambs which is to die at the earliest opportunity. In Crow's case that was on 8th May 2001 when less than three months old and barely weaned. One of the mysteries of life and death. I buried his little body under a tree in Badger's Wood clandestinely and after dark. We were in the middle of the Foot and Mouth outbreak of that year.

Honeylamb- born 20th February 2001 to April. April's second and last lamb was probably fathered by Tuesday as he was the prettiest creamy white creature sporting black freckles I'd ever seen since I met Gilly. He was a leggy, tall creature too, quite elegant as sheep go. Very much in the background of the flock, Honeylamb developed a maggoty foot and strip between the cleats in the summer of 2009. I managed to catch him and treat him for these relatively minor ailments. But when a few days later he developed "maggoty brain", as it is called in the farming fraternity of North Devon, or listeria, as it is known by the veterinary profession, he fell way beyond my powers to save. Listeria in sheep is a condition of the brain and causes the sheep to run about aimlessly and frantically until it collapses, exhausted, in a heap. This is what happened to Honeylamb on 28th August 2009. Beyond my help, I summonsed Mark West and his shooter to dispatch poor Honeylamb where he lay, by the hedge in Oasis field paralysed and helpless.

Layla, Roxanne's last offering, was deposited on 23rd February 2001. She was left with her tail on so that she could be distinguished from her cousins, but in hindsight this proved unnecessary. Layla was the result of careless interbreeding and destined for a short life. Slight and spindly, black and delicate, she went into rapid decline and died a mysterious but natural death on 25th September 2001 after only 7 months of an unspectacular life.

Pancake was born to Sundae on Shrove Tuesday 2001 during an unusual spell of perfect lambing weather; bright and sunny but cool. She was Roxanne's first and only, so far as we knew, great granddaughter. Pretty, white with mottled markings, she was almost certainly an offspring of Tuesday's, but her mum, Sundae, would have been less than a year old when Pancake was born. She stood out in a crowd of sheep because of her wonky tail, and indeed it was by her tail that we chiefly recognised her dead body near Orchard Gate in Boot Hill where Gilly found her at tea time on 11th September 2007. There was not a mark on her and she had displayed no signs of distress or ill health. Still warm to the touch, another mysterious and unexplained death. We had become used to this over the years, particularly with sheep.

Miracle was the tall and handsome lamb I delivered from Hortense; a first and only experience for each of us. Though big and beautiful in stature, Miracle was to prove timid in his relationships with others, not one to push himself to the forefront. But he did well, kept well and gave us no problems in his twelve plus years on Earth. And when he died, on 2nd July 2013, it was aboard Steve Parkin's quad bike as he transported Miracle to the Donkey Shelter following a short but unidentified illness.

Margarita was as much of a surprise to us as to her young mother, Consuela. Juanita's daughter was less than a year old when she produced little Margarita, just one day after she was sheared with the rest of the flock in the Stock Barn, on 16th June 2001. Now a sheep has a gestation period of five and a half months. Consuela must have been impregnated by a marauding Tuesday in mid-January, a few weeks before we left for Devon.

She was a pretty little horned lamb, cheeky like her dad, unassuming like her mum and grandmother. She lived to the respectable age of nearly 14 years before she started to lose condition in the spring of 2015. Separating from the rest of the flock she was clearly under the weather on 18th March when we brought her up to the Stock Barn, hoping to give her respite from the cold. But she finally expired in the afternoon while I was receiving training from Citizens Advice in Barnstaple. By the time I got home Gilly had buried her.

Angela Brimbles was our first trespasser. She came over the bank from neighbouring Harvest Farm three days before Christmas 2002, obviously in search of better digs and maybe some Christmas Fayre. We sort of rustled (adopted) her. Poor little thing was one of the inferior, skinny, spare little creatures farmer Jeff

Hutchins kept for the subsidies. Gilly named her after her habit of becoming entangled in the brambles that surround your average meadow grass in the autumn. In North Devon they're called "brimbles". Anyway, whether they're brambles or brimbles they were the undoing of Angela. Gilly was continuously extracting her from the vicious spiky things for the entire two weeks of her stay at Long Lane Farm. She died quite suddenly, likely of malnutrition, stuck in the brimbles (or brambles) in Oasis Field, on 6th January 2003.

Our association with Diana Lewis and her North Devon Animal Ambulance started in early 2004. We were to adopt our next six sheep from the NDAA and Diana became a regular visitor to Long Lane with her waifs and strays; Sweetheart, Cherub, Gabriella, Primrose and her lamb Snowdrop, and Venus came to us in this way.

Sweetheart arrived in the animal ambulance on 6 September 2004, an attractive boy lamb who'd been the victim of fly strike in three hooves in the late summer. He'd been treated for the fly strike and we put him in a loose box temporarily to recover from the treatment and tame him down before letting him loose on the rest of the flock. He grew to be a fine strapping and leggy sheep and he stayed with us for well over 10 years. And when he went, it was quietly, like the Sweetheart he'd always been. We found him on the evening of 15 March 2015, dead and mostly eaten, in the Donkey Shelter, where a badger had likely been feasting on his remains.

Cherub (aka "Maid") was a little white sheep of indeterminate age. Diana deposited her with us as abandoned on 15 October 2004. As with the other Diana deposits she arrived late in the afternoon and was incarcerated in a loose box pending recovery from her ordeal and during the short course on humanisation we'd formulated for arrivals such as hers. She soon joined the flock and merged into the background for seven or eight years. She went blind when older, a condition she found it hard to deal with. We found her dead in the Stock Barn on the morning of 16th January 2012.

Gabriella (aka "Hinky Puff") was a little orphan lamb who had clearly suffered from her abandonment by her owner. Diana brought her to us two days before Christmas Day 2004. We kept her in the maternity loose box next door to the goats' quarters, fed her from the bottle with replacement milk and weaned her onto creep nuts. But unfortunately she contracted joint ill, a condition which generally heralds the end of a young lamb, within the month. Her little legs became stiffer and stiffer and her gait more and more awkward, despite hefty injections of antibiotics in an effort to ward off the inevitable. By the time Diana retrieved her from our willing but useless care on 15th March 2005 she was all but off her stiff little legs and needed help to stand at all. We never saw her again.

Primrose the sheep with no fleece arrived at Long Lane Farm with her son **Snowdrop** on 5th. April 2005. It was a beautiful spring and the primroses were just replacing the snowdrops; these seasonal names seemed appropriate. This unlikely pair were dropped on us unannounced by Diana Lewis of the NDAA. She'd rescued (or perhaps just rustled) them from an unsuspecting hill farmer somewhere in North Devon. The lack of fleece on Primrose need not have been a sign of neglect. A sheep is prone to losing large chunks of its fleece, perhaps the entire thing, if it is given a substantial dose of antibiotics. But her appearance as half bald, added to the fact that she was not a pretty sheep, gave her the soubriquet "Moose", by which she was most commonly known. Snowdrop on the other hand was your classic pretty little lamb with mottled markings on a white as snow background. He was still entire, so I'd have to attend to his testicles as soon as possible if we were to avoid unwanted pregnancies the following year, but I'd learnt the art of castration by this time and seemed to get it right a day after Snowdrop's arrival. Mother and son were housed in a loose box in the Stock Barn pending familiarisation with our routines and procedures, and to allow Primrose to recover some of her coat. They soon joined the flock and rubbed along very well with the others for some years.

Primrose (Moose) was with us for nearly four years. She started to lose condition and weight in the New Year of 2009. I found her *in extremis* and on her side in the Stock Barn on the morning of 11 March. I had to summons Mark West with his pistol to put an end to the old girl. I was half way through digging her grave in the garden near to a primrose under the holly tree when the telephone rang.

"Hello my dear! Is all well with you? Where are you now, pray?" I enquired of Gilly who was travelling the Orient with a friend.

"I'm good thanks. We're in Pokhara. Walking around Lake Phewa. It's wonderful. How're you and the animals?"

"Oh everything's fine, thanks. Couldn't be better! Just cooking the Chillun's dinner."

After a few more pleasantries I hung up the phone and returned to the digging.

Little Snowdrop grew into a fine strong lamb and lasted well over ten years under our care at Long Lane. But for the last two years of his life he developed a pronounced sway in his gait, which we subsequently put down to his contracting listeria from eating the grass near mole hills. He finally went downhill as sheep are prone to do over a month or two. He died on 15 December 2015.

Venus appeared on the scene on 16 January 2006. Another of Diana Lewis' deposits, she was an attractive little ewe lamb we named after our visit to the Black Venus pub where we'd lunched that day. She sported a peculiar club foot or hoof, but trotted about the farm quite happily for over six years after her statutory week in the loose box. We found her dead in Donkery Down beside a fence the day after we returned from a visit to France on 15th September 2012 with friends Jo and Steve. Our house sitters had apparently overlooked her corpse in the field as she had been dead for some time. Gilly buried her in the reserve grave she'd dug for the house sitters by the Cosmic Ordering Service.

Marlene and Boysie were the next diminutive entrants to the menagerie of Long Lane Farm. We adopted this little pairing, naming them after the characters from *"Only Fools and Horses"*, on 5th and 9th February 2006 respectively. Both were orphan lambs received from Steve Parkin and were too expensive in terms of time and trouble for him and his wife Pam to care for. If we hadn't taken them on they would surely have been "dapped on th'ead" to use Steve's delightful expression. They'd lost their respective mothers (different mothers, they were not related) shortly after birth, and been brought up thus far bottle-fed. I collected Marlene in the Reliant and transported her bemused little form the short distance up the hill as she sat in the passenger seat. Perhaps the only sheep to have ever been transported in such a conveyance. Certainly the only road trip Marlene ever took. She'd been born just over a month before and would need to be bottle fed for a couple more weeks and then weaned. She joined Venus in the waifs and strays loose box.

Boysie joined Marlene in the loose box four days later on our fifth anniversary of arriving at Long Lane Farm. At first a little weakly and disinterested, he slept his first night in our bedroom, but he soon bucked up and took well to his bottle with Marlene and Venus as stable mates. I was responsible for the elastration of little Boysie and got it right again. He grew into a fine strong lamb and a fond favourite of the many visitors we had to our little country zoo. Late in life he had a battle with arthritis and began to waste away. Gilly had to lift him bodily to his feet for some weeks towards the end. He was a fighter though and didn't really want to die. He was finally dispatched by Mark West and his pistol on the morning of 21st April 2017, as he stretched out for another ginger nut.

Marlene made it to the ripe old age of fourteen. Another favourite of our visitors, she was much smaller than Boysie. She lost her sight overnight about two years before her death and while the sheep shearer of 2019 tried to restore this by a hefty application of antiseptic spray she remained blind and stumbling until she could stumble no longer. On the morning of 30th January 2020, while I was undergoing a "procedure" at North Devon Hospital, Gilly discovered Marlene expiring on her side in Boot Hill, near to Middle Gate. She summoned Mark West with his pistol, but the pistol was not required. Marlene met her maker naturally and in her own time. Mark kindly took her away for disposal.

Susan Dorothy was retired from active service by Mark West on 19th October 2006. Old, tired, a little underweight but otherwise quite tame and amiable, Mark deemed her no longer commercially viable but did not have the heart to send her for dog meat as she had rendered many years of loyal service. We adopted Susan Dorothy, naming her after Mark's wife and mother respectively. She joined the flock in Barn Field that evening. But her stay was short and she survived barely a month, expiring in the field she first inhabited on 16th November. Gilly and I were in Northam at the time of her death, as I was receiving treatment from a chiropractor following traumatic damage to my sciatic nerve. Mark retrieved Susan and committed her to the flames later that day.

I should perhaps here allude to the sciatic injury I sustained in the last paragraph. This was the result of an episode playing *Animal Rescuers* with Diana Lewis. A month or so previously Diana had contacted me with a request for help rescuing an abandoned and distressed sheep in a field a couple of miles away from Long Lane Farm. The sheep appeared injured and confused and most of her wool had apparently been flayed from her back. Always willing to assist the brave but diminutive Diana in those days I readily agreed to the adventure. She picked me up in the animal ambulance and soon we were speeding towards White Field Hill under flashing blue lights and a blaring klaxon. (Actually the klaxon wasn't working and Diana made me simulate the wail with a rendition of *"Greensleeves"*, the only song I could think of which when rendered in the club style gives quite a good idea of what a klaxon should sound like. And the flashing blue lights were actually orange, so we looked rather like a sickly and dissipated ice cream van. But we still sped towards White Field Hill.)

We found the "abandoned and distressed sheep" moseying distractedly about the field, looking a bit sad in her bedraggled and ragged fleece. Diana was determined that we capture the creature and bring her to safety. So we crept up on her adopting a sort of pincer movement, a tactic you must use when trying to catch a reluctant sheep without a sheep dog. It sort of worked, though my attempt at a rugby tackle last employed in my youth and at school was rather more clumsy than I had intended, and at age 56 in a muddy field and on a soggy sheep was probably not well advised. Anyway, I struggled to my feet, still grappling the sheep's rear end, as Diana reached the front end of the sheep and got her in a kind of headlock.

What happened next was to result in traumatic and excruciatingly painful damage to my sciatic nerve, a short spell in a supermarket wheelchair, several weeks on a crutch, three visits to a chiropractor and one to Jack the Back, a fierce little masseur in Ilfracombe. I realised of course that once the sheep evinced no intention of being caught, much less of being manhandled across a field, along a river bed and into Diana's Ambulance, I should have pointed out to the determined Diana that our rescue attempt was doomed and should be aborted. The sheep seemed, after all, extremely strong and not the least perturbed by her plight, only by our ministrations. However, Diana is a feisty and determined little woman. And determined she was to get the little beast into her ambulance and to safety. So we struggled to lift her bodily, me at the rear, Diana at the helm, and thus burdened we transported the amused animal across the field, along the bed of a shallow stream and up to the field gate. We were just about to contemplate the strategy necessary to get her over the padlocked gate when we heard the approach of a friendly welcoming call:

"Oi, what you'm a doin' of yer m'dears?" It seemed likely that this was the farmer, the probable owner of the sheep.

"We're rescuing this poor little sheep. She's in obvious distress. No doubt abandoned to her own devices. And she's lost most of her fleece. Must be very ill. Why do you ask?" enquired the belligerent Diana.

"Well that be moy sheep. Little bugger's allus away on her own. But she's voine. Well she ought to be after the dose of antibiotics I give 'er last noight. That'll be the cause of her losing 'er fleece today. Leave 'er be." I think the farmer was trying to keep his calm.

Diana and I put the sheep back on her feet. She scurried off, a touch indignant I suspect from the ordeal we had put her through. Diana gave the farmer a little homily on the proper care of the ovine species and we left. He retorted with something that sounded like

"Get orf my laaand!!"

When we discussed the matter later we both realised how lucky we'd been to have avoided allegations of rustling. I, however, was to be reminded daily for a couple of months of my folly by the excruciating pain and discomfort above described.

The next five members of our flock were introduced to Long Lane Farm by Diana and her ambulance.

Jaswinda and **Mumtaz** were as far as I am aware unrelated except in adversity. They made a bold and desperate bid for freedom together, leaping like some latter day Thelma and Louise from the halal meat lorry in the middle of Braunton High Street whilst on their way to ritual slaughter. This leap into the unknown took place on 18th January 2007 and the two escapees were gathered promptly in by Diana as she chanced by, fortuitously one might say, in the redoubtable ambulance. Diana brought them straight to us at Long Lane where they were ostensibly parked as temporary visitors in Donkery Up, with access to the Donkey Shelter. But they were soon and gratefully accepted into the flock where they spent the rest of their natural lives.

Mumtaz dropped **Mohammed,** the lamb she must have carried with her aboard the halal lorry when she leapt into the unknown, in donkery up, just outside the donkey shelter. Steve Parkin pulled him from his mum at 8.30 on the morning of 10th April 2007. A fine, strong lamb, with a blond Tony Curtis quiff, he's still with us during the Coronavirus lockdown of 2020. As is **Shadow**, dropped indiscriminately by Jaswinda on 21st April in donkery down. Shadow is our last remaining black sheep, proving beyond doubt my theory that a Jacob cross will always be black.

We hosted Jaswinda for just over four years until in the spring of 2011 when she went into a slow decline and we felt it was time to call the shots on her. We had become used to summonsing Mark and his pistol by this time. He dispatched Jaswinda with a single shot to the brain in the Marauder's Meadow (when it was still called the Orchard) on 28th March. Her mate from the halal lorry, Mumtaz, lasted precisely four months more. She'd always been on the scrawny side, despite producing a fine specimen in Mohammed. It was old age in the end that got her. She must have been ancient and was certainly toothless when we discovered her on the afternoon of the last day of July, quite dead in the Donkey Shelter. In the morning she'd been happily grazing on lush meadow grass. We buried her next to her pal from halal.

Wanda just wandered into Long Lane Farm from Diana's ambulance on the afternoon of 17th March 2007. Approximately six years old, having been born during the foot and mouth outbreak of 2001, Wanda had survived that pandemic though suffering from joint ill as a young lamb. She'd been a pet lamb, secreted away from daylight and the ministry vets and cured of her ailments as the gestapo marauded about the countryside. Partially blind because of her inauspicious beginnings, she'd been brought up by an elderly spinster who'd since gone into decline and could look after her no longer. Diana and her friend Pauline Bussell brought her to us in the ambulance's loosebox and she joined the "also rans", the elderly and sick of the flock: Jazwinder, Mumtaz and Dave the Fire in Donkery Down.

She didn't last long. Whether it was the change of environment, pining for the loss of her elderly mum, or just the fact that she'd had an unfortunate entry into the world we shall never know. Wanda was a heavy old girl, and always seemed to be confused at

Long Lane. After four months in our care she went off her food, contracted pneumonia in July and expired in the Donkey Shelter on the afternoon of the 26th.

Sky joined the fraternity of sheep at Long Lane Farm as an orphan lamb. He was almost an exchange for Fuchsia the goat. We'd summoned Diana and her ambulance to put a humane end to Fuchsia on 18th April 2007, shortly after my return from the Dark Continent. Diana duly arrived and administered the lethal injection to Fuchsia as requested, and promptly produced a fine little lamb from the back of her ambulance. He was, she explained, in need of a home and, if possible, a mother. His own had died in childbirth. So we took the dear little chap on, though we were at the time getting a tad overrun with sheep and the other animals. He'd need bottle feeding for some weeks, and would need to be kept alone in a loose box, which was not ideal for a newborn; they need company. That company was to arrive the very next day in the shape of

Pam . Neighbouring farmer Steve Parkin was and can be a grumpy sod. But this time he came up trumps in lending us one of his middle aged ewes who'd lost every one of her four lambs that year. Pam was black, good natured and quite tame for a commercial sheep. She'd obviously made a competent mother for some years but had been unfortunate to be carrying four lambs inside her as they're often stunted when they're crowded in the womb. Steve offered her to us on loan so that she could bring up Sky and also use the prodigious bag of milk she'd accumulated to feed her brood of four. Steve also showed us how to get a bereaved mother sheep to adopt a strange lamb.

Top Tips for Farmers No.10: How to persuade an adult sheep to adopt a strange lamb.

1.   First catch your adult sheep. The subject should preferably be female (called a "ewe"), used to motherhood by previous experience, bereft of her own young by accident or design and well "bagged up" (that is to say provided with a goodly supply of mother's milk), which she will only be if she is recently bereft.

2.   Place your adult sheep in a loosebox or other suitable enclosure from which she is unlikely to escape.

3.   Now place the strange lamb in the same loosebox or suitable enclosure so that the pair can become loosely acquainted.

4.   Get an assistant of reasonable strength and stature to restrain the adult sheep while you plug the strange lamb (who will not be quite so strange after her short association with it as described in 3 above) onto one of her nipples. Be careful now. Allow the strange lamb to drink its fill. The strange lamb should waggle its tail vigorously, denoting that it is receiving appropriate satisfaction and sustenance.

5.   Repeat step 4 above several times at different times of the day.

6.   By the time the mother's milk has passed through the strange lamb's digestive tract and the strange lamb begins to deposit its faeces about the loosebox or suitable enclosure the adult sheep will have become habituated to and accepting of the strange lamb and the strange lamb will be a stranger no more.

7.   When you have performed the above steps to your entire satisfaction you may release both sheep and lamb into the field. They will do the rest.

Pam turned out to be an efficient, dutiful and rather attentive mother to little Sky. And when Sky was grown and weaned, with a few years good grass inside him, he wasn't so "little". In fact he grew into the biggest sheep we ever had, with massive biceps, huge belly and a personality to match. At shearing time he was a nightmare and it took two men to deal with him, with a third to treat his feet. Sitting there on the Stock Barn floor like some great woolly Buddha he was a sight to behold indeed. Once, in my late sixties, I grabbed him from behind and turned him over so that I could attend to an overgrown hoof. I amazed the friends we had staying with us at the time, with my suave nonchalance in performing this truly Herculean task without help or assistance, just sleight of hand.

Sky suffered a bad attack of fly strike in the summer of 2016. His coat being so thick, and his body so massive, we'd failed to notice the telltale signs. Sheep should ideally be sheared in the late spring, when it is warm enough to do without their coat but not so warm that they attract the interest of the blowfly. Our sheep were sheared in the middle of June that year, so a tad late perhaps. And when it was Sky's turn for the shears he was found to be literally writhing with maggots. The shearer did his best to deal with them, of course, but in the process Sky lost a good deal of his fleece and the underlying skin. The maggot had been feasting on him, apparently, for some time. Duly sheared he was given a massive dose of antibiotics for his wounds and a week to recover from them. But we found him, still warm but quite dead, in Donkery Down on the afternoon of 21st June on my return from Citizens Advice.

Pam had died the previous year, on 25th January 2015, presumably of old age and natural causes. Gilly and Beauregarde discovered her at tea time under a hedge in the Oasis. Her eyes had been pecked out by crows.

Alfie was delivered to us on 18th June 2007, the same day and by the same ambulance as the two geese, Mick and Titch, of whom I shall write elsewhere. A sickly, fly-blown, maggoty and confused little lamb, he was in need of some love and attention, as well as castration by the elastrator, when Diana placed him in one of our looseboxes with the wool from our recently sheared flock. He spent most of his short life in the garden with Gilly and generally wandering around looking ever so slightly dazed. He was more than likely brain damaged, as some of our early charges have been. He never seemed to develop beyond the lamb stage, and was terminated by Diana in the old horse box, which had become a feed store since being vacated by Potter pig, three months after his arrival, on 27th September.

Lola just wandered over the hedge one day, on 27th October 2007 to be precise, into Oasis Field, leaving the rest of Farmer Hutchins' sheep behind her. A pretty, if mature, little sheep, she'd made a bid for freedom from the oppressive and quite mad Farmer Hutchins, and needed to be encouraged in her adventurous spirit. Pam Parkin helped Gilly rustle Lola and secrete her in Barnfield, where she would defy discovery. As she did. And on the following 17th March, St.Patrick's Day 2008, she presented us with two fine strong lambs which we named

Isolde, (born about 12.30 a.m.) and **Tristan** (3.00 a.m.) in Donkery Down. It was a sleepless night for us both.

Lola was to stay with us for nearly three years, but contracted what we believe to have been listeria in September 2010 and after an attempt at saving her Mark West finally had to dispatch her on 1 October. I buried her at the end of Iqbal's Lament. She overlooks the fields in which she spent the better part of her life.

Tristan wasn't meant for old bones, it seems. Gilly found him dead in Boot Hill near to Parkin gate on the morning of 6th November 2010, only a couple of months after his mum expired. He was only 2½ years old and there was no hint of him being ill.

Isolde is with us to this day (I'm writing during the Coronavirus outbreak in 2020). She's twelve years old, has a wonky ear and struggles a bit, but she made it to this year's shearing. She's currently residing in Donkery Up with the other three remaining sheep. Mark has just attended to the "dagging out" of her rear quarters to avoid fly strike during the unseasonably hot weather.

Carol lasted in our care for just three days. Introduced to us as a temporary measure by Diana on 9th December 2007, she was aged, unwell and needed significant attention. We placed her in the secure middle loose box in the Stock Barn but had no confidence she would last long. As expected, we found her dead on arrival back home after a visit to my sister Linda a mere three days later. Diana retrieved her for cremation.

Mini Bah Bah (aka Brittany) was a gift from Steve Parkin, and she arrived a few weeks before we left these shores with the Parkins on our first visit to Brittany, theirs to anywhere abroad. She was the tiniest lamb we'd ever seen, fitting comfortably into the palm of Steve's meaty right hand. She was born, one of a brood of four, on 23rd March 2008. Rejected by her mum as the runt of the litter, she'd been brought up on the bottle by Pam, but did not seem to be progressing sufficiently to make a viable lamb. Steve was of a mind to "dap 'er on th'ead", but he could see how entranced we had become with the little creature. So, when she was but three weeks old and still needing daily feeds with substitute milk, Steve presented her to us, on 13 April. She spent a week or more living in the house.

In fact, with a bit of care and kindness she grew into a fine, strong lamb and later into a rather rotund sheep. She'd become humanised under our tutelage, and would accompany us and the Chillun on afternoon walks around the Oasis. She had absolutely no fear of dogs or, well anything really. She was tame and yet feisty; from meagre beginnings to proud and characterful adult.

We had her nearly eight years and she appeared centre stage on one of our early corporate Christmas cards, standing on a bucket as the tiny lamb she started out. On 10th January 2017, after several weeks of strange behaviour when she appeared not to be eating but retaining her voluptuous proportions, with a full set of teeth and no warning, we found her dead, her colleagues quite unconcerned, in Donkery Down. There was not a mark on her. She was still warm.

Alambama was blind, either from birth or shortly thereafter; the result of ingrown eyelids that hadn't been treated. She'd been rescued by Diana at local beauty spot Heddon's Mouth where she'd been reported as aimlessly head-butting a wall. Diana brought her to Long Lane in the ambulance and she spent her first night with us no doubt terrified and confused in a loosebox.

The day after her arrival on 6th June 2008 I built her a field shelter out of pallet wood and she took up residence of the Orchard (now the Marauder's Meadow). She wasn't too impressed with my efforts to make her comfortable and refused point blank to enter the field shelter I'd so painstakingly made. And she must have been abysmally lonely in the Orchard on her own. So she soon joined the flock.

Alambama was to spend nearly ten years stumbling about in Boot Hill. She managed to keep up with the flock however, and though she had no particular friends the flock seemed to tolerate her. Bringing her in for shearing with the others could be a bit of a trial because she could not see and therefore understand the sheepdog. But averagely she'd fend for herself as sheep seem to do.

Zebrabah was the last of the sheep introduced by Diana Lewis. By the mid naughties we'd accumulated a number of waifs and strays, each of which has been detailed above. With the coming of the tiny Minnie Bah Bah Gilly was boasting a flock of 31½ pet sheep and we felt if we admitted any more we might become overrun and too busy to care for them individually. Thirty or so sheep is not a large flock by any means. But it is quite a large private pet menagerie. So we put a temporary stop on Diana with the arrival of Zeb; this stop was never lifted.

He was a pretty jet black sheep with a white flash on the forehead, very humanised and tame, almost certainly, I thought, a pet sheep gone astray. He joined in very well with the others and seemed quite happy in his new surroundings when Diana left him with us on 11th February 2009.

Something strange happened to Zeb after four years of innocuously walking around Long Lane Farm with his faintly aloof and regal manner. He developed over a few months a wonky head; a growth appeared to be appearing subcutaneously on the right side of his face. To the touch it was hard and bony. It grew to quite massive proportions, and though not as ugly as the Elephant Man's fibrous appearance, it gave Zeb the look of a *rictus sardonicus*. It also impeded the poor chap's eating. We took to feeding him massive quantities of rich tea biscuits (sheep love them) in our attempt to prolong his life. These we "posted" into the side of his mouth and he took them hungrily. Without them he would surely have wasted away. We found him dead on the morning of 14th November 2013 in the loose box.

Ptolemy just wandered in one day. A strange and slightly bulbous looking creature, black faced and heavily pregnant, she stepped in through Dallyn Gate on 10th December 2012 as Gilly opened the gates to let me drive through in the Nimbus (Reliant) on my return from swimming. I did wonder whether Gilly would let her stay; she'd imposed an embargo on new entrants from Diana and the provenance of this new interloper was completely unknown. I gave her the name. I figured if she had a name Gilly would find it much more difficult to banish her to the outdoors. The name itself was inspired by Ptolemy's peaceful and contemplative appearance. She took her place in the flock and I was right to have given her that name. She was to produce for us our last lamb and to hang around for nearly seven years. On 4th December last year, 2019, after a long and productive life and a battle with encroaching arthritis, she was off her feet for the last time and Gilly could no longer stand her up. She summoned Mark West, and his son Christopher, a licensed slaughterman, attended a few minutes later to administer the lethal bullet to Ptolemy's brain in the middle of Boot Hill. Chris kindly took the corpse away for disposal.

Twilight entered the world at twilight on 23rd February 2013 in quite dramatic circumstances. Gilly was trekking in Nepal with friend Alex Caley at the time and I was home alone caring for the animals. I was doing my rounds of the various animals and looking forward to a beer when I noticed something ominous protruding from the rear end of Ptolemy in the dim light of approaching dusk. I'd sussed that she was pregnant and on the verge of delivery before Gilly had left these shores, because she was "bagged up" ready for the birth of her lamb. I had been hoping she'd delay the happy event until Gilly's return.

Sneaking up surreptitiously on Ptolemy in the gloom of the Oasis I was able to confirm my suspicions that what protruded so ominously were a pair of lambs' forefeet. Twilight was on her way. But Ptolemy, though displaying no outward signs of distress, was in need of some assistance. Normally, about to give birth, a sheep will make itself comfortable and push the little chap out. But Ptolemy was still on all fours, trotting about with the rest of the flock. I would need to catch her and pull the little creature off.

Now, catching a pregnant sheep, even an old one, on your own at dusk and when you are a retired solicitor in his sixties is not a simple task. Here is how it's done.

Top Tips for Farmers No.11: How to capture a pregnant sheep and "pull one off" in your early sixties: old style method.

1.   First try temptation and guile. Armed with a number of rich tea (or digestive) biscuits, approach your sheep making attractive cooing noises and offering the treats quite generously. When your sheep is close enough, drop the biscuits (do not trouble

to put them away safely, there will not be time for that, just drop them) and make a dive for your sheep, as athletically as a sixty plus year old retired solicitor can, and grab it by the rear legs or any other part of its anatomy that presents itself conveniently.

2.   When that proves singularly unsuccessful, pick yourself up out of the sheep shit, swear a little, then a lot, then chase the sheep around the field hurling abuse, invective and the odd bucket or whatever else is to hand.

3.   When this also proves rather fruitless, consider summoning assistance. The assistance you choose will be whatever is available, but ideally it will be a large, grumpy but strong dairy farmer, ideally local to you and with a quad bike. Summons him by whatever method is available to you; telephone call or just a loud shout is probably quickest, letter, email, semaphore or aldis lamp probably not to be advised.

4.   When your assistance as described above arrives, mount his quad bike from the rear and adopt the pillion riding position. From this position you will find it is possible to give appropriate directions and instructions to the grumpy farmer on the piloting of the quad bike and the corralling of the sheep. If you have chosen well, the grumpy farmer may have some ideas himself on these issues.

5.   Your goal will be to chase the sheep around the field while the lambs' feet protrude from its vagina for as many times as it takes to direct the sheep to an appropriate location where it can be cornered and captured. Three laps of the field are recommended and should be sufficient. You should hang on tightly to the grumpy farmer if you are to survive this manoeuvre unscathed.

6.   When your sheep is sufficiently cornered, stressed to the eyeballs, tired and about to give up (as you may be yourself) leap as nimbly as you can from your position on the pillion, grab the sheep by its extremities, or perhaps its head, and gently pull the little lamb from its mother. If the grumpy farmer can be persuaded to carry out instruction 6 he will probably make a better job of it.

Twilight was "pulled off" from Ptolemy by Steve Parkin in the Orchard (now the Marauder's Meadow). She was a fine, strong and rather large lamb. Steve and I took mother and child and stabled them both in a loose box overnight. Both were exhausted from their ordeal. As was I. My, did that beer go down well!

Gilly returned from Nepal a few days later to be delighted by our newborn. Twilight grew into a veritable giant of a sheep, easily as big as the giant Sky. She's just over seven years old now and is locked down with the rest of us during the coronavirus pandemic of 2020. She's sitting in Donkery Up right now as I write this, with the three other remaining sheep, Mohammed, Shadow and Isolde.

Coconut was the last contestant for entry to the Long Lane sanctuary. She was sort of rustled. She'd been roaming around nearby fields for six months or so and had become a bit of a nuisance to Steve Parkin. Probably an outcast or an escapee from a flock of Patrick Kift, neighbouring and to the south, she was a rather scruffy, unkempt and unlikely creature in the Devon countryside. Because she was a Soay, just like little Beau, the first of our sheep to arrive at Long Lane in 2001. Coconut sported the same short brown curly coat and the same dark, soulful eyes. She lacked Beau's horns however. And her spirit. She'd been living rough for some six months and become quite wild and dishevelled by 9th April 2013 when Steve Parkin and I helped her through Parkin Gate and into Boot Hill late in the darkling evening. She joined the other poorly sheep for a while until we could get her cleaned and tidied up a little, then she joined the others and had free access to our fields.

It soon became evident why Coconut had strayed between Patrick's fields and Steve's. She'd probably strayed into Patrick's flock in the first place. As a Soay she really had no business in North Devon. She wouldn't have been out of place in the Hebrides or the Orkney Islands, but Devon? She was a serial escape artist, the only one of our sheep to escape over the wall from the Oasis field and into the main road. She only did this once, however. Ever mindful of her propensities, we contained her in Boot Hill and the Donkery for the rest of her stay.

Those reading this may have noted that I made no mention of the demise of Alambama above when dealing with the life of that blind creature. That is because I was leaving it to now. Blind Alambama and Coconut the Soay, both in their way outsiders from the main flock, died on the same day, in the same field (Boot Hill), a couple of hundred feet apart. The date of this mystery was 7th January 2018. Alambama would have been about eight years old. But she'd spent all of her life in the dark and much of it a tad stressed by her circumstances. In the days leading up to her death she'd been off her feet and at best stumbly. She probably hadn't eaten for days. We called on Mark West to do the dispatching and he sent young Christopher to do the unofficial slaughterman's duties with his high powered pistol. By the time Christopher arrived at the scene Alambama had given up her ghost; a bullet was unnecessary. But walking back across Boot Hill I noticed Coconut, lying prostrate and quite still. It seems she'd suffered what passes for a stroke, much as Beau had many years before. Coconut was speedily dispatched by Christopher using the bullet he'd brought for Alambama. Gilly and I towed one body on a sack barrow, while Chris brought the other on his quad bike, to a grave we'd been digging next to the remains of Mini Bah Bah. We buried the two together.

That almost brings to an end the story of our sheep. I have recounted their biographies in some detail because I know they are of a species close to Gilly's heart. She has continued to look after our flock and others for nearly a quarter of a century and her love, dedication and attention have been unstinting. I use the epithet "others" advisedly. We have had encounters at Long Lane Farm with numerous of our neighbours sheep which have been lodged with us on a temporary basis. And here Gilly's job, carried out uncomplainingly, has been to carry hay and water to nourish them daily, extricate the more ambitious from bramble entanglements, assist

Mark West with the dagging out of shitty arses, and generally tend to the whimsical beasts. We have had up to 50 or more sheep from Steve Parkin parked in the Oasis field over a couple of winters to eat down the grass. On one occasion Steve parked a dozen bullocks in our field, but two of these made their way into our back garden and caused havoc among the roses.

In the spring of 2013 Steve bought four young sheep for his daughter as a surprise for her birthday. He asked whether he might secrete them in the Oasis for a few weeks and we took them on board, calling them the "Box of Frogs", because they were as mad as one.

Gilly has also looked after Mark West's sheep which winter here in the Oasis and Boot Hill regularly now that we only have four of our own. As I write we have 23 of Mark's in Boot Hill. Or at least we *had* 23. Now we have 24 as one of the 23 gave birth to Jesus, a fine strong lamb, just four weeks into the coronavirus lockdown. When I informed Mark he had been delivered of child he expressed some surprise.

"That's impossible! They're not supposed to have been pregnant. How has that happened?"

"Well, Mark, far be it from me to tell you the facts of life. But I assure you there is a lamb with its mother in Boot Hill. And the lamb wasn't there last night."

"Something must have got in! Either that, or it's the immaculate friggin' conception".

"Nothing's "got in", I assure you."

"Well then, the immaculate conception it is!"

That's why we called her Jesus.

18. Bird Table Three, Goose and Gander

Geese. Large but stately, elegant and personable creatures. They lay wonderful eggs, well the females do. Eleven minutes to soft boil but you need plenty of soldiers because your average goose egg equals 2½-3 large hens' eggs. These are the geese of Long Lane Farm.

Mahatma was the first goosey applicant for sanctuary. She arrived rather suddenly and unannounced one Wednesday morning in late January, 2007, brought to us by Diana Lewis of the NDAA, who just thought we'd like a goose. I was busy with final preparations for my trip on the Plymouth-Banjul Challenge, but found time to settle Mahatma down in a spare bay at the end of the Piggery. She was a gentle goose, quite self-effacing really, and we called her Mahatma after Ghandi of course. We were never sure of her sex, though she acted with the grace and charm of an aloof young lady. We never had an egg out of her.

Mahatma may have been pretty lonely during her first six months with us. But she got on with her life in her own uncomplaining way, until she was joined by two boys who should have spiced up her lonely existence. Diana Lewis brought us two strapping male examples the following June. We named them Mick and Titch and placed them temporarily in the piggery bay recently vacated by Candace Marie (pig).

So we had a sort of ménage à trois, a mixed relationship in which the dynamics escaped me. Mick took the dominant lead. If, as I suspect, he and Titch were brothers, then Mick was the psychotic Ronnie to Titch's more pliant Reggie. Mahatma refused to have anything to do with either of them and I seriously began to doubt her sex, or perhaps her sexuality. Let us say she treated the two boys with indifference bordering on disdain. The three muddled along together in the piggery, with Mick harassing the pigs at every turn unless there was a human, particularly a male human like me about to harry and bully. What with Ashleigh Fuckwit marauding about the west end of the farm and Mick playing the tobacco baron down east, I would run the gauntlet between armed with broom handle, hoe and an anxious expression for a couple of years.

Titch died in my arms in the car park one February morning in '08 when I caught him in the log store to treat his bleeding feet. What had actually happened to him and Mick to cause their feet to be so bloodied is still a bit of a mystery. I suspect a rat. When a goose sits down to sleep its feet stick out at the sides and they are a little exposed to the chancing rat who'll take a nibble. The geese were clearly traumatised and would not enter the piggery bay until I'd cleaned it thoroughly and supplied it with a baited trap. I believe I caught the rat this way. But the problem of dealing with partially eaten feet remained. I used alamycin blue spray, a topical antiseptic agent, which did the trick for Mick, though he resented me picking him up bodily to examine and treat him.

Poor Titch however, always milder mannered and more retiring than Mick, was completely freaked out by my attentions. I managed to treat the feet, but he simply expired in my arms, presumably from shock or the goosey equivalent of a heart attack. We've only ever eaten two of our creatures and this when we could be sure of the cause of death. Iqbal the psychotic turkey Gilly curried, if you remember. Titch was roasted, and he was absolutely delicious with all the trimmings.

For the next couple of years Mick had to put up with his apparently frigid wife Mahatma for company. He got grumpier and grumpier, either just because he was a psychotic goose, or perhaps out of sexual frustration. We meanwhile continued to remain eggless

So we bought Lady Jane, a female Toulouse grey goose, from Nick Cooper, local hobbyist farmer and IT consultant, on 10th August 2010. We paid Nick £25 for Lady Jane. She'd been hatched in May and Nick told us she could live 25 to 30 years! Pretty bird, beautiful plumage, mild mannered too, she'd make an ideal partner for the frustrated Mick and perhaps provide us with an egg or two.

Three months later we invested in another of Nick's Toulouse Greys. Peaches joined the small harem we'd established for Mick and by April 2011 we were in full scale goose egg production. Mick was delighted with his wives and calmed down considerably. He even became a touch protective of them.

We had such a good supply of goose eggs for two years and more that I would peddle the surplus to friends and colleagues at the swimming pool. But the idyll that the piggery had become was not to last Nick Cooper's predicted 25 years. My particular favourite goose, and a prodigious layer, Lady Jane, died after a short and undefined illness and rehydration. We'd placed her on a bed of straw in the piggery to breathe her last on 23rd May 2013.

Mahatma the eggless left us in April 2014 after a short illness that put her off her feet. Diana Lewis, who'd introduced her to Long Lane Farm seven years previously kindly escorted her in the Animal Ambulance to a vet who diagnosed her with "egg sack blocked by dead egg". She probably hadn't eaten for days. She was humanely despatched and left with the vet for disposal. So Mahatma wasn't entirely eggless in hindsight, it's just that she was killed by her first and only, belated, egg.

Peaches carried on the good tradition of egg laying for another three years before she succumbed to a short illness and death in late March, 2017, perhaps also egg-bound. That left poor old Mick as our sole goose and indeed the sole inhabitant of the piggery, our last Pig, Mahlon having gone to the great piggery in the sky.

We had six months with Mick all alone in the east end of the farm, getting grumpier and grumpier by the day. I felt so sorry for him even though I'd have to pick him up bodily every couple of months and dump him in the road drain to cool his evil temper. Putting him to bed was a dangerous nightmare for both us and our house sitters if we went away. By September I could stand it no longer. We looked for an alternative home for Mick. And we found that home with Chrissie Gubb of Berrynarbour. Chrissie was looking for a husband for his two female geese on the pond at his place. He and his wife picked Mick up and bundled him unceremoniously into the back of his Land Rover late on the sunny afternoon of 18th September 2017.

The piggery was completely empty for the first time in its history. We never saw Mick again, though there's an open invitation to visit. I hear he's delighted with his new surroundings and company. I wish him well.

19. Donkey Tails

We've never really considered ourselves "horsey people". Though we'd lived all our married life in a village or other rural surroundings, we'd never hob-nobbed with the hunting, fishing and shooting fraternity. We'd sat on the odd donkey in Spain, even ridden the odd camel in the north Sahara on an ill-fated holiday in Tunisia. But neither of us had ever sat astride a horse. Still haven't. Then we met Blackjack.

I have told elsewhere of the coming of Blackjack, the black Welsh pony, and his adoption from Wendy DeMeur of Honeywick Farm. His antecedents remain largely a mystery to us, but we believe he was of gypsy stock; Wendy was a gypsy aficionado. Blackjack likely came into her possession as discharge of some debt or other she'd been due from one of the clan that proliferate in rural South Bedfordshire. Jack seemed much more knowledgeable than I about country pursuits and taught me in very short order how to drive a pony and trap. It's done with the voice, you know, rather than the reins.

He made it successfully to Long Lane Farm, but must have felt slightly redundant here. We'd left the trap Graham built for him out of a cocktail cabinet and two motorbike wheels back in Bedfordshire. So Jack just moseyed around the place looking not too disconsolate, not too disenchanted with his lot. But decidedly redundant. So he went into early retirement, trotted about Barnfield grazing, and slept (if horses can truly be said to sleep) in the Stock Barn. Indeed he had access to the Stock Barn all day, and that was perhaps his undoing.

Our progress westwards in February 2001 had been frantic, and although well organised, we had far too much furniture, junk and other accoutrements from 27 years living in Bedfordshire, the "stuff" you hang onto just because it might come in handy somewhere. Far too much, and too large to fit into the small rooms of Long Lane Farm. So we'd stored in the Stock Barn such exotic and otiose items as Gilly's mum's cocktail cabinet (a horror from the 'fifties), a shed in sections left behind by the former occupants, a couple of beds, gardening tools and a whole plethora of useful(less) items. The Stock Barn in those days was just a barn, with dirt floor, no electrics or water, and no proper loose boxes for the animals (these were all to come later). It was basically an untidy shambles; a messy accident waiting to happen. And happen it did. On the last day of August 2001, while I was away in Bedfordshire and London attending a masterclass on hypnotherapy techniques and generally carousing the evening away with Paul Wilson. We shall never know exactly what it was that freaked poor Blackjack out. Gilly found him in the morning as she did her rounds with the animals. The Stock Barn was a mess, she told me; items of furniture, old gardening tools, the famous cocktail cabinet were in disarray, as if the place had been ransacked and unsystematically trashed by some infantile burglar. Blackjack lay just outside the back door to the barn, on his side, his muzzle snuffling in the wet mud. He'd clearly broken a leg.

Well that was the end of Blackjack, and I imagine one of the first and most traumatic of the many losses Gilly has had to endure and deal with over the years. Of course a vet was summoned, as was my cousin Christine's husband Keith, to help Gilly through the emotion and the practicalities on that wet and misty Sunday morning. But the diagnosis was predictable. Blackjack would have to be destroyed. The vet handled the euthanasia. And neighbour Michael Johns attended with his JCB to dig a large hole in the corner of Boot Hill, drop Blackjack in and backfill. By the time I arrived home late in the afternoon that Sunday the deed was done. And Gilly, bless her, had kept me in the dark about her traumatic day until I was relaxing comfortably with a beer.

We still have Blackjack's shoes. I cleaned them up quite recently, gave them a coat of matt black and nailed them up in the Stock barn as a kind of memorial to him. And we still have the mound of earth and shillet that marks his grave, in the corner of Boot Hill from which it derives its name. A year was to pass before we had another equine.

My mum died in 2002 and left both Gilly and me bequests. Gilly thought she'd like to use part of hers to realise an unfulfilled ambition of my mum. Mum had always harboured this wish, it seems, to possess a "dear little donkey". She'd never told me about it, but she'd confided in Gilly. She'd been in a position to do that very thing for in excess of 10 years when she lived on her own smallholding in Cornwall. But she never put her goal to the test. Which is as well really as I cannot see her coping with the hard work and dedication animal husbandry can mean. Anyway, Gilly determined to acquire a couple of donkeys for Long Lane Farm and she approached the Donkey Sanctuary in Sidmouth on Devon's south coast for advice.

The Donkey sanctuary is, in charitable terms, fabulously wealthy. The grounds at Sidmouth are extensive and they are manicured to perfection. The many donkeys who live there are very well cared for indeed. There is a fully operational conference and training facility, souvenir shops and a restaurant. The donkeys could want for nothing. And the curious inquirer will be treated to masses of help, information and guidance on all matters donkey related. At least this is what we found on our visit to the Sanctuary in the spring of 2002 shortly after Gilly's mum had left us to take up residence in a care home and we were free enough to indulge the quest for a donkey.

Though they do not advertise the fact, the Donkey sanctuary operates an adoption scheme. If you wish to parent a donkey, and you have the means to provide accommodation at least as luxurious and well-appointed as that at Sidmouth, you may have a donkey or two on permanent loan. We applied immediately. Long Lane Farm would have to be inspected for suitability, but as suitable adopters we were accepted without demur.

Top Tips for Farmers No.11: What you need to do to make yourself and your property fit to accommodate two donkeys.

1.   First take one acre of decent grazing land. Divide it into two half acres and provide strong and durable fencing around the entire perimeter and along the dividing line between the two paddocks. Stout post and rail fencing should suffice.

2.   Each paddock should be provided with a ten or twelve foot gate. If your design is cleverly thought out one gate should suffice if it can be positioned so that it swings between the two paddocks. Affix the necessary gate furniture (hinges and catches as appropriate).

3.   Construct a square donkey shelter of about 10 feet by 10 feet and six feet high on the dividing line so that it is accessible from both paddocks. This should be of post and rail construction with a watertight roof provided with gutter and downpipe with water collection system. The floor should be of concrete or concrete slab. There should be an opening into the shelter from either paddock and both openings should be capable of being shut off by a simple moveable rail system. This donkey shelter will serve as the donkeys summer quarters and be accessible throughout the day in the event of rain or other inclement weather.

4.   The winter quarters should be in a barn which is provided with adequate loose box accommodation to house at least two donkeys. The barn should be provided with running water, electric lighting and a concrete floor. If your barn is not already provided with any of these facilities the provision of them should be put in hand before the donkeys will be released into your care.

5.   You will require adequate electric fencing so that the grazing of your paddocks may be rotated thus preventing overeating by the donkeys and the onset of laminitis in the elderly. You will also require a goodly supply throughout the year of fresh hay, straw, donkey nuts and chaff, ginger nuts and apples. Donkeys like to play so you should also provide a number of bats and balls, full cricket pads, croquet mallets and the odd jigsaw puzzle.

6.   Finally, at least one member of your household, preferably the farm foreman if you have one, should attend the one day training course in the care and management of donkeys, level 1, provided by the Donkey Sanctuary.

Well we did all of the above in the spring of 2002. Our fencing contractor Mark Dallyn of Paracombe handled the donkey enclosure and shelter. He followed my innovative plans and, using the best of materials, constructed a veritable palace for our new charges in what has become known as Donkery Up and Donkery Down. At the very modest price of about £3,000. Steve Blackman of Braunton and the Christian Surfers was contracted to do the barn conversion, adding water and electricity supply, a concrete floor and two commodious loose boxes to the Stock Barn which have stood the test of time. Much of the woodwork in the Stock Barn, which was added to later by our builder friend Derrick Hamley by the replacement of the decrepit old door by a purpose built new one, and three further loose boxes, has been eaten by a succession of donkeys. But the basic structure remains serviceable.

I attended the Donkey Sanctuary course in Sidmouth with my cousin Christine. After what turned out a relaxing and unchallenging day together, grooming and picking out feet, we both came away qualified in basic donkey care and husbandry. I've got the certificate to prove it. If the donkeys ever get fractious or rebellious I get out the certificate to prove my authority and this generally subdues them into docile acceptance of who's the boss.

Our first two donkeys arrived in a horse trailer from Sidmouth on the sunny afternoon of 22 July 2002. A mother and daughter duo, Frieda was white with attractive brown and black markings, about 20 years old, and had a slightly regal air about her as she stepped delicately from the box and down the drive to take up residence of quarters in the Stock Barn. Her daughter Heidi, standard grey or, as they are known, standard brown, sported the traditional cross on her back. As they all in fact do. It's just that a white cross does not stand out that well on a white background. Heidi was slightly less confident than her mum, and slightly more skittish. But she followed her mum into a haven of peace and respectability at Long Lane where the two were to spend several years under our care.

And the nature of that care, and its frequency, I'd learnt on the course at Sidmouth. Daily grooming is of course essential, and when we started we were good at that. Donkeys seem to like the attention. You're supposed to pick out their feet regularly for mud and stones, but I was reliably informed by Heidi early on that this would not be necessary as there was no mud and very few stones to watch out for at Long Lane. Mum Frieda wouldn't let me near her with the trusty foot pick.

For food your average donkey spends most of its day grazing. Older donkeys need to be strip grazed as they can over eat the lush meadow grass and are susceptible to laminitis, a painful and potentially lethal foot condition caused by too much protein in summer grass. We supplement the grazing with a dish of mixed donkey nuts and chaff, with a chopped apple as a treat (as it keeps the vet away) and of course a twice daily ginger nut. Donkeys love ginger nuts and we always keep an ample supply. Show a donkey a rich tea or a digestive and it will not be impressed. But wave a ginger nut in its direction and it'll be putty in your hands.

Donkeys, we were told, also need regular worming, though this seems to depend on whether your donkey regularly goes on excursions or holidays. It's not an easy matter to shove the contents of a donkey wormer down the average donkey's throat, so we used discretion in this and kept our eyes open for uninvited worms. They need tetanus and equine flu jabs too, but these are administered by a vet.

The most arduous task in the care regime of a donkey is the footwork, or, as it is called, the farriering. Of course the farrier, who is professionally qualified to carry out this task, does the clever bit of pairing back the hoof overgrowth with pincers and file every six to eight weeks. But the clever bit the farrier expects you to do is to gather in your donkeys, put on their halter and lead rein, and then get them to the stable ring for the farrier to do his clever bit. Donkeys are nothing if they are not stubborn. And strong. And heavy. And they literally have a kick like a mule. So you treat the rear end of a donkey with respect; never stand within kicking range. And you move a donkey towards its stable ring by a little persuasion and a lot of brute force.

Our farrier in the early days attending to Frieda and Heidi's feet was Clive, a middle aged chap with years of experience, a relationship issue and an apprentice called James. Being an apprentice of course James got the thin end of the wedge, the back breakers, the experience building little numbers such as treating donkeys. And when James qualified and went freelance he took us with him as customers. Now James was a powerfully built young man who needed little help with our two elderly donkeys. And if they did on occasion cut up a touch fractious he would simply wrestle them to the ground and hold them in submission while he had his farrier's way with them. I never did see him lose a battle with a donkey. In those early days James was a wealth of information on matters donkey and horse related. He once diagnosed an early case of laminitis in Frieda and suggested we keep her off grass for a month or two. Advice we were to accept gratefully. And it worked. Both donkeys, being of a certain vintage, had a touch of "seedy toe", which submitted over the years to James' ministrations.

Frieda and Heidi settled into the gentle rhythm of the countryside at Long Lane. The Donkey Sanctuary, ever mindful of their responsibilities to their charges, sent Nikki to inspect them quarterly. Nikki was a paramedic and a local volunteer with the Sanctuary. She'd appear once every three months to check on Frieda and Heidi, measure their girths with string and tape measure, confirm their injection records and look at their feet. Once a year we'd have a visit from Lionel, senior Donkey Inspector with the Sanctuary. Tall, tanned, avuncular and with a curious South African accent and sense of humour, we could always trust Lionel to find something wrong with our donkey regime, after all we were only amateurs, he was the true professional. But we rubbed along reasonably well with Lionel. He was never exactly caustic with his criticisms, and he could smooth over his visits with a charm I think Gilly found irresistible.

Christmas Eve 2006. The light was fading. Across the country excited children and even more excited adults were dressing Christmas trees, stuffing turkeys, decking the halls with boughs of holly. At Long Lane Farm we awaited, breath baited, Diana Lewis and her sidekicks Pauline and Norman Bussell in the North Devon Animal Ambulance, with their latest addition to the menagerie. This was an ancient and rather scruffy white donkey which I named Mistletoe as she shambled from the loose box, in honour of the season.

Mistletoe had belonged to an elderly lady who had fallen rapidly into dementia on her Cornish smallholding. The lady had a number of animals about her home and the ancient Mistletoe in a barn, which she'd completely forgotten about. Diana found the old girl knee deep in her own droppings and existing on the befouled bedding straw she'd been given to sleep on. Poor Mistletoe was emaciated, gaunt and looking distinctly nervous as she was bundled into her new lodgings in the Stock Barn for her first Christmas Day with us. Diana was doubtful she'd make it through the night.

We kept her separate from Frieda and Heidi in the early days, nervous that she might not be accepted by the resident mother and daughter team. But they seemed to tolerate Mistletoe and to bond rather well with her.

She looked noticeably better after a few days, but was reluctant at mealtimes and much of what she grazed came straight back out of her mouth in a sort of gunky green goo. We suspected Mistletoe's teeth could do with a looking at. A donkey's teeth grow throughout its life, so that attention from an orthodontist, particularly with an elderly animal can be a frequent necessity. Unattended, the donkey's teeth will become sharp, broken and rotten, and pretty soon your donkey will find it painful and difficult to eat. We summoned the assistance of ex-army equine dental technician Gill Spinney, and on the evening before Graham DeMeur and I left for Africa and the Plymouth-Banjul Challenge in early February 2007, we three wrestled with Mistletoe in the Stock Barn as Gill applied her tools to the clamped open mouth of the frightened creature. Gill was surprised that Mistletoe had survived the neglect of her recent past. She declared Mistletoe to be ancient in years, perhaps over 50, as she removed Mistletoe's remaining broken and jagged molars in an operation that was to make her life so much more comfortable. From that evening on she began to thrive, if a fifty-year-old donkey can be said to thrive. Gill had rendered her a toothless crone. She would have to drink her food and for the rest of her natural life Gilly would make a sort of porridge out of soaked donkey nuts which she slurped from a rubber feed bowl and seemed to relish.

I carried Mistletoe's molars throughout the dark continent on my travels. I like to think they brought Graham and me good fortune.

Frieda was the first of our donkey charges to leave us. Gilly found her dead and contorted in the donkey shelter on the morning of 18 September 2008. She'd clearly died of natural causes as she'd been fine the night before when put to bed. But her death appeared not to have been painless, judging from the twisted form of the corpse we found on the donkey shelter floor. The Donkey Sanctuary insist on a post mortem on donkeys that die away from home; we were to await the arrival of a local vet. Meanwhile we were to leave Frieda where she lay. This latter instruction from the Sanctuary was nothing to do with forensics or the opinion of Scenes of Crimes Officers, more the practicalities of mourning. Donkeys bond for life with their companions. Both Heidi and Mistletoe would require sufficient time to absorb the departure of Frieda, to come to grips with the loss. Twenty four hours is recommended for this bizarre process which is a bit like an equine lying in state.

The local vet duly attended and performed the post mortem in the donkey shelter, while I was signing copies of my book about the Plymouth/Banjul Challenge in the Combe Martin library. Frieda appears to have suffered a twisted gut, heart attack and near instant death. What caused the twisted gut we shall of course never know. I laid out her body in the pit dug for her by Michael Johns and his JCB in Boot Hill near the mobile field shelter Dungroamin.

Heidi got over the loss of her mother and returned to her usual good spirits and obstinate ways. Mistletoe, who was considerably her senior, no doubt took Frieda's place in Heidi's affections and the pair tolerated each other's foibles of behaviour for another three years.

The departure of Heidi was not so sudden nor so comfortable. In October 2011 she showed the usual signs of being off colour. Off her food, her stomach seemed to reject even the grass she seemed so avidly to munch. And when the green gunk started to ooze from her nostrils and to flow from her mouth is seemed time to summons the vet and to inform the Donkey Sanctuary. And informing the Sanctuary proved to be our biggest mistake. Because they have strict rules. Any fostered donkey displaying signs of illness is required to be treated by the Sanctuary vets. Heidi would have to be picked up, in her distressed state, and transported to south Devon and Sidmouth for treatment. The local vet was instructed to build Heidi up for the journey. To do this she would need to be fed, and force-fed if necessary, about a gallon of warm porridge. This instruction was issued sight of Heidi unseen. The Sanctuary apparently assumed she would be weak and emaciated from her illness. But in fact to the casual observer she was neither emaciated nor weak. She was just off her feed.

The local vet, Rachel, arrived at Long Lane Farm on 14th October with her instructions and her porridge, a full gallon of the stuff, which she'd been instructed to administer to the ailing Heidi. Well, Heidi was less than impressed. She just turned her muzzle up at the unappetising sludge. But the vet had her instructions, and she was intent on carrying them out. Gilly and I were requested to hold Heidi steady while she was intubated by the vet, who then poured the entire gallon of porridge through a funnel and into Heidi's complaining stomach. My did we all struggle. Gilly, Rachel, Heidi and I all fought valiantly to force the stuff down or keep it out. I'm afraid the humans won the struggle. But we brought poor Heidi quite literally to her knees in the effort. With an audible cry she sunk to the floor as the last of the porridge was poured into her stricken maw.

"Oh, she's all right. She's just taking a rest. It's quite an ordeal you know!" exclaimed Rachel, but I could see the doubt in her eyes.

"I don't think so. Never seen her do that before," I replied weakly.

I cradled Heidi's head in my arms as I sunk to the floor with her. I shall never forget the look of love, mixed with reproach, in the dear animal's eyes. I have always felt complicit in Heidi's agonising death throes; guilty for not following my instincts to prevent the force feeding of an animal I did not consider in need of such brutal action. But it's bittersweet really, those feelings of guilt. Rachel returned to carry out the statutory post mortem the next day. What she showed me was a liver one third of the size it should have been. Heidi was about to die of acute liver failure, probably induced years ago by eating ragwort on some less than ideal pasture. The point for me is that she did not deserve or need to die in agony. The vet Rachel should have known better than to force feed an animal that clearly did not need to be force fed. And the Donkey Sanctuary should never have issued such instructions without knowledge of her condition.

Heidi is buried close to her mum in Boot Hill. Michael Johns and his JCB did the honours. I acted as undertaker, laying out her body in the pit to best advantage.

Mistletoe was by now our sole surviving donkey. We were down to one goat and a few aging sheep, and the Chilluns of the day of course. The place was becoming a bit sparse of livestock, and Mistletoe remained the star attraction. We had her very nearly eight years in all, which for an already aged and toothless donkey was quite an achievement both for her and for Gilly.

I made the mistake of letting her get hold of a half apple on one occasion. Of course she couldn't chew it up with her toothless maw, so after a few sucks she tried to swallow it. The poor old girl nearly choked to death and went into an agonised paroxysm from which I felt sure she'd not recover. But recover she did, and she was to survive Heidi by exactly three years.

In the October of 2014 Mistletoe displayed the same symptoms as Heidi had three years previously. She suddenly lost interest in her porridge, which until then she'd slurped up with great gusto. Mindful of what had happened to Heidi we summoned the vet for an opinion. We didn't trouble Rachel, the vet who'd put an agonising end to Heidi. We'd rather lost faith in her and the practice of which she was a part, when she signed the postcard reminder of Heidi's flu injections a fortnight after she'd force fed her to death. We'd changed veterinary practices back to Mullacott Veterinary Hospital after Heidi. It was a delightful and most caring young lady who examined Mistletoe and diagnosed acute liver failure from her vital signs. So Mistletoe was spared the agony and the ignominy poor Heidi'd experienced. She was administered a sedative followed swiftly by lethal injection on the miserable afternoon of 13th October 2014 and Mistletoe lapsed quickly into oblivion. I have to admit to a flood of tears; these terminations have never been easy for me. The final glance from the depths of Mistletoe's sweet eyes joined the countless glances from animals of the past, and will be with me until I give my own final glance.

I'd only returned from France the evening before the departure of Mistletoe. My bags were still packed. But Mistletoe would be left in her loose box in the Stock Barn over night, where Aramis the goat, her mate since Heidi's demise, would be able to get used to his loss and start the mourning process.

The next morning Steve Parkin helped me drag Mistletoe on the back of his quad bike to Boot Hill near Parkin Gate. There, with his JCB and a face just solemn enough for the occasion Michael Johns dug a neat grave for her next to the other lost donkeys. Steve picked up Mistletoe in the bucket of his tractor and dropped her neatly in. I jumped into the pit and straitened the body into a semblance of respectability, then Michael backfilled with the JCB covering the body. The whole operation took about 20 minutes. We were becoming professionals in the disposal of equines.

The loss of Mistletoe, though swift and painless, hit me harder than I could have expected. And her loss coincided with the deaths of two of our beloved dogs, the Chillun of the day. I shall write about the Chillun later. But we were donkeyless at Long Lane Farm. I think I declined into a mild depression. I'd reached 65 that year, and with the decline in our animals and my own thoughts of mortality I just felt sad, flat and empty somehow. The mojo had gone out of my life.

Though it recovered in the first months of 2015 (after a disastrous and very lonely week in Cyprus) with my introduction to the Citizens Advice Service and puppy training with our new batch of Chillun. I began to find new purpose, or a set of new purposes in my life. Optimism soared, self-esteem rocketed, appetite for further experience and adventure was whetted. We should invest in a couple of donkeys; they're so much fun. Gilly felt the same way. Although we had made a conscious decision some years previously to run the operation of Long Lane Farm down and to devote our lives to fresh endeavours, the place seemed empty without them. So in the spring and summer of 2015, whilst I was further knocked back by contracting first type 2 diabetes and then early stage prostate cancer, we determined to locate a couple of donkeys in need of new lodgings.

We surfed the internet to begin with, looking for small donkey charities who might like to foster out a couple. But after considering our experiences with the Donkey Sanctuary we felt it would be rather nice to be free from the quarterly invasion by Lionel and his cohorts. The Donkey Sanctuary had rendered plenty of support and advice, but their requirements were sometimes a tad draconian and we could do without the constant feeling that we were under the scrutiny of the eyeballs in the sky. We decided we would go it alone. We'd buy our new donkey couple and be free of control and regulation.

We soon discovered Zoie (Welsh spelling) Burton, a young lady running an operation she styled, imaginatively, "*Donkeys in Wales*". Zoie specialised in the miniature variety and in miniature crosses. And she bred them in Wales. Hence her business title. Now a pure bred miniature will set you back a couple of grand. And there's always the risk that you get a duff customer that'll die in five minutes. So we went for a couple of mongrels, or half breeds. Zoie could let us have a choice out of three or four miniature cross standard donkeys at £450 apiece. They'd just been born in the April of 2015 and would be able to leave their mothers at six months old, or by October/November. Zoie sent us pictures.

Well we were both taken with the little fellows. We'd only had female donkeys thus far. Males would be a bit of a novelty; they're usually less decorous and a whole lot more naughty than females, but if they were miniature crosses they wouldn't grow very big would they? We should still be able to manage them in our advancing years. We chose one white and one standard grey. We paid Zoie a deposit and she promised to keep us updated on their progress through adolescence until they were ready to leave mum and make the trip to North Devon in about six months time.

We spent the summer of 2015 in preparation. Not that much preparation for the donkeys was necessary beyond laying in a stock of bedding and feed for our new charges; the preparations we'd made for Frieda, Heidi and Mistletoe would set us in good stead. Our attention in the summer of 2015 turned to my health. The strict regime of a sugar and carbohydrate free diet would attend to the diabetes and bring my sugar levels back to the acceptable within three months. For the prostate cancer I selected the radical option of prostatectomy by laperoscopic keyhole surgery. My operation was to take place in early November, at about the same time as we expected to receive our new donkeys. There was a lot to look forward to that year, and after the initial shock and dismay at contracting two potentially life limiting conditions within months of each other, the focus for both of us was getting back to rights and the arrival of the donkeys.

A couple of months after we'd made our selections from the pictures Zoie sent there was a tragedy at *"Donkeys in Wales"*. The little white foal we'd selected took a fall and broke its leg. He'd had to be destroyed. It was a tearful and a very apologetic Zoie on the phone in June. Did we still want the standard brown, or would we like her to return our deposit? She asked, between sobs. Alternatively we could have the brown and select from the remaining two whites whichever we would like, as neither had been taken. Gilly and I hummed and haa'ed for a bit, but not for a very long bit. We both knew we would be taking the brown and both whites. And when could we have them? Zoie cheered up immediately.

"The two whites are actually half brothers," she explained. "Same sire, different dames. I would love you to have them both. I wasn't looking forward to splitting them up actually. They've kind of bonded already. And they'll get on with the brown, as they were all born at about the same time. They know each other well."

So that's how we came to be the proud owners of a trio of donkeys.

Pedro, Pablo and Pancho entered our lives at 5.00 p.m. on the dark and howling evening of 28th November 2015, during a wild and woolly gale and a monsoon of biblical proportions out of the monsoon season. They had been on the road in a horse trailer towed by Zoie and her partner for over six hours as they'd battled their way from the wilderness of west Wales, over the Severn Bridge and around the corner into North Devon. Zoie and her partner were wet, weary and tired after their ordeal, but wouldn't accept the lightest of refreshment. It would be another six hours on the return trip in the foulest of weather and they needed to make tracks. The three young and frisky donkeys were unloaded onto our drive, one at a time, and led, wide-eyed and protesting, across the front lawn and into the Stock Barn. Zoie, cute, comely, almost coquettish in an impish way, brightened up on sight of the accommodation we had prepared for the three little chaps. The Stock Barn was brightly lit, with a loose box done out with straw bedding and an ample supply of hay and water. It would be a comfortable B&B for the newcomers. We assured Zoie that the three would stay in the warm for at least a week to get acclimatised to their new surroundings. And then they left. I don't think they even noticed my limp. I'd only been released from hospital the previous day and was catheterised as I led one of the donkeys into its new quarters.

We'd already decided to name them Pedro, Pablo and Pancho, "los tres amigos". Pedro; pure white, calm, aimiable, a bit of a philosopher on the quiet. Pablo; almost the same in colour but with the feint trace of blue markings on his back. More boistrous than Pedro and and with a tendency to be a bit of a bully. Pancho; standard brown, actually more of a grey, slightly smaller than the other two, charms with his cute and cuddly looks. All three were a bit spooked out by the drama of arrival, so after a few words of reassurance and encouragement we left them to their own devices. They could meet their stable mate Aramis and the few remaining sheep in the morning.

It has to be said that there was precious little evidence of "miniatureness" in los tres amigos. When they arrived they were bright-eyed and frisky, a little anxious perhaps, but cute and at six months fascinating creatures. Over the next six months they achieved adulthood and their full growth potential. Which was very much the same size as your average donkey. All three are powerful, strong, stubborn and completely endearing. They play in the fields and munch away at the grass all day and throughout the year. They give structure to each end of our every day. They can be hard work sometimes but we wouldn't be without them.

Anyone reading this should be aware of at least three things before investing in three adult male donkeys; their feet, their bollocks and their tendency to eat everything in sight.

FEET:

Your average donkey's hooves grow throughout their lives, a bit like our finger and toe nails. The subtle difference between a donkey and a human is that the former walk on their hooves, whilst the latter only use their finger nails as screwdrivers, nasal gouges and sometimes purely as a decoration. Toenails are not really used for anything at all. So that attention to a donkey's hooves is essential, rather than just as a hobby or a practicality, if the donkey is to continue to walk properly. Even donkeys that live on harsh rocky desert terrain need their tootsies attended to occasionally, though they rarely get this attention. Donkeys living on the lush meadow grass of England require attention to their hooves about once every six to eight weeks, because they will not wear down naturally on such terrain. I learnt all about this at Donkey School.

Anyway, it is not recommended that you attend to your own donkey's feet, unless by chance you happen to be a qualified farrier. A farrier is a person who has spent seven long years as an apprentice to a qualified farrier learning just how to treat the feet of a donkey, or any other equine for that matter. Farrier's come in all shapes and sizes. We chose James as farrier to our three donkeys, as he had done a stellar job with Frieda, Heidi and Mistletoe in the past. He had treated them firmly but fairly, and they had not given him much trouble.

James was young, handsome, and very powerful indeed. And very good at the task of farriering. We would gather the donkeys in, put on their head collars and lead reins and wait for James to appear at the appointed hour. When he appeared we'd help get each donkey to a stable ring where the donkey would be tied to the ring with its snout close to the barn wall so that there was little room for movement. Then James would do the business. Each foot in turn is examined, then the overgrowth paired back with a massive pair of pincers, and the bottom of the hoof rasped flat with the biggest industrial rasp I've ever seen outside a steel foundry.

This procedure worked very well to begin with. James had qualified apprenticed to Clive Ley (of whom see above) and gone freelance. To start with he was most professional, polite, firm but kind to the donkeys and an allround personable guy. He was a bit of a chauvinist, however, and seems to have had a rather low regard for women. Gilly didn't like being called "dear", but brushed off the insult in the interests of getting the job done. I quite liked James' visits. We'd pass the time of day in idle banter as he struggled with the donkeys and he surprised me with stories of his other interests, which included being an ebay trader in antiques, and ballroom dancing, at which he had won several medals.

But over time something happened to James. He began to be less reliable, to attend several hours later than promised, sometimes not at all, leaving the donkeys roped up in the barn fruitlessly all day on one occasion. And when he did attend he seemed to have lost the edge of his charm offensive. Mistletoe, the most elderly of the donkeys, gave him the most trouble. I believe Mistletoe had been abused by a male person at sometime in her early history and she was always more comfortable in the presence of women. She was wary of me and absolutely hated James. Because he became a bully. His interest in the ballroom was exchanged for one in cage fighting. I do not know where he practised this barbaric sport but James boasted to me once that he'd like to chase the bulls through Pamplona and show them a thing or too.

James once, in a fit of temper, wrestled Mistletoe to the ground and treated her feet while she lay supine and whimpering on the barn floor. I think it was a control thing; James had begun to have as little respect for the female donkey as he had for his girlfriends. It was not a pretty sight and I feared that the old girl might just expire there on the floor. I began to have more than second thoughts about James, whose entire personality seems to have changed, the Hyde in him taking over the Dr. Jekyll. He did start to farrier los tres amigos and could handle the strong and stubborn brutes very well, but when his unreliability became more than an irritation, I decided to dispense with his services and look elsewhere for equine podiatry.

Keith the farrier was recommended to us by a couple of our neighbours with horses. He's slim and slight, towers above me at 5 foot 5, surprisingly powerful at fifty five or six, and has spent his entire life in and about North Devon. He's also a very good farrier, probably coming towards the age of retirement (as the work plays havoc with the back). He is firm but kind to los tres amigos and he's as reliable as they come. He's taken on our donkeys and it's always a pleasure to host his eight weekly visits, sometimes accompanied by another farrier to help with handling them. Though he is a great farrier he does need that little bit of help getting the donkey to the stable ring. In the absence of his younger pal, which is most of the time, Gilly or I have to pull each donkey by the lead rein while Keith shoves them by the rear. We manage in this comical way to achieve the objective of treating the donkeys' feet. But at 71 years old (as I write) I wonder how much longer I'll be able to render the assistance I do.

We're right in the middle of the Coronavirus outbreak of 2020. I've just finished assisting Keith with the farriering. How ever much you try you just cannot maintain two metres of social distancing when two of you are trying to move a donkey to its ring, because your average donkey is not two metres from snout to tail. So I manufactured my own species of personal protective equipment to cope with this task and protect the three of us. It consists of a decorator's dust mask, a pair of swimming goggles and a nose clip, a strimmer's mask, teddy bear ear muffs and a snorkle. Can't say it was the most fashionable or alluring of looks, but I think it turned Keith on a bit.

BOLLOCKS:

Male donkeys should of course be castrated within the first two weeks or so of birth, if they are not going to be put to stud, that is. If caught during this window of opportunity the operation can be carried out by the owner in much the same way as a sheep farmer will elastrate a male lamb in its first week of life, by the application of a tight rubber ring at the base of the scrotal sack, as I think I have described rather tastefully elsewhere in these adventures. If the bollocks are allowed to accompany their owner into and beyond adolescence however, as was the case with the Long Lane Farm tres amigos, then do-it-yourself castration is most inadvisable. It's a potentially bloody affair, and definitely an expensive one if you do get the professionals in. Here is how it's done:

Top Tips for Farmers No.12: How to castrate three donkeys.

1.   First make sure your donkeys are in need of castration. You should check in particular

- That your donkeys are of the male rather than the female sex. Look out for the tell-tale penis and a couple of large dangly things that accompany it. You'll find these averagely amidships your donkey and a bit towards the rear. You will notice the penis as it is rather large, particularly when the donkey is aroused. The miner of old, it is said, would use the penis of a recently dead donkey as one of the tools of his trade, hence the words of the miner's anthem

    "Hi Ho, Hi Ho, it's off to work we go,

    With a shovel and a pick and a donkey's dick,

    Hi Ho, Hi Ho, Hi Ho, Hi Ho!"

    If you find no penis your donkey is probably of the female persuasion and will not require castration anyway.

- You'll recognise the donkeys bollocks because they, too, are rather large. If you have your own bollocks you can compare them for size but do not become discouraged. These are, after all, "donkeys bollocks", an expression used all over the world, well all over Ireland anyway, to denote something stupendously large and to be envied and admired. If you find no bollocks at all your donkey is either of the female persuasion or it has already been castrated. In either case further castration will not be necessary.

- The behaviour of your donkeys with each other, especially if they all turn out on inspection to be male, adult and entire (fully supplied with bollocks, or at least two thereof). If, for instance, your donkeys are calm and dispassionate at all times and appear to take no more than a passing interest in their colleagues, they probably do not need castrating and can be left to mosey around the fields together as chums in the countryside are wont to do. If, on the other hand, they are prone to chasing each other around the fields with massive and uncontrollable erections, taking it in turns to mount, bugger and ejaculate into each other on frequent and rather alarming occasions and this behaviour is seen to be indelicate, possibly unbecoming the gentleman donkeys you expected, then probably your donkeys need to be castrated.

2.   Once you are sure that a donkey castration scenario has presented itself, assemble your team of vets. You should ensure in particular

- That you select at least two. As we shall see you will require one vet to act as anaesthetist and one to carry out the operation.
- That they are beautiful, at least easy on the eye, well qualified and experienced, kind, efficient, understanding of the needs of both you and your donkey, pliable and ready to accept instruction.
- That they accept and respect your judgement and many years of experience in donkey and general animal husbandry, so that they will if necessary bow to your superior knowledge.

3.   Next prepare your operating theatre, if this is to be done at home. Pay particular attention to the following requirements:

- A dry, reasonably clean and disinfected concrete floored barn with weather protection.
- A loose box in which to coral your donkeys pending their operation(s).
- Couple of straw bales to prop your donkeys up with.
- An adequate supply of hot water, towels and soap
- A selection of kitchen knives, bottle openers, razor blades and sticky plasters for use if necessary by your vets. In fairness the vets will probably bring their own tools.
- Select a day in early spring or late autumn for the operation(s) when the blow fly is not so rampant.

4.   Procedure on the day of the operation should be largely as follows, but terms and conditions will apply:

- You should instruct one of your vets to adopt the role of anaesthetist, the other being the surgeon. Your vets may probably be trusted to select the role most suited to them. Once this is decided you will probably be able to let the vets carry out their respective roles without much direction or assistance from you. That is, if you have vetted your vets well.
- The anaesthetist should be told to sedate the first donkey intraveinously and that donkey should be led to the operating area, where the anaesthetist should be told to administer an appropriate dosage of anaesthesia.
- When the donkey begins to totter and to sink to the floor you should assist him and cushion his fall with bales of straw. This could be left to the vets but even if you are nearly seventy years old and they are in their late twenties and

gorgeous you should show willing. After all, they will be duly impressed with your manliness and fortitude, if not with your clumsy shambling gait.

- Now comes the difficult bit. The anaesthetist will merely have to ensure that the donkey is topped up with appropriate levels of anaesthetic throughout the operation so that he doesn't wake up. And the surgeon has the even easier bit of washing the donkeys bollocks with alcohol, slitting each scrotal sack in turn, extracting the testes, cutting (carefully please!) through the semen tract, and sewing up the hole in the scrotal sack leaving a drainage hole. You have the infinitely more difficult and delicate task of protecting the surgeon's head from any badly aimed kick from the hind leg of the donkey should he wake from his induced slumber mid operation. This you may like to do by sitting on the straw bale by the supine donkey and holding the hind leg at a safe distance out of range of the surgeon's head with a lead rein tied to its fetlock. If you are sensible you will have tried this procedure on your wife long before the operation so that you will at least look professional on the day even if you do cock it up.
- Once the operation is concluded you should stand by for your donkey to recover from the anaesthetic, which it will do in ten minutes or so if the anaesthetist has done her job well. Which she probably will have, even if she is French Canadian, beautiful and with an accent to charm the birds from the trees.
- Once you have assisted the donkey to its feet and he is steady, you may return him to the loose box and repeat the same procedure with the other two donkeys.

The entire procedure should take about three and a half hours. You will have earned that beer and a bottle of wine tonight.

TENDENCY TO EAT EVERYTHING IN SIGHT:

We hadn't noticed this with the lady donkeys. Of course they had been ladies of a certain age and respectability.   Since elderly donkeys are prone to laminitis if allowed free access to lush meadow grass in the spring and summer months, we had always to be wary of the state of the grass and to strip graze the donkeys if it looked too long or too lush. But at least the ladies stuck more or less to grass, supplemented by a daily feed of donkey nuts, chaff and ginger nuts. And they behaved themselves. They were decorous.

Los tres amigos did not display the decorous ways of their predecessors at Long Lane Farm. They were boistrous, naughty and as stubborn as they'd been allowed to be. And they soon evinced an inordinate apetite for wood.

We noticed at first little chunks being taken out of the fence rails that secured Donkery Up.Then the gates seemed affected by this strange malady. Could we be under the attack of an aggressive woodworm? I mused. Is there a death watch beetle that is attracted to the outdoors? A sort of foraging Ray Meers of the coleopteric world? Then I caught Pablo one afternoon having a jolly good munch on a fence rail and the mystery was solved. A few days later I spotted Pancho chewing contentedly on the gate. The habit was catching on. I couldn't see the problem really, I mean what's the odd fence rail between donkeys? But those rails had been in place for about fifteen years and had survived all weather conditions, hail storm and tempest, without complaint.

The wood chewing became more of an inconvenience when it was translated to the interior of the Stock Barn. Little bits nibbled tentatively out of the back door, teeth marks on the loose box supports. Soon the entire barn was under seige; I could envisage the donkeys eating their way out of the back door and making a bid for freedom. But as those long, wet and dreary days of winter passed by I did not have the heart to put in preventive measures. I thought, when the spring comes I'll have all their teeth extracted, they can live on gruel for the rest of their naturals, like Mistletoe had to. Or something.

Well the spring did come, and so did the Coronavirus. Lockdown! A concept frightening to many, more frightening than contracting the deadly virus itself. As the months wore on and millions upon millions of people bemoaned their lot, locked down in a two bed semi or a one bedroomed flat, with a couple of bored dysfunctional kids to feed and furloughed from their means of livelihood, well I do not wish to sound smug, but I was having a ball! Locked down on a 12 acre smallholding in a five bed house with the missus for company and the fabulous and unending weather of the spring of 2020, to me it was like heaven on Earth. The time, the opportunity, the weather and the wherewithal to make some improvements were with me. I commissioned local and recently qualified carpenter Luke Caley, son of my mechanic Neil, to undertake those improvements. I'd already replaced the fence rails that had all but disappeared from the donkery in a rare spark of enthusiasm that occurred with the first blush of spring and that glorious weather (which I swear did not accompany the lockdown as a matter of mere coincidence). I asked Luke to attend to the eaten rear door of the barn and to do what he could to restore sanity to its chewed structure. Luke did all this in less than a day, replacing the ruined door with one of his own construction and even repairing a couple of annoying leaks to the roof which had let in the rain like some sort of Japanese water torture for the donkeys for a couple of years.

That brings us up to date on the donkeys. They live a life of unbridled (see what I did there?) pleasure in and around the Stock Barn. They're fed daily and receive copious quantities of treats from visitors to the funny farm. They are now the stars of our show; they give back more than they receive in terms of affection, fun, general naughtiness and entertainment. And they are provided for in our wills.

20. A Walk on the Wild Side

In twenty years of living on a smallholding in rural North Devon you are bound to have a few encounters with wildlife, both indigenous and not. Mostly it's harmless, if aloof, preferring to keep its distance and its essential mystery. But there are a few species that the farmer and the smallholder must regard as the enemy, if only because of the damage and loss they cause. If you've ploughed your way even halfway through the Bird Tables above you will already have discovered that the fox is inevitably the enemy of the chicken farmer, duck fancier and goose fanatic. We have lost countless fowl to the fox. He'll even have a go at a new-born lamb if the lamb is weakly and its mother unaware. The only practical solution to keeping your fowl safe in the countryside is to invest in an alpaca, an animal that will keep the fox at bay and even attack it without compunction; the alpaca detests the fox and faced with one will become defensive to the point of belligerence. But a decent alpaca will set you back a couple of grand, and you'd need a pair for company. So as chickens and ducks are much cheaper than that they become expendable.

The fox is perhaps Public Enemy No. 1 to the smallholder. But there are other pests less damaging but no less irritating to deal with in the countryside. If asked to enumerate in descending order of irritation the enemies the smallholder may confront my list would look like this:

Foxes, because they kill or abduct your chickens and ducks. You can shoot these if you have a shotgun licence, a shotgun, a steady eye and a bit of luck. I possess none of these.

Moles, because they burrow underground and make a mess of your fields with their molehills. It is also believed that the subterranean dirt from these molehills can cause listeria in sheep grazing nearby. In any event moles are not farm- or farmer- friendly You can catch these if you have a supply of moletraps, a spade, some marker sticks, flowerpots and training in mole psychology and logistics. Because your average mole is a wily fellow, adept at dodging the moletrap and sarcastically mocking in the extreme when the score is Moles 10, Me Nil. A professional molecatcher will be a good investment if you are seriously at the mercy of Mr. Mole. He'll set you back about £180 or £10 per mole. And on no account should you believe a word of what Kenneth Grahame tells you.

Voles, a bit like mice really though slightly bigger and they burrow under the ground in tunnels. They don't leave hills like the moles, but they play havoc with your lawn and need to be encouraged gently away from it. If this doesn't work try proprietary mouse traps but use three at a time, baited with chocolate, around each volehole. Disguise the traps under an inverted bucket to simulate night hours. Collect your dead voles at first light if you are lucky. Or don't bother with traps and just get used to a ruined lawn.

Rabbits make short work of burrowing into and through your ancient Devon banks, so that they subside and slip gradually into the field. You can shoot these if you have the same equipment as for a fox (see above) and you can be bothered to portion and cook them into a stew. You'll need some carrots, parsnips, potatoes, peas and a few other veg. for this. Oh, and the odd rabbit or two.

Rats, which will eat their way through feed bags, feed, tools, wheelbarrows and most other agricultural equipment, without so much as a beg-your-pardon. Their urine can pass on Weils Disease (orse. Leptospirosis) too, which can be a killer. If they decide to take up lodgings in your ancient Landrover they will eat the seats, the wiring loom, the windscreen washer bottle and most other edible parts, even if those parts don't look tasty to you. So they need to be banished from your smallholding, though they'll always be present. Catch them using baited rat traps, then hurl the dead bodies into the road where you might catch a passing cyclist. Alternatively catch them alive in a humane rattrap. And then drown them in a suitable bath of water. They'll thank you in the end for saving them from a life of perdition and guilt.

Crows are mainly a problem to the arable farmer as they are voracious thieves of grain. If you are indeed an arable farmer you'll need to set up a bird scarer when you've sewed your crop, or be prepared to stand vigil with your shotgun in all weathers for a couple of months. If you're not an arable farmer but just a smallholder with an ancient Landrover and a couple of other cars you'll just need to keep an eye on your windscreen wipers, door trims and any other naked and unprotected rubber items about your place. You can try tying the feathers from a dead crow to the front end of your car. Looks a bit like voodoo, but it might save you a visit to Halford's.

Mice are more of a problem around the house and during the winter, when they will try to find a warm snug billet in your loft. If you hear the gentle scrabbling of tiny feet above your head one stormy winter's night as you ponder the meaning of life abed, be prepared with your mousetraps in the early morning. For if you leave the mouse to his mousy doings you might find the entire lighting circuit of your house compromised.

Squirrels are really just bushy tailed rats. They might look cute as they leap from tree to tree and nick your entire annual crop of hazelnuts just before you can get to them. But in reality your average squirrel can be as destructive as your average rat. It's just that they are more athletic. So that if you find that the entire lighting circuit of your private leisure suite has been eaten one day and that you no longer have reliable cinema lighting, it may just be that you have a squirrel family or two that have taken up residence in the loft of that building. You should try to block up any gaping holes in the roof or under the eaves of your leisure suite before you replace the lighting circuit. This may be expensive.

Flies, (esp. horse flies) are the bane of the smallholder's life, particularly in the summer. They lay eggs, which grow into maggots, which pupate and then turn into more flies. And all the time they're failing to note the reality of life which is that they do not provide a useful service. In fact they have no point. And as such they should be killed at every opportunity. Try proprietary fly papers, fly sprays or wield the trusty swat. Horse flies are the worst. They live in hedges and emerge to catch the passing smallholder a resounding bite when he is least expecting it. Horse flies should be against the law, or at least they should be made to wear stout boots so that the unsuspecting can at least detect the arrival of the horsefly before the beast sinks its not inconsiderable gnashers into you. My advice for horse flies is that they should leave my premises forthwith. Failing which they will be subjected to a sound thrashing.

Now that I have got all my rantings out of the way I can let the reader know about the few occasions upon which we have become the caring hosts to wildlife.

We had become early acquainted with the Veterinary Animal Hospital at Mullacott and in those first days at Long Lane Farm were frequent visitors. We'd also become known as a little eccentric in North Devon terms, so that it wasn't a great surprise to be asked, on 23rd October 2002, whether we could accommodate a squab, or young baby pigeon that'd fallen out of its nest. Speckledy Jim, whom we named of course after Lord Melchit's (*Blackadder*) only childhood friend, joined the flock at Long Lane the very same day.

Now racing pigeons, on their way back home from having been released somewhere "oop north", have often stopped off at Long Lane for a couple of nights rest and recuperation before the last leg home. They seem to know they are welcome to feast at our bird table and roost in the trees of our wood for a kind of country farmhouse holiday. We've always felt a little sad in the knowledge that they're in for rebuke and an almost certain "necking" when they get home for having lingered in the countryside and lost the race. But Speckledy Jim was of a different ilk. He must have been hatched in North Devon as a wild pigeon. He soon took to the comfortable quarters of a budgie cage in our dining room and a diet of corn, millet and birdseed. We did try to teach him a few words, but found him an unwilling student of linguistics and having an unusual predilection for the telly. His particular favourite was a showing of Alfred Hitchcock's *"The Birds"*, during which I caught sight of his wistful gaze at the telegraph wire over Tipi Hedren's shoulder.

But of course Speckledy Jim was destined to be wild. And in an effort to liberate him to his proper surroundings I began to take him on short walks in the country. Rides more than walks really, as he'd sit aboard my shoulder while I did the walking. Teaching him to fly was another treat I'd not bargained for. I think he was more than a trifle amused at my lumbering attempts to simulate flight, running as coolly as a 53 year old in wellington boots can manage whilst flapping outstretched arms and coo-ing into the wind. He seemed to get the point of it all though and I must say when he eventually did take off his style had learned a lot of my natural grace and charm. Those first few flights were ground-breaking stuff really, especially for Speckledy

Jim. At first he'd return to my shoulder and make for home, the fireside and his telly. Later on he'd disappear for hours at a time and just return at tea time, rapping on the kitchen window for his corn, particularly the night they showed *"Psycho"*, another of his favourites. When he began to stay away all night we rather thought we'd lost him to the wild. But then there he was again at early light, pecking at the kitchen window. Gilly would open the window and beckon to him, calling "Speckledy, come home, it's Heathcliffe!"

Of course it was Speckledy's tameness that was undoubtedly his downfall. He just wasn't accustomed to the denizens of the big outdoors. One day he didn't come home at all. All we found, on 7th February 2003, was a pile of tattered feathers and his little head, in Boot Hill. Victim to a sparrowhawk, we believe. I buried the head in a tiny grave in Badger's Garden by the old chicken shed.

Norman the hedgehog hailed from Woolacombe. At least that's where the family on holiday staying at the Woolacombe Bay Caravan Park found him looking a bit sorry for himself on 15 August 2003. Norman was clearly very young, perhaps he'd been ejected from the nest. He was also dehydrated and quite ill. The family from Woolacombe had been put in our direction by Diana Lewis of the NDAA. They handed little Norman to us in a cardboard box and helped us make him comfortable in a loose box in the Stock Barn where he could receive personalised attention and recuperation from his exposure. The family from Woolacombe were fascinated to look around Long Lane Farm; it was apparent the children had never seen pigs, goats or sheep up close and personal.

Norman only stayed with us three days. Gilly offered him tinned dog food and I dug him up some worms and the odd slug. It's difficult to say whether he took to us or his new surroundings as he was a prickly little character. On the morning of the 18th August he was dead in the loose box, probably a victim to dehydration and internal injuries.

It was more than three years later that we were to host our next batch of wildlife. A small flock of wild duck, mainly Mallard, had taken up residence on the outdoor swimming pool of the plush Barnstaple Hotel, where they'd swim majestically about and generally harry the guests. The Barnstaple Hotel is quite posh by North Devon standards and it caters for business conferences, wedding receptions and romantic weekends away throughout the year. Even though it is situated on the edge of an industrial estate it enjoys a 5* reputation and clientèle. This was April 2007, early in the year for outdoor swimming pools and just as well. But the management of the hotel saw it as their duty to rid the pool of its invaders before they became too entrenched, and certainly before the season was in full swing. Diana Lewis was asked to intervene, as the management felt it would not be seemly for them to don plus fours and deerstalkers and lurk about the undergrowth with their 12-bores. Diana, assisted by her colleague Pauline Bussell, was able one fine spring afternoon to capture the little brown Tulip, as she nestled down on her clutch of 15 eggs for an afternoon's hatching. Tulip and her 15 "bulbs" as we named them arrived at Long Lane on 14 April. Gilly formed a nest out of hay and placed the eggs and Tulip gently on them in Hagrid's House in the wood to await the hatching.

Two days later Diana roped me into her quest for the Hotel Ducks at the Barnstaple Hotel. She explained that she'd only been able to catch Tulip because she was on dry land at the time but that there were more ducks and ducklings to be "rescued" poolside.

"There are half a dozen adults and some sweet little ducklings that the hotel management really must get out of there. Trouble is, they stick to centre of the pool. Pauline and I haven't got a hope of catching them. Any ideas?"

"Have you tried *International Duck Rescue?* Their *Sub-Aqua Branch* should be able to help."

"Who? What?" chanced Diana.

"Mainly they chase and capture escaped ducks, from wetland sites. Should be just the job. I'll give them a call."

And so it was arranged that *International Duck Rescue: Sub-Aqua Branch* would meet Diana and Pauline poolside that very afternoon. I hastily put the little organisation together. It consisted of me, dressed in some ageing and rather baggy old swimming trunks, an elderly shrimp net (for effect) and my Reliant Regal three-wheeler, to which I had added appropriate signage (something like "*International Duck Rescue: Sub-Aqua Branch; your ducks rescued from wetland sites and swimming pools in a trice!*"). Thus attired and transported I presented myself poolside at the Barnstaple Hotel on the afternoon of 16th April 2007.

Now the event itself was far from spectacular. There was a bunch of six or seven ducks in a huddle in the centre of the pool. These needed herding, or coaxing rather than catching, towards dry land where they could be grabbed and boxed in a crate for transport. As it happened the *Sub-Aqua Branch* was not strictly speaking necessary as the water was only a couple of feet deep; it was a child's pool that had been invaded. But I like to think that I struck a proud and athletic figure as I strode manfully into the chilly water that April afternoon, my shrimp net held aloft, my cunning pincer movement not missing the cameras. For the local press and a small television crew were present to record the occasion. I made the early evening news on *Spotlight!* And though I wasn't interviewed sufficiently to give me celebrity status I still like to think I went down in the annals of television natural history to warrant some sort of minor recognition in the New Year's Honours List for services to, well, ducks I suppose.

For my troubles I was rewarded with Daphne, Deirdre, Dandelion, Dolores and Daniel, orphan ducklings all, in need of a roof over their beaks until old enough to fend for themselves. I somehow got the little blighters into the Reliant and, still dripping from the pool but radiant in the afterglow of the hero worship I'd had heaped upon me by the residents of the Barnstaple Hotel, I left for home. The newcomers were placed in Hagrid's House with Tulip and her Bulbs (which we suspected she'd given up on).

Tulip left us a couple of weeks later. She had clearly given up on her brood and really wasn't interested in fostering the ducklings. So it was time for her to be released back into the wild. I took her to the Hidden Valley and let her fly free there on 28th April during the NDAA Open Day. On 12th May the other wild ducks Daphne, Deirdre, Dandelion, Dolores and Daniel followed Tulip and the many others Diana has released at this delightful bird paradise just off the A361.

We've never had much luck with other, wilder, birds. Steve Parkin once delivered an injured baby buzzard into our care, but he didn't last the afternoon. On 16th May 2007, just after the departure of the wild ducks, Steve brought us Plucker, a pheasant with a broken leg he'd found beside the road, probably struck by a car. We put him in Hagrid's House but he only survived a couple of days. Nowadays Gilly would have plucked and eaten him. Back then we weren't so pagan. We put him in the fox's larder in Oasis Field.

Plucker was the last to date of our attempts to nurture ailing wildlife. Perhaps we know better now.

21. House Guests

William blinked at the tiny shaft of light that pierced the intense darkness. He could barely make out the feint outline of Elsie's cap in the grey gloom where she stood, just inches away. It had been this dark for hours, and yet when the blackness had come it'd been so sudden. Just after daybreak in early February as the day had begun to dawn it seemed that the daylight had been squeezed from the sky; just as William was beginning to open his beady little eyes he had been told by nature to close them again. And sleep. And now these many hours later the memory of hazy light reasserted itself for a brief moment.

The big rear doors of the furniture van swung back on complaining hinges and hit the door stays with a resounding clang! The young man in jeans and jumper leant into the back of the van and took William and Elsie's cage in one hand, Pearl's in the other. The driver's mate, older, taller, gaunt and perhaps a little careworn, followed with Barney's cage in one hand, the ferret hutch under his arm. The ferrets were destined for the empty greenhouse; Barney was to join his mates indoors. These four little birds were to be the first house guests to enter Long Lane Farm.

For the canaries William and Elsie, thrown together by the tragic loss of William's mate Clarice, 9th February 2001 was probably the biggest adventure and certainly the most momentous event of their lives. They had travelled the 250 miles from rural Bedfordshire to North Devon in the back of a furniture van together cheek by claw with the pungent ferrets, the irascible cockatiels, and a lifetime's worth of our miscellaneous junk and memories. The rest of their lives was going to seem pretty tame compared with that. The truth is, the life of your average canary is pretty tame when all said and done. Mundane even. As Ogden Nash famously put it:

"The song of canaries, never varies. But when they're moulting they're pretty revolting."

There's not much to be said about canaries really. William was a yellow Roller canary, probably. Elsie was a Gloucester Corona, sporting as she did a little fringe-like cap. She was named after Gilly's mum who had a penchant for berets but didn't look particularly French. William was named for my dad. They lived together in a standard budgie cage and Gilly fed them Trill, with sprigs of millet and the odd bit of greenery for a treat. They can sing quite sweetly if you're lucky. But they're not particularly amusing, interesting or diverting company. Nor are they high maintenance. Then one day they suddenly, without prior announcement, die. William died on New Years Eve 2002, of a short and mysterious illness, after nearly two years at Long Lane. Elsie soldiered on alone for a few months. Then she succumbed to the same non-specific and mysterious illness that is probably called old age, on 4th April 2003.

With the departure of Elsie the capped canary we were left with the two cockatiels Barney and Pearl as our house guests. We had decided by this time that to encourage the keeping of small caged animals and birds just wasn't our thing really. I for one, as a life coach, felt that little creatures could hardly be expected to achieve their full potential in life whilst cooped up in the tedious surroundings of a caged enclosure. The cockatiels could at least enjoy a modicum of freedom and socialisation; a cockatiel can be a very good and even life enhancing pet for the housebound, lonely or disabled. But canaries are really for the enthusiast. We'd decided in short not to host any more small birds.

Which is what made the arrival on the scene of Blue, Bruce, Cobber and Sheila, four domestic budgerigars complete with cage, on 2nd August 2004, a touch surprising. These four charming and varicoloured little parakeets were basically foisted upon us by my cousin Christine, who made her living then as now by house- and pet-sitting for native Devonians wishing to holiday abroad (or in Cornwall, which for a Devonian is the same thing). They'd become surplus to the requirements of one of her Braunton customers in the early stages of Alzheimers or some other deadly disease, and needed a billet in which to rest their weary beaks. Bruce was green, Sheila yellow, Cobber pure white and tinier than the rest, and Blue, predictably I suppose, was blue. The cage that accommodated them was chromium silver and stood on a blue enamel stand. It's fair to say that the little chaps did receive some attention and admiring glances from our other, human, house guests of the time. But Budgerigars are not known for their longevity. Five years is about right if properly cared for. Canaries can do three times that. The precise age of our four was unknown, but when they started to leave us it seemed to be a bit of a race.

Blue had only been with us a couple of months when he was found, after an astonishingly short illness, dead on the cage floor on the landing window sill on the morning of 11th October 2004.

The remaining three of the feathered quartet carried on their daily routines for a couple of years before they started to make their exits as if in obeisance to a monthly regime. Cobber (the white) succumbed to a short illness, possibly avian 'flu or pneumonia, and even made it to the vets at Mullacott for a tiny shot of antibiotics before he expired on 13th September 2006. Four days later Gilly adopted a replacement for Cobber in the person of Steve, another blue budgie from the NDAA. I'd been attending the NDAA Open Day with Black Betty, my steed for the Plymouth-Banjul Challenge, in search of sponsorship for the trip. I think Gilly was surprised to see me return with Steve as all I could raise that day from the fans of Diana Lewis and her NDAA. Steve took Cobber's place on the communal perch in the cage on the window sill and I'm not sure the others even noticed the change.

A month later, on 18th October, Sheila (the yellow) was found dead in the cage which by this time had been repositioned in Banjul Base Camp, operational and logistics headquarters for the Challenge (and later my bedroom). Bruce (the green) lasted into November, when he too was found dead on Sunday morning the 19th.

All of the Australian Quartet were interred in the Toad Garden, close to the fence, in tiny unmarked graves, the unknown warriors. Which just left the newly adopted Steve, our solitary budgie for the ensuing three years. We quartered him for company with Barney, of whom I shall write below. Steve and Barney were not particularly fond of each other, but they seemed to tolerate each other in what could have been an uneasy relationship, sharing a variety of quarters together in that time. When he eventually passed, on 16th October 2009, no doubt having reached his statutory five years, Steve was buried with the other budgies.

The cockatiels settled happily into the routine at Long Lane Farm. Pearl was a particular favourite of mine and of our frequent house guests. She'd never been taught to do impressions, but in her own way she was the singer who stood up while she played the piano. She'd often take centre stage at our little gatherings, amusing the guests quaffing red wine and gin, nibbling at the cheese and onion crisps, sucking the odd olive. She was a party girl and added to our soirées with her little quips and anecdotes, her sideways glances and her gestures of appreciation. She adored her head being stroked and tickled and would reciprocate with real affection. Pearl was a real lady, a perfect companion, a friend.

I believe Pearl was about middle aged when we adopted her in September of 1998. As she got older she developed an overbite and excessively long claws. There was a monthly spot for her with me in the task diary where I'd trim her top beak and each of her eight claws with a toenail clipper. She moulted from time to time and I've still got a couple of her tail feathers in a pot on my desk as I write this, some thirteen years after her death.

But of course Pearl did die. Exactly nine years to the day after we'd adopted her from the lady on the corner of the Orchards in Eaton Bray. On 17th September 2007 she died in her sleep over night in her cage in the Brewery Tap, where she'd been placed for the peace and quiet, and the red wine of course. I buried her under Gryffindor on Badger's grave in his garden.

Barney was probably quite a young blade when he escaped from his original owner and flew into the hands of Wendy De Meur in Bedfordshire. Wendy, you will recall had passed him on to us to be a boyfriend, or perhaps more realistically a consort to the regal Pearl. They each inhabited their own dome-like cage and though we did try to get them to cohabit for company's sake, if not for sex, neither Barney nor Pearl were up for it. So Barney was celibate for all the years we had him. He was a sociable little fellow really, and had been keen to tread the boards when with Wendy, who had a knack with parrots, parakeets and all avians. But Barney would not come out of his cage to socialise with us or any of our house guests. He even shunned the outside world when Wendy visited Devon on a couple of occasions in the early years. Barney seemed to be a home boy. And for him "home" was the generously proportioned, if enclosed, dome cage next to Pearl's.

Cleaning the cage periodically was a bit of a trial for Gilly. She had to negotiate for the appointment first, and this would have to fit in with Barney's busy social round. Even then she would have to put up with Barney's critical eye and supervision, not to mention his frequent attacks, shrieks and the general hullaballoo he'd put up over the intrusion. But in all other respects Barney was, like Pearl, delightful low maintenance company about the house.

We nearly lost Barney in 2010. He seemed to contract some evil illness, perhaps the avian 'flu that had been circulating at the time. He went rapidly downhill, off his seed and millet and extremely down in the beak. Our builder Derrick was busy constructing the Sun Room which now adjoins our lounge, and he would enquire after Barney daily, in fact Barney's health became quite the topic of conversation in the spring of 2010. Each morning I would get up early, walk quietly along the landing to the top of the east staircase and peer down at Barney's cage where it rested on the window ledge at the bottom of the stairs. For some days I expected the worst really. But Barney just stood there on the perch with his little head bowed, his eyes barely open, his beak besnotted. One morning as I passed the cage he seemed to look up at me blearily with an expression on his beak as if to say "Help me, please help me." I bent down, opened the cage door and put my finger in and up to Barney's chest. For the first and only time in his life he climbed gingerly onto my finger and I took him out of the cage for a little fuss and attention. I did think about necking the little chap there and then, putting him out of his misery, or so I thought. But I couldn't do it. I kind of knew I'd get it wrong. And I couldn't have born the grief of giving him pain. So after a couple of minutes of stroking his little head and under his beak I put him back in the cage and withdrew to let nature take its course.

Which it did, the very next morning. I got up earlier than usual to visit the toilet. As I passed the east stairwell I heard a gentle chirrup. I stopped in my tracks, swivelled around and galloped down the stairs. Barney was fine. He'd shaken off the torpor induced by his illness and very nearly managed a smile. He was back in the land of the living.

Barney was the last of the house birds at the time and the very last of the Bedfordshire crop of creatures to survive when he finally shuffled off the old mortal coil on 6th December 2015. We'd had him for nearly sixteen years, probably the longest we'd ever had a creature in our company. Old age had evidently caught up on him. He'd been acting out of character for some weeks, sleeping late and eating very little. This December evening as I sat in my armchair in the Snug sipping vodka and cranberry, I stroked his little feathered head on one of his rare excursions from the cage. This was my last contact with him. He died in my hand the following day at 1.30 in the afternoon. He's buried under the hedge in the front garden, close to Felix the cat.

We had decided years before this that with the leaving of Barney we would not have any more caged birds. It's just a shame that we didn't inform Chick Rumson, our tenant and friend, of this strategic and well-intentioned decision. Because six days after Barney's departure Chick bestowed upon us two bright yellow canaries, each in a paper bag, presents intended to soften our grief. Now I'm sure Chick's gifts were as well-intentioned as our decision not to entertain them. But I was not best pleased. Gilly was incandescent with fury.

"They cost an arm and a leg!" exclaimed the triumphant Chick as he lay the tiny paper bags on the kitchen counter, opened them gingerly and showed us the two sweetly innocent birds.

"Yes, they're lovely," replied Gilly between clenched teeth and false smile, "I'll have to clean out Barney's cage a bit sharpish. I was going to get rid of it." She disappeared in the direction of the Ossie, steam and smoke billowing from her ears. Gilly is not famous for her acting abilities. Feigning delight does not come easy to her. But cleaning out cages of recently deceased birds in a downpour on a dark, wet December afternoon with the prospect before her of 15 years caring for canaries she didn't want comes easy. Not.

The clue is in the names Gilly bestowed on the newcomers, I think. Bug and Fuck were stationed in the east hall for the duration of their stay at Long Lane Farm. Which was less than two months. They disappeared while I was on holiday cruising down the Nile with Chick in February 2016. On the 6th to be precise. Gilly gave Bug and Fuck to Pauline Bussell of the NDAA who reassured her that there is a lively interest in adopting these creatures. I am sure that they enjoy bijou accommodation and are truly loved and respected by their new owners.

By far the most exotic of our house guests was six feet long, six inches wide and green. Frederick Chappell-Pugsley was a handsome gentle giant of a green iguana, native to South America but resident when we met him in Ilfracombe on the North Devon coast. Fred came to our attention through a line dancing acquaintance of Gilly's. In conversation on the dance floor in the early days of 2004 Gilly was told that this lady's brother, Steve, was host to a six foot iguana that he wanted rid of. Apparently the iguana, Fred, had been brought home from school as a youngster by Steve's son some years previously and housed in a tank in the boy's bedroom. Eleven years later the boy had left home to pursue a career that does not involve iguanas. So Fred was at a loose end and Steve wanted the bedroom back. Would we be interested?

Now I'm sure six foot green iguanas are not the pet of choice for most suburban households. But we visited Fred in his billet, and to see him was to want him. Neither of us had seen anything so magnificently quirky and prehistoric at close quarters. And we both do quirky big style. There was no consultation; we agreed on the spot that we'd take him. There was just a matter of Fred's housing to consider. We wouldn't have been happy to have him contained in the glass tank he'd been existing in. And we needed the bath from time to time. Preparations would have to be made.

I consulted the internet, a pile of books from the library and our builder friend Derrick Hamley, researching the needs, wants and aspirations of green iguanas. Between us we came up with a design for a palace fit for this veritable king of lizards; Derrick's job was just to build the thing. He set to work with a vengeance, saw and screwdriver and a month of spare time later saw construction complete. Fred's "palace" was built to fit snugly in the Snug, the little sitting room at the eastern end of Long Lane Farmhouse which had also been constructed by Derrick. So it was 7 feet from floor to ceiling, 5 feet wide and about 3 deep. Built of dark stained wood with double glazed doors and a commodious compartment for storage of iguana paraphernalia, the construction resembled a huge display cabinet, with a sunken bath and, my idea, a thick beech log for Fred to rest on. Because iguanas are arboreal creatures; they live largely in trees. Derrick delivered the palace to Long Lane Farm in two pieces and I helped him put the thing together and manoeuvre it into position. By the middle of March it looked ready to go.

Iguanas are tropical creatures and have to be kept warm. They also need light on the subject; at least a semblance of both daylight and sunshine would make Fred feel somewhat at home and help him with his studies. And I felt that some ambient background music, reminiscent of the sounds of the rainforest, would relax the old chap and make him a happy and contented iguana. In short, the palace required some fitting out with all the mod. cons. available to the space age lizard. And this is where Steve Chappell, he who wanted his bedroom back, came in.

Steve was a whizz with all things electrical and electronic. He also liked his red wine and strong black coffee. So, over the next six weeks or so I supplied him with the latter while he attended to the former. Evenings and weekends he worked, often long into the night. I kept the flow of caffeine and alcohol as constant as my anecdotes of derring-do as he tinkered in the cabinet with wires, switches, thermostats and all sorts of electronic gubbinses. By May he had finished. Installed within Fred's palatial cabinet were the following:-

- Thermostatically controlled central heating with wall heaters set at equidistant intervals and calibrated to the ambient temperature of the tropics.
- A timed lighting circuit to simulate daylight hours at or near the equator with automatic dusk and dawn settings.
- Ultraviolet ray bulbs set at basking height to provide the simulated suns rays so necessary to the digestion and wellbeing of the green iguana.
- A music system providing ambient sounds of the rainforest, timed to commence with the dawn and subside at dusk. (I provided this little delight).

Frederick Chappell-Pugsley took up residence of his new quarters in the Snug at Long Lane Farm on Sunday 16th May 2004. And he seemed very happy about that. He soon found his way up on to the comfortably smooth and undulating beech log and just sat there for many hours, soaking up the ultra violet. Gilly fed him a daily diet of exotic fruits and leaves, with seasonal vegetables and crudités (for iguanas are vegetarian; do not be led by the cretins who feed them dog food) with the occasional treat of nasturtium leaves and flowers. He had a sunken bath from which he was supposed to drink, but he was prone to using this as an ad hoc toilet and Gilly had to clean it out daily. And there he sat, day after day, a life of luxury and indolence stretching out before him.

On Saturday nights he'd come out for the evening, sit on my shoulders and sometimes on my head, dig his claws into my scalp and take in a movie. *Crocodile Dundee* I and II were his favourites. I did toy with the idea of letting him range free in the back garden on Bank Holidays, but as your average adult green iguana can do a nifty 40 m.p.h. on the straight and climb trees it seemed an experiment too far. So Fred spent most of his time on the beech log basking in the ultra violet, sometimes entertaining our friends by falling off it with a thump, and in occasional excursions to the theatre on my head.

The following year he was joined in his tropical paradise by Sonic, the tortoise. Sonic came to my attention on a visit to Brian Ford's emporium in Barnstaple. There on the notice board I spotted the following, or something like it:-

"WANTED—Home for young tortoise. Believed male. About five years old. Comes complete with furnished vivarium and full instructions. Owner going up to university which will not accommodate. Will travel. £80 ono."

A south Wales telephone number was given for enquiries. So I made some. It seems that Sonic the tortoise (so-named apparently on account of his remarkable speed and agility) had been the childhood pet of a young girl who had recently accepted the offer of a place at Lampeter, and the university authorities were not prepared to accommodate him either on the course or in the halls of residence. The parents of this young girl were not prepared to commit to a caring responsibility of in excess of perhaps one hundred years, and had informed Sonic that he must make alternative arrangements. Hence the notice in Bridgemans, though I'm sure he had some help with that. Gilly and I discussed the issue over tea and decided that Sonic deserved to be rescued. He'd probably not be excessive in his needs for care and attention. And only a modest codicil would be required to our joint wills to provide for Sonic's care and accommodation post our joint mortem. So we'd take him on.

I must say I rather expected Sonic to take several months to reach us in North Devon. It must be about 250 miles from the Gower Peninsula, and I estimated that Sonic wouldn't, even with his reported speed and agility, be able to manage more than a couple of miles a day burdened with a couple of suitcases and a portmanteau. I hadn't bargained on the fact that Sonic's owner's uncle was in fact a delivery driver for Bryan Fords in Barnstaple and lived in Lynton; Sonic was to arrive taxi-driven and in style. He fetched up at Long Lane Farm on the evening of 8th February 2005, an early 54th. birthday pressie for Gilly. I paid for him cash-on-delivery.

There was no settling in period for Sonic; he'd arrived complete with his own home. We did rename him instantly. We called him Tarquin, because that begins with a "T", which had rather a nice ring to it. Also because he looked a little upper class with his dropped lower jaw and cravate, and very possibly just a bit gay. Anyway Gilly felt he deserved a name more in keeping with his sedate and good-mannered appearance. So Tarquin it was. Tarquin's vivarium was stationed in the Snug, within reach of Fred's palace. The two would be lively company for each other, we thought, and they could exchange views on vivarium heating and lighting systems if bored with the company.

As with Fred, Tarquin was to spend most of his life inside the heated and illuminated vivarium. Shy at first, he soon came out of his shell. He would busy himself about plumping up the straw bed, nuzzling his tortoise food and generally relaxing with a book. Occasionally I'd take him out of the vivarium and let him exercise on the carpet of the Snug, where he could get up a fair speed over a short distance. He didn't seem as interested in the television as Fred though. And he had a remarkable facility of letting you know he was bored with your company. He'd just retreat disdainfully into his shell and send you to Coventry for a couple of hours.

Though they lived only a few feet apart, Fred and Tarquin never actually met at close quarters. I had thought to put the two together, if only to save a little on our burgeoning electricity bill (unit consumption more than doubled for Long Lane Farm between '05 and '08 on account of the continuous heating and lighting of the two vivaria). However, I was unsure of the degree to which these two vegetarian reptiles from different continents could be expected to cohabit; I certainly didn't want the one to eat the other. So the two cohabited in the Snug but at a respectable social distance. Their lives had other similarities too. They both visited the vet on one occasion. And when they died it was in sudden, tragic and unique circumstances, both in the year 2008.

I noticed Fred's tongue sticking out the side of his mouth early into the New Year. He looked almost drunk or dissipated as about half an inch of tongue lolled uselessly out of the right side of his mouth, though the mouth itself seemed closed. I kept my eye on the situation, but when the tongue began to turn black I thought to consult the medical profession before things went too far. I called Simon, our small animal vet at the time, on 8th January. Simon told me to bring Fred into his surgery on the Roundswell Industrial Estate in Barnstaple on the very next day.

Now transporting a six foot long green iguana to your local veterinary surgery is not as straightforward as you'd think. We still had the four foot fish tank in which Fred had made the trip from Ilfracombe to Long Lane Farm three years before. That would have to do. I picked Fred up in my gauntleted hands as gently as I knew how and bundled him into the tank in a blanket. Gilly drove us the ten miles into Barnstaple and across the Taw River Bridge, where I showed Fred the sights and some of the population of that town, much to the bemusement of said population.

Simon took one look at Fred and diagnosed simple tongue rot. He obviously had bags of experience with exotics such as Fred and I took Simon at his word.

"This condition," explained Simon with an air of authority, "is common in the elderly Green Iguana. It should respond well to surgery. But I should take blood samples. There may be something else going on like renal failure. I'd like to at least rule that out before I do any work on him."

So Simon took blood samples, told us he'd know the outcome in a few days, and dismissed us from the surgery. Fred went back into the tank. We travelled back across the Taw River Bridge. Gilly went out to her line dancing class leaving me to keep a watchful eye on the slightly surprised looking Fred.

I looked in on Fred at about 8.00 p.m. He was quite dead. I do believe I shed a silent tear as I turned off the lights and heater in the palace.

When Gilly arrived home a few minutes later I was in the middle of a flurry of frantic telephone calls. First I phoned the vet to put a hold on those blood tests. I really wasn't interested in the cause of Fred's death and didn't fancy springing for the cost of abortive blood tests on a dead iguana just to satisfy the curious. In fact we haven't used that particular vet or practice ever since. He's a little too "experimental" for my liking. My second call was in search of a taxidermist. I found in my travels through the phone book one of the only two practising taxidermists in North Devon, who happened to also be a publican. To this day I am not sure which was the profession and which the hobby; taxidermy or the purveyance of beers wines and spirits. At any rate the interim advice of this gentleman was to put Fred on ice. Literally. I was instructed to wrap Fred, all six foot of him, in newspaper, and stick him in the deep freeze. I should then bring him to the publican (taxidermist) in three weeks' time, for an inspection and estimate.

So we chucked out about a gallon of ice cream and some elderly frozen vegetables, made room for Fred and, during a macabre midnight ceremony, consigned him to the depths of our chest freezer.

I'd like to say that is the end of the story of Frederick Chappell-Pugsley. But the truth of the matter is that there is no end. Fred was taken to the taxidermist/publican and left for treatment about three weeks later. He's probably still there. We've lost his address. And neither of us can recall the name of the pub.

And what of the palace? Well it did give service as a temporary home for Barney and Steve for a while when we tried to get them to share digs and each other's company. But eventually we disposed of Fred's palatial residence. It was dismantled about three years after Fred left us and sold to a budding amateur herpetologist.

Now if Fred's departure was a story of medical melodrama mixed up with a little good old fashioned farce, Tarquin's was straight out of gothic murder mystery and redemption.

It was a Friday afternoon in November (the 7th to be precise) and we were chatting over coffee to Chick Rumson in the kitchen of Long Lane Farm. All was quiet and peaceful. I'd let little Tarquin out for his constitutional on the carpet, the Chilluns were relaxing in the lounge.

"What's she got there?" asked Chick as he gazed smilingly at Calypso, the little springer cross collie pup we'd recently adopted from The Dog's Trust.

"Looks like a crusty pork pie. That looks tasty…" he carried on.

"OMG!" I stumbled. "She's got Tarquin. Quick, stop her!" I was on all fours in a trice, well as quickly as I could manage. Prising open the puppy's eager jaws and risking life and limb myself, because to come between a young spaniel pup and her dinner can be fatal.

Most of the damage to Tarquin was to his shell, but it didn't look exactly superficial. And I did detect the ominous signs of crimson blood.

"Call the vet!" I shouted, "Tell them I'm on my way with a damaged tortoise!"

With that I was out of the door, tortoise in one hand, car keys in the other. I was in the ancient Ford Escort and racing the five miles to Mullacott and the Animal Hospital in a cloud of dust on two wheels. Well, I got there as soon as the Escort would allow.

"What can you do for this little chap?" I chanced. "He's had a sort of an accident with a puppy and come off worse."

The vet gave a quizzical look, turned the tortoise upside down, rattled him a bit, tapped him on the desk, felt for a pulse.

"The problem is," the vet became all serious and meaningful at this point, "the skin has been broken and Calypso has eaten a little of the soft tissue. Whilst the injuries themselves may not be fatal, if they were caused as you describe, by a dog, this little chap will potentially have a massive infection. So I could pump him full of antibiotics. But the trouble with that is you're not going to know if he's infection free for weeks. A tortoise has a very slow metabolic rate. Antibiotics are only absorbed into the blood stream very slowly. Meanwhile we'd have to sew him up before he bleeds to death."

"What are you saying?" The truth was dawning on me rather quickly.

"Honestly? I think I'm going to have to put him to sleep before he is in the painful misery that he will almost certainly suffer."

I was feeling pretty miserable myself by this time. Miserable, and guilty, for having so negligently left Tarquin in temptation's way.
"All right. Go ahead I suppose"

"I'll administer lethal injection when you've gone. You can pick him up in a week's time."

"Can't I wait for him?"

"Well you can, but he'll take about a week to die. It's that slow metabolic rate, you see. I should leave him with us. Give me a call in about a week's time. He should be dead by then."

So I left little Tarquin with the vet. Picked him up a week later when he was dead. Probably. I buried the little pork pie shaped creature outside Camelia Cottage, the old pump house. He's commemorated by a concrete likeness a few feet away from where he lies.

22. Tales from the Tank

My Christmas gift to Gilly in 2007 was an aquarium. She had taken a fancy to keeping fish at Long Lane Farm and as there is no pond here and no convenient watercourse an aquarium seemed the most plausible option. The aquarium I purchased from Pets World, the big new emporium in Barnstaple, is about two feet square and 8 to 10 inches in depth. It was fully fitted out with an oxygenation pump, lighting, gravel, exotic looking fronds and weeds and toys that approximated sunken castles, crashed cars, etc. A tiny glass prism of a world, quite separate from the kitchen and the bustle of its guests, it was to provide hours of colourful fascination. I left it to Gilly to stock the aquarium in the new year of 2008.

It was stationed in the kitchen on a work top, which it was to share with a reproduction valve wireless radio of yesteryear. The comings to and goings from the Tank, as it became known, were the subject of daily news briefings on the radio.

(Crackle crackle) "This is the BBC Home Service. Here is the News for the second of January 2008. There is excitement in The Tank at Long Lane Farm today as new residents Bilbo, Merry and Samwise take up occupation. The three albino clawed toads hail from sub-Saharan Africa where apparently they proliferate in ponds and watercourses. They look a lot like little naked men as they plunge around acrobatically, playing in the gravel and weeds in their new surroundings.

"Albino clawed toads are so named because they are albino, and therefore pure white, and they have three toes with claws at the end on each of their four limbs. With which they tear and claw at their food. They are also voracious eaters. And not too discerning with their choice of diet. Observers of the toads are wondering how they'll get on with the other new occupants of the Tank.

"The other new occupants are three apple snails who've been employed as cleaners. Algernon, Ernest and Lady Bracknell did look a bit nervous when we interviewed them at the Tank today. They haven't done this sort of work before, which involves sucking the algae from the walls of the Tank and generally keeping it clean. They report that they are looking forward to taking up full time duties, but are not sure how they'll get on with the toads. We wish the little community well and we'll keep listeners posted. And now for the shipping forecast…" (Crackle crackle).

(Crackle crackle) "This is the BBC Home Service on the twenty-seventh January 2008. Breaking news this morning is the sad loss of Bilbo, one of the albino clawed toads in the Tank at Long Lane Farm. Bilbo was found dead at the bottom of the Tank this morning. There are not believed to be any suspicious circumstances, though these toads do not normally drown; natural causes are assumed. Bilbo will be buried in Iqbal's Lament later today at a private ceremony. The bereaved Pugsley family request no flowers, but fronds and pondweed gratefully accepted. Other news today…" (Crackle crackle).

(Crackle crackle, fizz) "This is the BBC Home Service with the news on seventh February 2008. Headlines today—there's a new toad on the block for the Pugsleys of Long Lane Farm. Frodo, the replacement for Bilbo who sadly died recently, joined his new friends Merry and Samwise today in the Tank. We at the BBC wish him many years' good luck and happiness."

(Crackle crackle, fizz, pop) "This is the BBC Home Service with the news on sixteenth February 2008. Tragedy unfolds at the Tank today as it is revealed that the albino clawed toads of Long Lane Farm may have been practising satanic rites and indulging in cannibalism. The first signs of strange goings on in the fishy hotel that has become known to the nation as The Tank were noted yesterday, when the dirty condition of the Tank indicated that the Apple Snails had not been performing their essential cleaning routines. On investigation by the Management in the course of disciplinary proceedings it

became apparent that the Apple Snails, Algernon, Ernest and Lady Bracknell, were nowhere to be seen. All that could be found of them were three shells and Lady Bracknell's handbag. "Missing without trace", manager Gilly Pugsley declared. "This is a scandal. The contract cleaners have done a bunk. I shall have to get another crew in."

"Keith obtained fresh contract cleaners in the persons of Bex and Bissel, earlier today. They are Siamese Flying Foxes, noted for their superior cleaning skills. They will be employed on cleaning duties at The Tank for the foreseeable future."

"STOP PRESS!!! There's an update on that last item of news. We have just been informed that Bex and Bissel lasted just an hour in The Tank. They have just been eaten by the toads. A full investigation will be mounted and a public enquiry is to be held. But post mortem will not be possible in the circumstances. And now the weather…."

(Crackle crackle fizz pop bang) "This is the BBC Home Service with the news on first March 2008. We regret to announce the sad loss of Merry, one of the original albino clawed toads of The Tank at Long Lane Farm. Merry was found floating face down on the surface this morning. Foul play is probable. Relatives of the deceased report that he will be buried on Bunter Hill in a small private ceremony. Other news today….."

(Crackle crackle, burrrp.) "This is the BBC Home Service with more sad news nine days after the last lot. Samwise, third of the original three albino clawed toads was found floating on the surface today. Management of The Tank are quoted as stating that they regret that they do not appear to be having much luck with albino clawed toads. Samwise will be buried with his brother Merry on top of Bunter Hill at dawn. And a replacement for him is expected to be sourced as company for Frodo. But management are seriously considering diversifying from its policy of albino clawed toads as they may be carnivorous by nature, and even cannibalistic by belief. ….."

(Crackle crackle burrrp hum) "This is the BBC Home Service with the news on third May 2008. Developments at the Tank have been rapid since we last reported. Management have changed their suppliers of albino three clawed toads to BJ's Bargain House in Barnstaple. It is hoped that the new strain of toad will be of hardier stock, as the toads are of a lower social class and expectation than those provided by the elitist Pets World. The first toad from the new supplier is Gimli, who joined the Tank on 22 March from The Bargain House. Management of the Tank have been in negotiations with ACAS and the Sucker Fish Trades Union (SFTU) with regards to cleaning arrangements for the Tank. We are able to confirm that a variety of Hypostomus Plecostomus, or sucker fish, by the name of Mrs. Zambesi, has been successfully installed in the Tank as resident cleaner. Experts assure us that Hypostomus Plecostomus, more commonly known as the common pleco, lives predominantly on algae and is, culinarily, less than interesting to the albino three clawed toad. And now for the football results…."

(Crackle crackle, whizz pop bang) "This is the BBC World Service with the one o'clock news on 31st May 2008. It has been a month of mixed fortunes for the albino clawed toads of the Tank at Long Lane Farm. Frodo was found floating on the surface on the eleventh. Gollum, donated by a Mrs. Jill Hunter of Bletchley, Bucks., joined the Tank on the sixteenth. Gimli suddenly suffered heart attack and died during the cleaning out routine earlier today. The deceased have been buried on Bunter Hill, which is a tradition for albino clawed toads, at least in North Devon. Gollum, the sole survivor, shares an uncertain future with the cleaner Mrs. Zambesi. And now a brief interlude with some kittens playing with a ball of wool…."

(Crackle crackle, fzzzz, ting) "This is the BBC Home Service bringing you Monthly Roundup, the news and views of the past month. On 31st July 2008 we're looking first at the events in the Tank at Long Lane Farm. Tragedy as the last of the albino three clawed toads, Gollum, was found floating on the surface of the water by Gilly Pugsley early in the morning of the 26th. He will be buried with the others that have passed this way, on Bunter Hill. Management of the Tank report that they are done with the little creatures and Gollum will not be replaced."

However, Mrs. Zambesi, the cleaning lady, was joined in the Tank earlier today by Molly, Captain Haddock and Mr. Guppy, three random and very different fish (supplied by Pets World of Barnstaple) for her to clean and care for. Management are keeping an open mind on the new arrangements.

There are as yet unconfirmed rumours of strife and turmoil within the Tank and Mr. Guppy is said to have come to grief within the hour. We will keep listeners posted on events as they occur over the next few weeks. Other news from the regions ......"

(Crackle crackle, fzzz etc.) "This is the BBC Home Service. Here is the news at 1.00 o'clock on 23rd September 2008. The Minister of Agriculture Fisheries and Food announced today that an investigation is being launched into mysterious deaths in the Tank at Long Lane Farm. It seems that Molly, one of the random fish introduced to the Tank at the end of July, was found floating in a pondweed "bush" on 9th August, little over a week after her arrival. At the time nothing particularly sinister was thought to have happened. However, this morning Captain Haddock seems to have suffered a similar unexpected demise. The departure of these two randoms leaves the faithful cleaner Mrs. Zambesi alone again and with no one to clean for. The Minister reports that she is bearing up under the strain of loneliness. "I don't mind really," she told our reporter, "I shall 'ave a little 'oliday I expect. I likes me own company". So we shall leave Mrs. Zambesi to her little holiday and return to other news....."

(Crackle crackle fizz pop bang) "This is the BBC Home Service. This is a news flash timed at 21.33 hours on Tuesday 22nd June 2010. Mrs. Zambesi, resident cleaner and sole occupant of the Tank at Long Lane Farm, died this evening. She appears to have suffered a fit or mental accident a few minutes ago while Tank Management was on the telephone. Attempts to revive her with mouth-to-mouth resuscitation proved both difficult with a Plecostomus sucker fish, and fruitless. Mrs. Zambesi will be buried in the morning at a small private ceremony in Iqbal's Lament. The Minister of Agriculture Fisheries and Food said "This is the end of an era. A sad loss for the Tank and the Pugsley family, Mrs. Zambesi will be a hard act to follow." The BBC would like to pass on its own condolences. And now for the shipping forecast..."

(Crackle crackle etc.) "This is the BBC Home Service. The news at 1.00 o'clock. The Tank at Long Lane Farm has stood dormant for over three months since the death of Mrs. Zambesi. Tank Management report the arrival today, 2nd October 2010, of the Golden Arrows, five goldfish supplied by the independent pet shop in Ilfracombe's High Street. The goldfish, which have been named Taylor, Goldie, Chalkie, Adam and Mandela, took up residence today. They have taken to their new quarters on the counter in the kitchen of Long Lane Farmhouse. We will keep you up-to-date with developments. And now for the weather, with Michael Fish..."

(Crackle, whirr, humm) "This is the BBC Home Service. And now for a special edition of Life on Earth with Sir David Attenborough, who's spent the last four years studying the very small aspects of life on earth as they occur in the Tank at Long Lane Farm. Over to you Sir David."

"Yes, well thank you, Raggy. As Raggy mentioned, I've spent the last four years exclusively studying life and events in the Tank, the aquarium at Long Lane Farm that has become beloved by the Nation. Much of that time was pretty fruitless really, unproductive. Goldfish are goldfish after all when all's said and done. They can be calming, attractive, even pretty creatures. But not too exciting. Not a riveting watch. Nothing much to write home about, as it were. Gilly Pugsley would dutifully clean out the Tank at more or less regular intervals, using a magnetic cleaning pad to replace the eponymous Mrs. Zambesi. And water changing times were of some interest as the Arrows had to be scooped out with a ladle while this was done. But nothing truly earth-shattering or mind-blowing transpired during these years.

"Things did seem to jazz up a little towards the back end of last year. I began to sit up and take notice. It all started with the sad loss of the biggest and most impressive of the Golden Arrows, Taylor. He had the most magnificent sweeping tail and big eyes. Taylor was found floating on the surface on 7th October s2014. He'd clearly gone to meet his maker in the great fish tank in the sky. Bereft of life, he was buried discretely in the wood.

"There was nothing too surprising about Taylor's death. Goldfish just do die. Sure, they can live 20 years and more but when they wish to shuffle off their mortal coil they just do that, without so much as a suicide note. But when Goldie disappeared some three weeks later on the 24th, she did just that. Disappeared without trace. Not a trace of her remained. Gilly Pugsley reckoned she'd been a bit off colour for a couple of days, but was just as surprised as me and the film crew when she just disappeared into thin air. Gilly began to question whether goldfish might not be cannibals?

"Well of course they are. Everybody knows that. Gentle and placid as your average goldfish appears, when it's big enough it'll eat anything that will fit in its mouth, and even some things that won't. The trick is to keep goldfish of approximately the same size. As I told Gilly at the time. (It's no good relying on Google to tell you these things, especially when you've got an expert in the house.)

"So when Chalkie disappeared without trace three weeks later on 13th November she shouldn't have been so distraught really. Three weeks is about the time it takes one goldfish to digest another I should think. We both suspected Mandela the Murderous, as he had a monobrow and the look of the psychopath about him. And he did seem overly interested in Adam, the remaining Golden Arrow.

"Adam had survived an over-indulgent Christmas and well into the new year when he was found floating on the surface in that tell-tale way on 17th January 2015. We cannot be sure that he was a victim to Murderous Mandela, as there was not a mark on his body when I helped Gilly fish him out and bury him near the laundry, well out of way of the puppies. Keith was on his way back from Cyprus of course, and I helped Gilly ready him for the shock.

"Mandela the Murderous (we can only assume, as we have no eye witness evidence) was now a very lonesome fish in the Tank. Was his solitary confinement of his own making? Was he the author of his own isolation? We shall never know. But he was to spend the rest of his life on his lonesome ownsome. Gilly did not dare introduce any more fish to the Tank, to be lambs to the slaughter.

"Mandela went blind over the last few days of his life. He stumbled clumsily about the Tank during the first few days of October, and was found floating near the bottom of the Tank on the afternoon of 8th October 2015. Gilly buried him at the back of the old chicken shed.

The tank was once again empty of life. It was decommissioned, emptied and put for sale in the Ossie. The fish history of Long Lane Farm had come to its natural end."

23. The Chilluns of Long Lane Farm; my "other family"

Lest this work fall into the hands of anyone who is not acquainted with the writer or his wife Gilly, I should point out that we never had children, at least human ones. Never really felt paternal or maternal. Gilly would tell you that if she could have given birth to a lamb, or perhaps a puppy, even a giraffe, things may have been different. We have always regarded the dogs in our lives as our children, and, again for those who do not know us that well, we refer to our dog or dogs of the time as "The Chilluns". That's just the way it is. This is the story of the Chilluns of Long Lane Farm.

Badger Arthur Maradona "Bonecrusher" Pugsley (aka Whistbrae Country Boy) celebrated his fifteenth birthday on 19th January 2001. Gilly will have made him the usual birthday sausage cake; a pile of mashed potato with fifteen sausages stuck in the top to resemble a pale-skinned hedgehog. The old boy would have snaffled his way through the mound of mash and enjoyed a game of "In the gooaal!" with Gilly and I at the foot of the stairs of our house in Eaton Bray. The long walks of his youth had gradually become truncated over the years. Badger was an elder statesman, still in reasonable health and with a good appetite, but pot-bellied, hard of hearing and slower to enthuse than in his early days.

His relationship with Jason Whippet was uneasy, put mildly. Badger had spent his entire life until his fifteenth year as the indulged sole heir to the Pugsley estate. His first few years as a latch key kid while mum Gilly was still at work first full- and latterly part-time, he'd learnt to be quite independent and to put up with his own company. When Gilly retired from employment to start up Black Pig Farm he was already 10 years old and his mum's essential companion. Jason first encroached onto Badger's splendid kingdom in early 2000, when Elsie, Gilly's mum, in the early stages of dementia, came to live with us from down the road. Because Jason belonged to Elsie. Badger didn't take too kindly to the territorial incursion and showed his displeasure in a regular baring of elderly teeth, the odd snarl, the occasional skirmish. We kept the warring hounds apart as far as was practicable when one's mother/mother-in-law is sleeping in one's lounge.

On the evening before our departure westwards Badger had what I think is officially known as "a funny turn". The entire contents of two houses had been packed into a commodious furniture delivery van. Gilly and I were preparing to camp on the floor of our bedroom. Elsie was on the settee in our lounge with her companion Jason. It was about 10.00 p.m. on a dark and drizzly February night. Badger wanted to go out.

Well I wasn't sure whether the old boy wanted a pee or just to say farewell to his old haunts, the neighbourhood where he'd grown up and spent his entire life. So I followed him out into the night. He walked slowly and with a little stagger into the middle of the road, turned and looked at me obliquely. I couldn't figure what it was he wanted. I realised later he was having the equivalent of a mild stroke or perhaps a heart attack. I picked him up gently and took him back indoors.

The first contingent in our epic move westwards left for Devon and Long Lane Farm early the next morning. Gilly and her mum Elsie and friend Julie Carter left in the tiny Rover Metro with Badger in the tailgate and Jason in the back seat with Elsie. Badger, who was likely profoundly deaf by then, barked pretty well continuously for the entire 250 miles.

Those first days at Long Lane were frenetic. The unpacking, organising, cleaning and reorganising left precious little time to attend to the needs of the ailing Badger. It was a week before I had the chance to consult the Mullacott Cross Veterinary Hospital some four miles distant. Badger was diagnosed with a heart condition, not unusual for a bearded collie of his advanced age. He was prescribed medication that was to stabilise his condition and give him one more year of life.

That first year at Long Lane Farm was to prove difficult for all of us, not the least for Badger. In Bedfordshire he had had a sort of right to treat Jason as a trespasser on his patch and get all proprietorial about the territory. Here at the farm he'd entered the place on the same day and presumably on the same footing as his nemesis. The situation between Badger and Jason was delicate at best, sometimes stretching into volatile. Sleeping and eating arrangements were unusual. Badger had to be confined to downstairs, to which he had been accustomed in Bedfordshire. Jason shared a bedroom or the lounge with Elsie. Somehow we managed to hold the show together without too much mayhem.

But in September (2001), just after the momentous events at the World Trade Centre, Badger and Jason got into a ruck which somehow cost Badger a torn cruciate ligament. Without surgery, he was destined to limp badly for the rest of his time on Earth. We were both extremely anxious at the time. I feared for Badger because of his extreme age, and the implications of putting him under general anaesthetic. But I couldn't bear the thought of seeing him limping and in pain for the rest of his natural. In the end I committed him to the tender mercies of Simon at the Veterinary Hospital and Badger lived to tell the tale.

When Badger did eventually die, on 9th January 2002, ten days before his 16th birthday, it was just as if he'd taken that decision. He had eaten his dinner, served to him on the lounge floor as Jason ate in the kitchen. Then he just lay down on the rug. And died. And I shall always be grateful to the old chap for taking that decision out of my hands. It's a decision I've had to take many times on behalf of an old or ailing animal. But Badger, God bless him, made up his own mind.

It was with heavy heart indeed that I dug the grave the next day, in what has become known as Badger's Garden. His grave is fourth from the left, marked by 2001's Christmas tree and the statue of Gryffindor.

Jason ("born in a basin") Whippet

The bitter-sweet departure of Badger came at the end of a dramatic and difficult year for us both, but for Gilly the loss, though not unexpected, was cataclysmic. In that twelve months she'd experienced the upheaval of moving house and farm, the decline of her mother into dementia, the onset and management of foot and mouth disease with the inevitable fear for her animals, the machinations of a psychotic lunatic of a neighbour, caring for my mother until her death in April 2001, the tragic loss of Jack the pony, and now the loss of her (second) best friend and soulmate Badger. The stress and distress finally got to her and I believe she suffered a minor nervous breakdown. She began to search for him in unlikely places, imagining him lost or stolen. We searched the countryside for him. And though I'd buried him with my own bare hands I found myself humouring Gilly with extensive forays into neighbouring Somerset and Cornwall. All these searches were accompanied, of course, by Elsie (who had developed her own form of mental illness) and Jason, probably the sanest of us all.

Jason had a checkered history, with a reputation for being a bit of a Jonah to his owners. His first had been an elderly gentleman who'd promptly upped and died, leaving the young Jason homeless. His second, a well-meaning adopter, went away on holiday and deposited the middle aged Jason with Wendy de Meur for safe keeping, fell either ill or into dementia and left Wendy as third owner to manage Jason with the other ten or twelve dogs that roamed indiscriminately about Honeywick Farm. Elsie, the fourth owner, took the mature Jason on after the death of her second husband Stan had left her without someone human to care for. She treated Jason well, rather too well as it turned out. For Jason became the son Elsie never had. She took to smothering him with motherly love, dressing him up in swaddling clothes, feeding biscuits up his bum (because she couldn't tell one end of Jason from the other). In fact she lavished upon Jason all the affection that'd been so wanting in the childhood of her only daughter, Gilly.

Jason was a sweet little whippet in white and tan markings. Friendly and willing to please, he seems to have weathered the changes in his fortunes and living conditions without resentment or attitude. Wary at first, he had to tread carefully in Eaton Bray when he moved with Elsie to live with us in the last year before the move west. Because he had moved into Badger's previously undisputed domain.

He was to be more relaxed at Long Lane Farm where he enjoyed equal rights to residence, but there was the odd skirmish between him and the much heavier Badger. The two rubbed along reasonably well until Badger left us in January 2002, when Jason became pack leader and formed an especial attachment to me. The problem for Jason was that as Elsie slipped quietly into dementia so she clung ever tighter to the reins attached to Jason. She'd always been a controlling parent for Gilly; that control now manifested itself in an obsession with Jason. On the couple of occasions Elsie "escaped" from the prison camp she imagined Long Lane Farm to be, she disappeared into the distance with her knitting and Jason in tow, heading back to the Luton Town of her youth.

When I eventually unloaded Elsie in the Belmont Grange care home in Ilfracombe that fateful Thursday afternoon after a mornings negotiation and arm-twisting with Social Services, I had to unload Jason as well. So Jason left our lives on the same day as Elsie, 11th April 2002. The date is emblazoned on my memory, as it was for me the first day of the rest of my life, a life in which I was to recover and rediscover Gilly from the clutches of her mum. And to begin to live the veritable idyll that Long Lane Farm without her proved to be. I am afraid to say that thoughts of Jason and his fate were not uppermost in my mind as I enjoyed the gleeful moment.

But our paths did cross again. We never did visit Elsie; the pain would have been too much for Gilly and as it was she spent the last four years of her mother's life in a sort of irrational fear of her return. About a year after Elsie left us for Belmont Grange she was moved to the more secure accommodation for the elderly and confused at Instow. This had become necessary as a result of Elsie's leanings towards escape. But she was not allowed to take Jason with her; the accommodation was intended for human rather than canine escape artistes.

Jason had a lucky escape of a different kind. For at Belmont Grange he had met and befriended the kindly and avuncular Jim Beamer, resident chef and general handiman. On Elsie's departure to Instow, East-the-Water, Jim took Jason on as owner number five and the last man standing. Jason was to spend the rest of his life as the adored pet of Jim and his partner Anne, in their flat in Ilfracombe's High Street and later at The Candar. I was a regular visitor as unofficial pedicurist to Prince Jason. I'd attend to his claws at six weekly intervals with my claw clippers and permanganate of potash. When I first performed this function it was after a year's separation from Jason, but he remembered me with much wagging of the tail and a friendly greeting. And though Jason didn't particularly enjoy the experience, he always greeted me with the same doggy smile and wag.

Jim kept Jason in luxurious quarters for nearly seven years, the best years of his life. When his time finally came, Gilly ferried Jason and Jim to the vet in Highfield Road Ilfacombe, where Jason was humanely dispatched, a victim to old age. Gilly brought his little body back to Long Lane Farm and I buried him in the back garden, marking his grave with a concrete bird bath. So, after an absence of nearly seven years, the wanderer returned.

Mr. D'Arcy McGregor, heir to the Beardie tradition

I am very fortunate in that I am able to process my grief with great speed. I never forget the dead, but I can get over the immediate loss of the dear departed in very short order. In the case of Badger the beardie the decision to leave the stage was taken by Badger himself and at an acceptably great age. So that celebration of his life rather than grief for his loss was easy and appropriate. Gilly took the loss less well, though with everything else that was going on in her life at the time that is understandable. In any event, having come to terms with the situation, Badger's death did apparently seem reasonable enough after a couple of months. She was on the lookout for a replacement beardie as soon as possible. We were still in telephone contact with Badger's breeders, Alan and Viv Stevens, and as I'd called them religiously on every one of his fifteen birthdays, I'd already called them to inform of his death just before his sixteenth. A few weks later I was back on the blower asking after recommendations for beardie breeders in the south-west. Alan gave me the contact details of a likely couple, two ageing ladies in Cullompton, who had a fine reputation for the breed.

We made contact the same day with said ladies, Celia and Una. They had a female beardie in pup and about to produce a litter. We reserved a male. And Mr. D'Arcy McGregor Pugsley was born, the smallest of a sizeable litter, on 11th March 2002. Celia sent us a photo of Mr. D'Arcy on his actual birthday, in which he can be seen struggling for place amidst the sibling battle for an available nipple. She had selected the smallest (generally known as the "runt") for us as he was her especial favourite and she knew us to be childless. Her thinking was that the little chap would avoid all the bullying and childish pranks the other, stronger, siblings would be subjected to in families with young and boisterous children. So we were the safe option. I like to think she chose us well.

Puppies need to be weaned from mother's milk and to have their first innoculations before they can leave the nest which means they cannot leave mum until they are eight weeks old. We were able to visit Celia, Una and the brood that included Mr. D'Arcy, twice in this period, travelling along the A361 the forty odd miles to Cullompton with the bewildered Elsie and the surprised Jason in the back seat. So we visited our new puppy at age two and six weeks, but on both occasions Elsie refused to get out of the car, so that neither she nor Jason were to meet Mr. D'Arcy in the flesh. By the time we travelled for the third and final time to Cullompton to pick up Mr.D'Arcy and bring him home, on 5th May 2002, Elsie and Jason were long gone in the debacle described above.

There is no doubt that Mr. D'Arcy was the cutest, most adorable and beautiful creature either of us had ever seen. In that first year we took him everywhere with us, to puppy exemption shows (as he would be too young until six months old to be entered formally), to places such as Lynton and Lynmouth, and as far afield as Minehead, just to show the little fellow off. Before he was "street legal" with a full set of innoculations I'd take him into Barnstaple or Ilfracombe for a carry through the crowds. And the population, particularly young girls, were utterly entranced. As a young pup he looked more like an elaborate stuffed toy. I would carry him aloft with pride, or sit him on my shoulders to the envious sighs of passers by. And of course if you tell anyone enough times how very beautiful they are they will begin to believe you. Mr. D'Arcy did. He simply glowed with self-esteem.

At Brendon show that year he won First Prize in the puppy exemption. And at a show in Beaworthy he was the cause of my rekindling an acquaintance with Mark Betambeau, a Town and Country Planning Officer colleague of mine from the Dacorum Borough Council days. It seems the show was taking place in his back garden.

In 2002 Gilly and I went on holiday. We were celebrating the departure of Elsie, and the arrival of Mr. D'Arcy. We ate too much, drank a little and partyed on down. We were basically having a ball with our new-found freedom. But once the music and the dancing had died down, at the end of that first year it did dawn on us that there would be times when we would have to leave Mr. D'Arcy at home while we attended to the other things we wanted to do with our lives. I still had a busy practice in hypnotherapy in Ilfracombe. Gilly was attending line dancing and other classes in Woolacombe and Barnstaple. There were regular shopping trips to consider. We needed a companion for Mr. D'Arcy, but not a love interest. As Badger before him, we'd kept Mr. D'Arcy entire; we did not want the patter of little paws to disturb the domestic idyll we'd discovered since the departure of Elsie. And we thought it'd be kind of appropriate for a rescue operation to give a rescue dog a chance.

Just outside Ilfracombe on the A361 to Braunton and Barnstaple the Dogs Trust (formerly, and at the time of our visit, the National Canine Defence League) have a large and impressive establishment dedicated to the rescue and rehoming of dogs unwanted or abused in Wales and Ireland. We repaired there one dank Saturday afternoon in February 2003 with Mr. D'Arcy in tow, on the offchance that something suitable might be available.

In those days the dogs available for rescue were housed in two large round carousel cage affairs, so that prospective owners could view them from the outside whilst the inmates could be fed, watered and generally serviced from the centre. We left Mr. D'Arcy in the car and walked slowly around each carousel viewing the possible companions for Mr. D'Arcy and reading about their antecedents and temperaments on the postcard sized notices outside each cage. I believe we were trying to be quite focused and responsible in our approach. Even scientific, weighing up the various pros and cons of the different breeds and ages on offer. We'd thought perhaps a Jack Russell would fit the bill, and at the same time be up for catching the odd rabbit for our dinner. Or perhaps a St. Bernard, complete with brandy barrel, to help us weather the mountainous snowdrifts that frequent North Devon from November onwards. In truth we did not know what we were looking for.

Towards the end of the second circumnavigation what we were looking for came out of the back room, and we were chosen.

Puff the Magic Whippet

She was tall, tanned, svelte, elegant with a sweeping tail, the most soulful dark brown eyes and a manner that was as calm and unassuming as it was engaging. She approached us with a warm smile and lifted her delicate front paw as if to welcome us into her life. We had never for a moment considered a whippet lurcher as an appropriate companion for Mr. D'Arcy, but we tacitly agreed that we were both smitten and so would Mr. D'Arcy be. As we left the NCDL we were told that there were others interested in Jess, but that we could reserve her and take her subject to "introductory visit". We agreed to the introductory visit in one week's time.

The introductory visit was one of those very good ideas invented by the NCDL in recent times, something that would have avoided the embarrassment we'd suffered many years before with Sam, the Airedale Terrier, from Battersea Dogs Home. The idea was that you were trusted to borrow the dog for a day to see how it got on with other members of your household, other pets in the house, the natural and home environment etc., so that any necessary adjustments could be made, such as getting rid of the kids, putting down the mother-in-law, etc., before a firm commitment to take the adoptee is made. Well it worked swimmingly well for Jess. She was one of the more delightful guests at Long Lane Farm and fitted in with both our expectations and Mr. D'Arcy's. She'd been speyed, so there'd be no hanky panky. And her injections were up to date. She could move in straight away.

Except for the kennel cough, which she contracted on return to the NCDL, which delayed her actually taking up occupation of her new quarters by a couple of weeks. And of course her name would have to be changed. With every other dog in North Devon having the monicker "Jess", that would have to go. It was me who came up with "Puff". And whilst I told everyone who enquired after the derivation that it was on account of it being short for "Hufflepuff", one of the four houses in Harry Potter's Hogwarts, in fact it was on account of a curious idiosyncracy. Whippets and whippet derived crossbreeds have a tendency to puff out their cheeks on the exhale, perhaps because of their relatively narrow mouth. Puff's name was actually inspired by her outbreath.

Puff eventually came to stay at Long Lane Farm on 3rd March 2003. Her actual birth date being unknown, that date became her official birthday. She was estimated to be five years old by the NCDL when we adopted her. Bred somewhere in Wales, we supposed her to be an outcast, or perhaps an escapee from some gypsy encampment. But that's just because we're romantic fools.

When you have more than one dog in your household a pack dynamic establishes itself, and the dynamic is different from the different points of view of pack members.

For me the pack order was clear from those early days at Long Lane Farm. The descending order was Gilly, Mr. D'Arcy, Puff, me. I have always known my place.

The pack was a perfectly harmonious little family for five years. We went everywhere together. Popular with the locals in Ilfracombe and Barnstaple, we, the pack, were well known to Tourist Information as favoured local attractions for seasonal visitors. And it was with the arrival of Puff that the junior Pugsleys first became known, affectionately, as "the Chilluns". Mr. D'Arcy continued to attract the female of the human species. Puff, with her long legs and elegance, appealed very much to gentlemen of a certain age. I seemed to have a particular bond with Puff, sealed on day one when I picked her up from the NCDL during one of Gilly's line dancing sessions.

Both the original Chilluns enjoyed good overall health and though both were insured, we made no calls on the policy during those years. Mr. D'Arcy had two traumatic collisions with wheelbarrows in his early formative years and developed therefrom a fury with anything wheelbound. He'd attack wheelbarrows in particular, especially those in motion, and try to eat the wheel. But this fury extended beyond the confines of the farm; he'd think nothing of full frontal assault on a moped. Anything wearing spandex passing our front gate was fair game. Puff, temperamentally, was calm, stoic and accepting. Unless fresh roast chicken was in the offing, when she'd shift excitedly from foot to foot in anticipation. Her only appearance before the vet was occasioned by a disagreement with the dysfunctional sheep shearer's dog who'd attacked her unprovoked and opened a gash in her side. The sheep shearer cost us £45 that particular year, the vet setting us back a further £75.

Five years passed by. Eventfully, but peacefully. We begun to think about succession planning. With Mr. D'Arcy a middle aged 6 and Puff a dowager aunt at 10, it seemed reasonable to consider how we would best cope with the loss of one of them. One sunny spring afternoon in 2008 we moseyed down to the Dogs Trust (which the NCDL had by then become) just to see what was on offer. The premises were much improved; the change in title had clearly been reflected in an enhancement in the facilities. By this time I had become acquainted with the branch manager and her husband, both of whom I'd had occasion to treat hypnotherapeutically, both of whom lived on site. It was a most convivial afternoon. But we came away empty-handed. There were that day no suitable compatriots for our Chillun.

Calypso, a very special Sprollie

We were head-hunted by the Dogs Trust. I know this because it was a first for me. I'd never been head-hunted before. When we received the call from the manager of the Dogs Trust, a lady who I'd had occasion to help with her apparent lack of confidence, there was a note of anxiety in her voice. Anxiety mixed with tones of both desperation and determination.

"Dr. Pugsley," she said (we had not breached the boundaries of formality as yet, and she must have got the title from my credit card as I don't use it much) "we have a little puppy for you. She's springer spaniel crossed with border collie, what we call a sprollie in the trade. Dear little thing. Last of a litter. There's no mum, so she's on her own in this vast puppy compound. Must get her a loving home pronto. You'd be ideal. And you wouldn't need a house check. Your place, and well you really, would be ideal. Whaddya think?"

Well what I thought was two things:

1. The confidence building has worked well. She's not the little mouse she was when I saw her a couple of months ago. Quite pushy now, in a pleasant sort of way. Make a good sales person.

2. Let's look at this little sprollie shall we?

We tripped along to the Dogs Trust that very afternoon. It seems we were minor celebrities with the Trust; we were trusted with the keys to the puppy compound and told to help ourselves.

As we let ourselves into the compound's exercise yard we were greeted by this exhuberant bundle of black and white fur, a tornado of joyfulness and love that just jumped into my arms as if she'd known me all her life. We called her Calypso, on the spot, in recognition of her essential blackness, her soulful rhythm, her big brown eyes. She was all alone in that massive yard and compound, quarters big enough for six or seven litters with their respective mothers, and yet she seemed so happy, so willing to please, and so carefree. Once again, we were smitten immediately. We would have to have her. And we were told we could pick her up whenever we were ready. We scuttled away and made the minimal preparations you need to accommodate a third dog when you already have two.

Calypso joined the pack at Long Lane Farm on 2nd June 2008. Her recorded birth date was 4th April, so she was barely two months; just old enough to leave her mother, of whom we'd seen nairy a hairy. She would need house training, speying and an injection or two. The Dogs Trust would spring for the spey and injections, but we'd have to attend to the house training ourselves. June is a good month for this, especially if you live in a remote country farmhouse. Simply leave the back door open at all times; your new puppy will train itself to use the big outdoors for its toilet needs in a trice. Speying could wait awhile. Nine months, or just before the first season is a good rule. And the injections against parvo virus would follow at timed intervals.

Calypso, soon reduced in length as familiarity allowed to "Clippie", edged her way gently into the pack. She probably supplanted me at fourth place to start with, relegating me to number five. But at mealtimes she soon assumed the lead and would be first at the dinner plate. She was avid for her treats too. If we bought the

Chillun bones from the butcher she'd have all three at her command within minutes of their allocation. And she'd protect all three with blood-chilling snarls and a baring of teeth. Clippie was soon to be dubbed the "Bone Collector" on account of her acquisitiveness on the bone front. We soon realised that she was going to have a battle with her weight if we didn't keep a close watch on the calories. And in her early puppyhood Clippie's diet was not confined to the eatable. As with many puppies going through the teething stage she'd chew at most things soft and chewy. Tablecloths were her speciality, particularly plastic tablecloths. She'd chewed her way well into the plastic kitchen tablecloth (rather an ornate, lacy lime green affair) before Gilly caught her at it and bade her stop. We still have the tablecloth, or its remains, to remind us of little Clippie.

The dynamic between the pack didn't alter much. Though the Chillun got on very well together and were protective of each other's dignity, except at mealtimes, we did not venture abroad nearly so much with three as we had done with two. All three enjoyed trips out in the car and were good travellers, but we learnt that three are not as manoevrable as two, unless you have the extra set of hands that a guest brings. In the summer, afternoons with all three Chilluns in Oasis Field were a delight. Sometimes I would walk around the field and think how lucky I was to live in such a beautiful, idyllic place, with three such wonderful and delightful characters for company. And Gilly, of course, leader of the pack!

Calypso began to have her problems before she was a year old. One morning in November she seemed reluctant to accompany Gilly to the piggery as was her custom. I noticed she was walking with a peculiar, laboured gait, as if she was in pain. Ever the constant companion she'd become for Gilly, she struggled to make it stiff-legged to the gate and could go no further. She'd always been a joyful little soul, eager to please. This was out of character and needed proper veterinary attention.

We hurried with her into Barnstaple and Simon, in whom we'd put our trust for so many animals. Simon looked her over, felt her about a bit, and diagnosed possible meningitis. He could give her a full C T Scan, which might highlight the issue. That'd cost about £1000, but it'd be covered by the pet insurance, he explained. So I had to explain to Simon that we had lost faith in pet insurance schemes as they never seem to cover what has happened to the pet. We were self insuring at that time and have done ever since. Would he please treat Calypso for the suspected meningitis and quit trying to get his expensive C T Scanner subsidised by unsuspecting clients or their insurance companies. Well if I'm honest I didn't say that last bit. But I thought it. Simon dosed Calypso up with the appropriate antibiotics and she responded to them within 24 hours. We had overcome one trauma. But I think that was when I lost faith with Simon and his expensive posh practice. For future treatment we moved our custom to Market Vets.

The following spring we were considering having Calypso speyed. She couldn't stay living under the same roof as an entire male (Mr. D'Arcy) or trouble could be on the point of brewing at any moment once she became sexually mature and came into oestrus. Unfortunately we were just a tad late in our deliberations. We took Calypso into Market Vets for an examination prior to this life changing operation only to be told that her first season had in fact commenced. We would have to wait for the oestrus to drop before Calypso could be operated on, but had we considered giving Mr. D'Arcy the chop? Well, perhaps it was a little unfair on Mr. D'Arcy, who'd hung on to his bollocks for 7 years without a murmur. But it did seem to be the simplest solution to our dilemma, and castration of the male is far less intrusive (and expensive) than speying of the female. So I'm afraid Mr. D'Arcy was separated from his crown jewels within the week. I'm sure he didn't feel a thing, though I smarted a little at the thought.

Everything was now on an even keel. The three Chilluns settled into a steady routine. Peace reigned. Except when the bones were distributed and Calypso insisted on commandeering all three.

Then the fits started. There was no warning. Calypso simply keeled over one morning and lay in a shivering heap. I had witnessed epileptic fits in humans on a couple of occasions and knew there is nothing sensible you can do for the patient but keep them as warm and comfortable as possible until the fit passes. And Calypso's fit did pass. But it was an alarming experience for us as her parents and an extremely tiring one for her. We consulted Market Vets of course, and had her checked over. But the prognosis for epilepsy is much the same in a dog as it is in humans. Nothing much you can do about it. Medication is available for severe cases, but if the fits are infrequent, as Calypso's were, they are best left to take their course. Calypso was to suffer similar fits at six monthly intervals.

When we look back the writing was on the wall for Calypso. We just hadn't spotted the obvious clues. She was a lone pup when we first saw her. No signs of her mother. She'd come from Ireland. She was barely eight weeks old. She was, in hindsight, clearly the product of one of those infamous Irish puppy farms, force bred and quickly reared for fast profit. If we'd known this at the time we'd still have adopted little Calypso, but we would perhaps have been more prepared, both financially and emotionally, for the problems that were to beset her.

The Tragedy of 2014

I found this bit too painful to write and have been putting it off for some time. In the end I thought it best to put it in the words of my journal, as this was written contemporaneously with the events of that terrible summer, six years ago. So the following are edited highlights.

"22 June Clippie seemed a little off colour today, off her breakfast. I removed an engorged tick from her right shoulder. Made an appointment with the vet. Took her in this afternoon. She's very anaemic it seems. Vet's put her on a massive dose of steroids. Says it should boost her immune system. Trying to keep upbeat about it.

"23 June Puff pissed on my bed last night. Unlike her. We took Clippie for another blood test today. Her red blood cells are down from a healthy 35% to 11%. If they drop below 10% she'll need a transfusion. I was asked (instructed) by Craig, the vet, to search for a donor dog. The donor should be over 1, under 7, in good health, weigh 25Kg. I asked Steve Parkin about his Badger and Mark West about one of his several dogs. Both are considering, but neither particularly keen. Clippie's weight has soared to 27.3 Kg. Should be no more than 22. She's on antibiotics, streoids and anti-sickness meds.

"24 June Puff pissed the bed again. Don't know what's wrong with her. Clippie visited the vet again today. Red blood cells down to 8%. Vet has a volunteer donor—a Rottweiler. Trying to distract from all this. We took Puff and Mr. D'Arcy down to visit Badger. I've ordered incontinence pants for Puff. Clippie's had that transfusion from the Rotty. Blood count's up to 22% now. She's still got a canula in her little front leg for tomorrow's transfusion.

"25 June We lost Mr. D'Arcy today. I took him to Tesco for an early morning shop at 6.30. Then travelled on to Bridgemans for feed, with Mr. D'Arcy in the back. He got out of the car after quite a long wait and had the staggers. He fell outside the Witch's Tit. Tried to tempt him up with a sausage. Made another appointment at the vet's for 2.30. Had to carry him to the car. I noticed there was nothing of him. I think we'd both quietly noticed his weight loss over the past months and put it to one side in our minds. The vet confirmed our worst fears. Mr. D'Arcy was terminated in the back of my car.

Clippie's blood count up, but only by ½%. We travelled home with one dead dog and one deteriorating. I dug Mr. D'Arcy's grave while Gilly went off to Slimming World. We informed all those interested by phone this evening. Jo Wilson almost as devastated as us.

"26 June Puff didn't piss the bed last night. I wonder if her condition wasn't stress related. The incontinence pants arrived, but I don't think she'll need them.

I buried Mr. D'Arcy at dawn. Marked his grave with the statue of Mr. Grimli. Many condolences arrived by telephone. Clippie seems to be making progress.

"27 June Puff has not pissed the bed for 2 days. We returned to the vets for further blood test. Clippie is up 2%. We played cards a little, drank some, cried a lot.

"28 June Puff hasn't pissed again. I think it was a temporary stress related abberation. Not surprising with all this illness about. Perhaps she thought she was going to die as well?

Chick brought up a wooden cross he'd fashioned for Mr. D'Arcy's grave. Characteristically well made but badly spelled. But that's Chick, all heart no grammar!

Gilly left for France today with Laraine. I'm on my own for a few days in this crisis.

"29 June *Clippie seems a little slow today, breathing a bit hard and heavy. Perhaps she's tired.*

"1 July *I'm still putting heavy duty steroids in Clippie's breakfast. Then we were all off to the vets for Clippie's blood test. It took us an hour to get there, following a typically nightmarish North Devon traffic diversion. Test satisfactory but blood count still has a ways to go and it's a slow recovery. Steroids have been increased in number and strength. Puff's enuresis seems to have settled.*

"2 July *I think the situation's getting to me, particularly because I'm coping on my own right now. I'm getting increasingly irritated and annoyed, to the point of being angry, at four particular people in my life right now because they have not come up to my very high expectations. I've got to deal with these situations and yet keep a lid on the anger.*

Meanwhile Clippie's developed dry eye, poor little creature. I called the vet about it and apparently it's caused by the steroids. I tripped into Ilfracombe for eye drops. I'm treating Clippie's eyes at regular intervals throughout the day.

"4 July *Working like a demon on the garden and other projects. Trying to keep my mind off more immediate matters. Clippie's eyes a tad better.*

"5 July *Gilly arrived home from France. But she arrives home to a mess. Either Clippie's been sick or Puff's pissed on the carpet. Either way I was in the hot tub, so unaware. A spat ensues. I'm in the wrong again. And a bit fed up.*

"8 July *I fear little Clippie is not going to make it. At the vet's today Craig confirmed her blood count's down again despite a further week on steroids. I have feelings of impending doom. It feels as though I have an egg-sized lump in the middle of my forehead, and another in my throat. Clippie's weight has ballooned. She can no longer climb the two steps from the kitchen into the lounge.*

"9 July *She's not the happy dog she once was. We are drowning in Bombay Saphire and red wine.*

"10/11 July *We've been working all day mixing cement for Chick to work on the Snug wall. Clippie's stayed by us for company. She looks pretty desperate.*

"13 July *Gilly's sleeping downstairs with Clippie now, as she cannot get upstairs to bed.*

"14 July *We've been working with Chick all day on the wall. Clippie reminds us of her illness by sticking close by, looking forlorn and a little frightened. We seem to be doing all these things to divert us from the stark reality. I think we're going to lose two of our three Chilluns in a matter of weeks. Clippie has another blood test tomorrow.*

"15 July I cannot recall feeling this degree of apprehension since the days of my school exams. The abject despair, tears and an inexpressible feeling of loss as we are advised that Clippie may have lymphoma or leukaemia. At home in the meadow I cried alone and bitterly, at the feelings of helplessness and uselessness, and the unfairness of this happening to Clippie. I had to escape into Ilfracombe to walk around and vent my despair. I visited Nana Sue's where Steve Adair comforted me with a cuddle and a Bach's flower remedy. Later, at home, I tried to rationalise the situation. My goal it is to live for 117 years. Clippie may have to settle for just 6.

"16 July A day of desperation, pointlessness, distraction. We prepare for the worse. All focus is on Clippie.

"17 July It's over now. It was clear from the dawn's first light that she was on her last legs. She wanted to die today and she told me so. Then she asked for my help with pleading eyes and a soft moan. Three times she spoke to me. And I understood. Clippie lay under her hedge in abject misery.

Once more we tripped back to the vets. Clippie was dispatched in the back of my car on precisely the same spot in the vet's car park as had Mr. D'Arcy just three weeks ago. She gave a little cry as the lethal injection pierced her skin and that cry pierced my own heart such that I shall never forget it.

I spent the afternoon digging her grave, right next to Mr. D'Arcy. It's marked with the Easter Island statuette.

Puff is acting strangely. She seems free of responsibility, somehow livelier than of late, happier. Is she relieved to be alive?"

(There is a postscript to Clippie in all this. A couple of months after her passing Gilly sought out a clairvoyant specialising in the bereaved pet owner. She needed closure on Clippie, or at least some guidance on what had happened to her own dear girl. This was an unusual step for Gilly; she'd never consulted a clairvoyant before, though she'd acted as one many years before in a tent at a school fête where she'd trod the boards as "Madame Gibbo". This North Devon clairvoyant took telephone consultations. Gilly was on the phone to her for about half an hour during which time she told Gilly nothing very illuminating from beyond.

Suddenly she exclaimed in a tremulous voice "Oh, Clippie wants you to know that there is an old lady up there who has promised to look out for her until you arrive. And she's sorry about the tablecloth!")

The Aftermath, and new birth

We were emotionally drained, all three of us. Puff took to wetting my bed again, momentarily, I guess not really understanding what had happened and whether it was all over. She seemed to share her time between us equally, moving from my bedroom to Gilly's and then back again. It was almost as if she were trying to hold the two of us together in our grief, whilst at the same time trying to understand the fate of her two comrades. Chick arrived a couple of days later bearing a cross he'd made for Calypso's grave. Puff gave him such a greeting as she'd never given him before, palpably relieved to see him. One evening, well after dark, she dashed out the back door into the gloom and ran wildly about the Oasis, as if in search of something.

On Sunday afternoons in July the local town brass bands entertain in the bandstand at Runymede Gardens in Ilfracombe. We'd often attended with the Chillun the musical soirées in the park. Now we were just the three of us. Puff particularly enjoyed the attention of the tourists, and I believe found solace in the company of other dogs. Her old tail began to wag again. Encouraged by the signs of her emotional recovery I'd take her down the lane to visit three-legged Badger at Steve Parkin's place.

While we only had old Puff to lavish our attention on, lavish it we did. But Gilly decided, within a matter of days of losing Calypso, that we would have another beardie. Once again the search was on and I approached Una Cornthwaite from whom we'd had Mr. D'Arcy twelve years ago. Una had ceased her breeding operation, but she was in the know of matters beardie-related. She gave us the contact details of a breeder who had a bitch in pup somewhere in Somerset. Pups were due in about 7 weeks, so with luck and if we were quick in making our reservation we could be in pup ourselves in about 15. I made the call, reserved a male, bought Puff a single bone, sat back to wait.

But Gilly was still restless for doggy company, both for herself and for the ageing Puff. We visited the Dogs Trust only a week after Calypso's death in search of a possible replacement. Finding nothing suitable and available at the Dogs Trust, and perhaps a little wary by now of taking on a dog without being acquainted with its mother, we surfed the internet. And there we found, on 26th July, just nine days after the end of our tragedy, a Borderpoo, a breed unknown to us, aged just six weeks old, 78 miles to the south near Newton Abbott. We were compelled to visit, and drove those 78 miles that very day. We took Puff with us for the ride.

"She was a mistake really,"admitted Tina Pickford shyly on the lawn as we played with the tiny black fly-footed creature. " My daughter was out for a walk with a friend and her mum. They're both 16, you know, my daughter and her friend. Engrossed with their phones of course. Her mum (she's a border terrier, you know) was in the last week of her season, still very much up for it. Neither of them noticed the miniature black poodle stud dog loitering about. He was on the last day of his vacation, up for a bit of holiday romance. And he got lucky. The first I knew of it was when my daughter and her friend come galloping in with the two dogs tied together. They didn't know what to do. Well, of course, the damage had been done. The little poodle chap had a smile all over his chops."

We called her CoCo Chanel. She was the last of a litter of three; her brother and sister had already been reserved. CoCo was clearly waiting for us to be totally entranced with her. And though she was not at all what we were expecting (we thought a Border Collie/Standard Poodle cross would be significantly larger) we decided right there and then in the tiny hamlet of Caton, just outside Ashburton, near Newton Abbott, South Devon, that she had to come home with us. Puff wagged her old tail by way of agreement.

For the next couple of weeks we just got on with the stuff of life here at Long Lane Farm. Radical gardening, mending fences, cutting up logs for the winter. Puff became my constant companion and seemed to enjoy the extra attention she was getting. She was over her urinary problem and taking in the sights, sounds and smells of Barnstaple, a sausage at Friendship House where we went for tea and toasted tea cakes, sharing herself between us at night.

Gilly went off to France again, this time with her mate Sally, leaving me and dear old Puff to care for the farm and the animals. She was, as always, a helpful and resourceful companion, and very good company indeed during the floods I'd had to endure in the laundry and dairy, when she travelled with me to Bridgemans for sand and cement.

Gilly and Sally returned from France on 14th August. CoCo Chanel arrived on the scene the very next day.

CoCo Chanel, aka Baby Oleg, aka Raggy Omar, aka Flyfoot, aka Blackie, the Gorillapoo.

She's actually a cross between a border terrier (tan brown, wire haired) and a miniature poodle (black, curly). We named her for the renowned fashion icon and producer of fine fragrances, because she looks like she's wearing a slinky, albeit hairy off-the-shoulder-number. But she's been dubbed Baby Oleg by our friends and house-sitters Jo and Steve because of her similarity at two months old to that diminutive meercat character, and Raggy Omar because of her cute dishevelled looks and ability with the local news. Gilly calls her Flyfoot, because of her tiny hirsute feet and long skinny legs as a youngster, and her habit of catching flies on the wing. I sometimes call her Blackie just because it's common and working class and she thinks that's fun. Many's the unsuspecting tourist I've kidded she's actually a "Gorillapoo"—crossed miniature poodle and small South African gorilla. Many's the tourist that has believed me.

Whatever her looks, she has character in spades and personality by the bucketload. And she's our little girl. From the moment we picked her up from Tina Pickford's at lunchtime on 15th August 2014 to travel back to Long Lane in the palms of Gilly's small hands she's been a wonderful traveller, eager to get in a car, wherever it's going. And her wonder and excitement at the prospect of living at Long Lane Farm is palpable. As the words in my journal for that day testify

"I can feel happiness, tangible happiness, seeping back into the walls of this place"

Those first days with CoCo were great fun. She was to be shown off in Ilfracombe, paraded shoulder high in Barnstaple, socialised with the local shopkeepers in the High Street. At only about a foot long and eight inches tall she'd scoot for cover behind the sofa, lie on your lap for a tickle on the tum, play kitten-like with needles for teeth and razors for claws. Introductions to the other animals were always comical. I could almost hear her exclaim "What the fuck!" when she first set her eyes on Mistletoe the donkey. Her vocabulary and vocal expression went far beyond mere surprise, even in her first weeks. When she first heard the theme music to *"Lost"*, a post apocalyptic serial we were watching on DVD, her expression was one of deep distaste and disapproval, proving that she is a highly cultured and infinitely discerning creature, like me.

She slept in a cage in the kitchen until house training was completed. Then she took to Gilly's bed, where she spends an inordinate amount of time to this day.

The regained happiness in our new generation family was marred for a while at the end of the month by an ailment of Puff's, that worried me not a little at the time. She had taken well to our new addition, and adopted the mantle of fairy godmother to the still tiny CoCo Chanel. Quite suddenly the aged but still athletic Puff could no longer make it onto the sofa, where she had been in the habit of spending much of her wakeful life. Whether accident, injury or illness be the cause of this sudden lameness, I rather hoped it was not the harbinger of her end. On 30th August in that eventful year we consulted the vet about old Puff, expecting the worst. Spondylitis was diagnosed as probable cause of her distress. This condition, an inflammation of the vertebrae, is difficult to confirm, but rather simple to treat. Puff was put on painkillers. One of us was to sleep downstairs with her during recovery as she would find it near impossible to mount the stairs. We took it in turns. Fortunately Puff responded well and quickly to the medication. A few days into September she was back to normal, jumping onto the bed, sprinting down the stairs. I went off to France with Chick to attend to some work on the houses there and left Gilly with the girls to do some further bonding.

Beauregarde Fortescue Tit, latest in the Beardie Tradition

On the plus side, on the very same day as Puff was diagnosed with this complaint our new beardie was born, just outside Taunton. We visited him when he was just two weeks old, on 13th September on my return from France. We left Puff and CoCo in Chick's care for the visit, thinking that to impose these two on the little fellow so early in his life might be an experience too far.

John and Mal Lee lived in a posh house in the hamlet of Curland, just outside Taunton. A couple of retirees, Mal had her own litle art studio and John his woodwork shop in the back garden. To the rear of the property was a spacious paddock, and in the paddock a commodious summerhouse with veranda. And in the summerhouse with veranda lived Beauregarde Fortescue Tit, our new beardie, with his siblings and doting mother.

Forgive me the name, for it was I that thought it up. It was inspired of course by his fine good looks (Beauregarde), his aristocratic demeanour (Fortescue) and the fact that he is a bit of a tit (Tit). But at first sight only the first of these names was apparent and obvious. And once again, the choice was obvious and we just had to have him. We reserved Beau (as he became known on a daily basis), paid our deposit and left the Lees in peace.

It was going to be another month and two further visits to France before Beau would join the Pugsley household. CoCo received her final innoculations and became "street legal", taking her first steps in Ilfracombe's tourist bound High Street, guided in the ways of the world by an admiring Puff. We had one visit to Barnstaple as a foursome when I wandered into Halford's and lost the lot of them for a couple of hours. CoCo took permanently to Gilly's bed. Puff resumed her position as my bedmate. CoCo commenced a series of six weeks puppy training at the Barnstaple branch of Market Vets at which she excelled in the classroom from day one, and I, the doting father, beamed with pride.

On 18th October we journeyed to Taunton to pick up our new son and hair Beauregarde Fortescue Tit. Unlike CoCo, he is not enamoured of the car or car journeys. In fact he threw up his breakfast before he reached the end of John and Mal's drive and Gilly was picking bits of dog vomit out of her hair for the next fifty miles home.

But Beau was an instant hit with the ladies; our New Generation was complete. The two puppies played together and under Puff's expert tutellage grew into adolescence. Beau was much smaller than CoCo when he arrived; he could leave CoCo behind as he scuttled behind the sofa in our lounge. But in no time at all he outflanked her in both size and decibels. Beau followed CoCo with the puppy training regime and Gilly played the proud mum, conducting him to sessions. He enjoyed the training but hated the journeys to and fro. On more than one occasion Gilly had to have help from the trainer and some of her clients to manhandle him back into the car for the return journey.

Beau lost his manhood out of pure pragmatism. The operation was just cheaper and less intrusive than a speying of CoCo. So he was separated from his testicles before the year was out. It's not made him any less attractive to CoCo however, and we did find the two of them once in the bedroom tied together in back to back passionate embrace. More CoCo's fault than Beau's, I think. Not sure Beau had any idea what it was all about.

Puff was a master of pragmatism too. She'd taken over the reins of surrogate motherhood to the New Generation with aplomb. Kindly and forebearing with her new charges, she put up with their playfulness and Beau's rowdiness (he's quite the noisiest beardie we've ever had; will bark at the drop of a pin or the swat of a fly) with gentle humour and good grace.

In September 2015 Gilly and I were bound for St.Lucia in the Carribbean for what was to be an eight day rum-and-reggae-soaked holiday in the sun. House and pet sitters Jo and Steve had arrived to look after Long Lane Farm and its dwindling stock of inhabitants, our bags were packed, we were ready to go. We awaited our taxi to the airport and the jet plane. Puff had just had her lunchtime snack. Then she had a stroke.

She just collapsed in a heap in our lobby. I let her stay prone on the floor for a few moments to collect herself. Then we helped her to her feet, opened the back door and encouraged her into the daylight. She seemed dazed, only perhaps semi conscious. Aware that we had a plane to catch and that our house sitters wouldn't have a clue how to dig a grave, Gilly grabbed spade and mattock from the Witch's Tit and made a bee-line for the wood. There she dug, in next to no time, a three by four four foot deep grave, adjoining Calypso's. I tended to Puff and generally supervised the digging.

Puff rallied a little, and seemed to recover full consciousness over the next half hour. The taxi arrived. We bade a meaningful farewell to Puff and the other Chilluns, and the housesitters, and we were off to St.Lucia for the rum and reggae.

The holiday in St.Lucia was wonderful, laced as it was with the expected reggae strains and so soaked in rum cocktail that a massive gout attack forced me into a wheelchair at the airport on the way home. We'd called home every day enquiring after the health of the Chilluns, especially Puff. Our house sitters had reassured us every day, as they had been instructed to do, that everything and everybody was fine, that Puff was still in the land of the living. But secretly we did both wonder whether the house sitters were being tactful and pragmatic, indulging in white lies rather than spoiling our well-earned and longed-for holiday.

However, when we arrived back home dear Puff greeted us as excitedly as did CoCo and Beau. She'd seen out the duration of our holiday, I believe, as her parting gift. For one week later, on the evening of 14th September 2015, Puff suffered two more attacks. She was dispatched by the vet Craig at 12 noon the following day. She was 17½ years old (estimated). She is buried next to companions Mr. D'Arcy and Calypso in Badger's Wood and marked by one of Chick's traditional crosses.

Six years have passed since the passing of Puff. I still miss her. She was the most elegant and graceful, the most unassuming and self-effacing, the most placid and the most generous hearted of the Chilluns I have had the privilege to have known. And though Beauregarde has replaced her as my bed partner and general go-between, and I love him dearly, I shall never forget my Magic Whippet.

Epilogue

It is September 2020. We are six months into lockdown.

I know I'm not supposed to write this, and that to do so will make me sound ever so slightly smug. But I, for one, have really enjoyed the lockdown. Of course I have great sympathy for those whose lives have been damaged, destroyed, inconvenienced or just put on hold. I feel for the bereaved and their families and those who are lonely, frightened or ill. I feel for those that have lost their jobs or have been furloughed. I feel for those who have had their education disrupted. As a volunteer Citizen's Advisor I've done my level best two days a week to alleviate the problems and the difficulties encountered by those less fortunate in these unprecedented times.

But the truth is I am one of the fortunate. I live in a beautiful and remote corner of England, here in rural North Devon. I am reasonably fit and healthy even if HM Govt. deem me to be "vulnerable". I am financially secure, with plenty to eat and perhaps too much alcohol to drink. I have the company of the lovely and resourceful woman I have loved for over 50 years to sustain me. And I have 12 acres of land and gardens in which to roam and recreate.

Above all, perhaps, I have plenty to do and to occupy myself with. I have yet purpose in my life, a reason to get up in the morning. I have Long Lane Farm and its illustrious band of inhabitants to care for and to amuse me, and I have had the time, at last, to write about them.

To remind those readers who have faithfully flogged their way through over 100,000 words to this point, there are three donkeys, one aged goat, four prehistoric sheep, five middle-aged ducks and two young Chilluns still resident at Long Lane Farm in September 2020. Pedro, Pancho, Pablo and Aramis all had their ginger nuts and a cuddle this morning. Isolde, Mohammed, Shadow and Twilight enjoyed rich tea with their morning coffee. Penguin and his four wives produced one egg between them and are paddling about under the bird table. CoCo and Beau are resting after a long bark.

The lockdown for me has become an opportunity for peaceful reflection and remembrance. An opportunity to collect my thoughts in an unhurried way and to put into words the feelings I have for this place, and for the many characters and personalities I have had the privilege to encounter over a lifetime of association with animals.

Over that lifetime my observations have drawn me to more than one conclusion. In my Prologue I mentioned that there are **8.7 million species** of creature in the known world. I ask you to accept my observation that every one of the creatures I have come into contact with and that are mentioned in this book has displayed, at least to me, its own unique, distinguishable character and personality that sets it apart from the rest. And if I may extrapolate from that suggestion the obvious conclusion that there are, in the known world, at least **8,700 million** separate and distinct individualists, I am sure it is a conclusion that must be shared by the most learned and eminent in the fields of psychology and zoology.

With that thought I must leave you, dear reader. The donkeys need mucking out.

THE END

Acknowledgements

I would like to thank personally all those whose names appear within these pages who have contributed towards the success of Black Pig and Long Lane Farms. Particular thanks are due to

- Graham DeMeur for teaching me how to dig a hole
- the RSPCA at Blackberry Farm and Diana Lewis of the North Devon Animal Ambulance who contributed many of the waifs and strays who were to become our inmates
- the Wests of Indicknowle Farm for their encouragement, hard work and support in Devon
- Keith the Farrier for wrestling with our unruly donkeys every six weeks
- Market Vets and the Mullacott Cross Animal Hospital, for just being there
- And all our guests and visitors who have enjoyed with us the inhabitants of Long Lane down the years.

Printed in Great Britain
by Amazon

87671174R00121